THINE OWN SELF

THINE OWN SELF

INDIVIDUALITY IN
Edith Stein's
LATER WRITINGS

Sarah Borden Sharkey

The Catholic University of America Press
Washington, D.C.

Designed by Kachergis Book Design of Pittsboro, NC
Printed by Sheridan Books of Ann Arbor, MI

Library of Congress Cataloging-in-Publication Data
Borden, Sarah R.
   Thine own self : individuality in Edith Stein's later
writings / Sarah Borden Sharkey.
      p. cm.
   Includes bibliographical references and index.
   ISBN 978-0-8132-1682-9 (pbk. : alk. paper)   1. Stein,
Edith, Saint, 1891–1942.   2. Individuality.   I. Title.
   B3332.S674B66 2010
   193—dc22
                        2009022586

FOR MOM AND DAD
Whose gentleness called forth my self

AND FOR SHARK
Whose wisdom and joy bring it more fully to be

Contents

Preface

What it means to be a human being is a critical question, but it is also important—in an even more personal way—to say what it means to be an individual, to be a particular human being. There is increasing concern, in both our philosophical community and our more general society, for difference, and there is a worthwhile emphasis on respecting difference and on recognizing and being ethically responsible to alterity. Yet this concern for alterity can run the risk of making others so inaccessible and unintelligible to us that we lose all sense of our commonality and membership in a common community. Questions of both commonality and difference are philosophically important, and all substantive accounts of the person ought to be able to account for both.

Plato and Aristotle both account for our commonality in terms of *form* and our differences in terms of *matter*.[1] Although each presents an elegant account, many thinkers have worried that such an approach inadequately appreciates our differences, our individuality, and our personalities. John Duns Scotus's thought has been attractive to many for precisely this reason: Scotus posits not only a common human form, but also a *haecceitas* (individuating form) for each individual, and thus he places individuality at the level not of matter (which is precisely the unintelligible in which the intelligible comes to be), but of form.

1. Their respective understandings of *form* and *matter* differ, but both nonetheless place the responsibility for commonality on our *form*. In Plato's case, at least in the most common interpretations, this is a Form separate from this world, which, in some sense, is "stamped" upon matter and thus made into many items of the same general type. According to Aristotle, the form is not separate from material items, but comes to be in and through matter. Each member of one species has the same (structurally, not numerically) form, but will differ in terms of the matter in which that form comes to be.

Scotus was, however, a medieval thinker, and his positing of such a formal principle of individuality was in the context of medieval debates regarding individuation. He certainly was not writing in the light of more recent research into personality theory, philosophical personalism, or the contemporary sense of the value and uniqueness of each individual person. Although perhaps his notion of *haecceitas* might be compatible with such contemporary concerns, Scotus did not explicitly address these issues.

Edith Stein writes about individuality with more modern sensibilities. Like Scotus, Stein appreciates the medieval scholastic tradition, and her later works reveal a deep interest in Platonic, Aristotelian, and Thomistic thought. Further, like Scotus, Stein is thoroughly committed to a substantial understanding of our human commonality, positing a common human form. Unlike Scotus, however, Stein addresses concerns regarding individuality from a number of quite different angles and discusses explicitly not only the question of individuation, but also questions of individual uniqueness, personality, and who each of us as an individual ought to be.

～

Stein was born at the end of the nineteenth century and was in the last years of her schooling when World War I broke out. Her initial studies were in psychology, which was then forming itself into the discipline as we now know it, but she turned to philosophy, tempted by the call to a new method in Edmund Husserl's *Logical Investigations*. Stein studied at Göttingen with a number of the early phenomenologists, including Adolf Reinach (who was then Husserl's *privatdocent*), Theodor Conrad, Hedwig Conrad-Martius, Max Scheler (who was then lecturing in cafes around Göttingen), Hans Lipps, Roman Ingarden, and Fritz Kaufmann. Stein followed Husserl to Freiburg, finishing her dissertation in 1916 and working for eighteen months as Husserl's private assistant. Stein attempted to habilitate, writing a second dissertation necessary for academic posts in Germany, but—in part because she was a woman—was unsuccessful. She turned instead to high school teaching, and eventually accepted a position at an educational institute in Münster. She lost the position in 1933 because of her Jewish heritage and entered the Carmelite order in October of that year.

None of Stein's writings were done from a position as a university professor, but she was nonetheless actively involved with an academic community, keeping in regular contact with her fellow phenomenologists, writing essays for Husserl's *Jahrbuch,* continuing her efforts to habilitate, and attending academic conferences. Stein published a translation of Thomas Aquinas's *De veritate* as well as a volume of papers by John Henry Newman, and was a regular speaker on the Catholic lecture circuit. After she entered the Carmelite monastery, she wrote at least two books, including her magnum opus, *Finite and Eternal Being,* and a substantial text on St. John of the Cross, *The Science of the Cross.*

Stein's philosophical formation was in phenomenology, but she developed an increasing interest in the medieval philosophical tradition and the spiritual writings of Teresa of Avila and John of the Cross. Her discussions of individuality reflect her interests in psychology, phenomenology, medieval scholasticism, and Carmelite spirituality. They provide a rich and multifaceted picture of human individuality, while also insisting on our common humanity and a common human form.

In this respect, we can see Stein as our contemporary Scotus, preserving much in the Thomistic tradition but challenging the Thomists to consider again the nature of our individuality. Much of the following text will be dedicated to laying out Stein's claims regarding our individuality, presenting her key arguments for positing such individual forms, and considering the concerns that prompted her to depart from the Thomistic position. Stein has, I believe, rightly recognized the need for more substantive philosophical accounts of our rich and varied humanity and individuality. She has rightly understood the great value of the person and the need to articulate philosophical positions, which, unlike classic Aristotelianism, fully defend the dignity and value of each individual person *as an individual person.* Although I find Stein's account of the individual beautiful and deeply, deeply attractive, I have in the end become a convinced, if modified, Thomist, and the final chapters will defend—however imperfectly—a more Thomistic view of individuality that attempts to appreciate Stein's concerns and challenges, while also remaining more Thomistic.

~

I am grateful for the aid of many scholars and friends as I worked through these thoughts. The personalities of so many in the Stein scholarly community itself have given me plenty of material for reflection on individuality as well as encouragement and friendship. I am particularly grateful to Marianne Sawicki, who provided the initial motivation, friendship, and intellectual guidance that made this study possible; Sr. Josephine Koeppel, whose many conversations and clear love of Edith have provided much wisdom and insight; the late Fr. Michael Linssen, who courageously welcomed me into the archives of the monastery at Würzburg; Ilse Kerremans, who introduced me (when I was so very green) to so many in the German and Belgian Stein communities; Sr. Waltraud Herbstrith, whose writing and conversation both have deepened my understanding; John Wilcox and the Edith Stein Center for Study and Research for the preservation of and access to so many important documents; Mette Lebech for sharing so freely of herself and her learning; Fr. Nicholas Madden for his extremely kind and beautiful comments on a related talk; Freda Mary Oben for her very kind encouragement and generosity; Augusta Gooch, who blazed a trail through Stein's *Finite and Eternal Being*; and especially Terry Wright and Tony Calcagno. Terry's great love of individual forms in Stein and his acute criticisms have profoundly shaped my thought on this topic, and I am very grateful for his many critical comments and suggestions. Tony read this manuscript very carefully and provided extensive criticism, without which this would be a much weaker book. I wish I could have taken all of his suggestions and insights into account.

I also owe a great debt to many others, especially Rev. Phil Kenyon for that fateful phone call, Fr. Joseph Koterski, the late

Fr. Norris Clarke, John Drummond, Fr. Chris Cullen, Dana Miller, Kathryn Rombs, the *Deutscher Akademischer Austauschdienst* for a short-term research grant which made work in Germany possible, Jan Aertsen and the Thomas-Institut in Cologne, the Husserl-Archiv (both in Cologne and Leuven), Fordham University's Teaching Fellowship and Alumni Dissertation Fellowship which supported original research on this topic, Wheaton College's Alumni Junior Faculty Development Grant, the late Thomas Kelly, Keith Egan, Derek Jeffreys, Gilbert Null, Mary Veeneman, Joshua Miller, James Kruggel, Ellen Coughlin, my parents, and my colleagues and students in the philosophy department at Wheaton College. I am most especially in the debt of the one with whom I share my life, heart, and mind, my husband, Michael Sharkey. We have had innumerable conversations about individuality, individual form, intelligibility, being and essence, cognitional theory, Thomas, Scotus, Husserl, the early phenomenological context, Lonergan, Heidegger, and Stein; this manuscript (as well as my heart and mind) has been immeasurably improved by his breadth of thought, insight, wisdom, encouragement, and love. I am profoundly grateful for him and our shared life.

Introduction

Stein's position on individuality is of interest because she attempts to offer a substantive and nuanced account of individuality that compromises neither the unique irreproducibility of each person nor a common human form. She follows the Platonic and Aristotelian tradition in claiming a common human nature based in a distinctly human form, and yet she also insists that that which makes us unique is not an afterthought or anything secondary to that which makes us alike. She values both the uniqueness of each individual person and the species-form which makes all of us part of one group.

In order to account (at least in part) for our individual uniqueness, Stein posits an *individual form* for each human being.[1] But she also claims that we genuinely share a common human form which retains its distinct character, even when united to an individual form. Although the notion of individual forms is not new in the history of philosophy, Stein's account of their role in making us unique presents a distinctive, and possibly new, account of them. The primary focus of this study will be Stein's understanding of individual forms and their place in her broader metaphysical account of essence and being as articulated primarily in *Endliches und ewiges Sein,* translated as *Finite and Eternal Being.*[2]

---

1. (Finite) *persons* have individual forms, and thus both human beings and angels would individually possess an individual form.

2. Edith Stein, *Endliches und ewiges Sein: Versuch eines Aufstiegs zum Sinn des Seins,* Edith Steins Werke 2 (Louvain: E. Nauwelaerts, and Freiburg: Herder, 1950), and Edith Stein Gesamtausgabe 11/12 (Freiburg: Herder, 2006). Translated (from the 1950 edition) as *Finite and Eternal Being: An Attempt at an Ascent to the Meaning of Being,* trans. Kurt F. Reinhardt (Washington, D.C.: Institute of Carmelite Studies Publications, 2002).

INTRODUCTION

The idea of "form," sadly, has not had universal acceptance in philosophy in recent centuries. Stein's primary (although not exclusive) understanding of form is simply as a principle of intelligibility, as that which makes each of us intelligible *as* human beings or *as* this particular individual. We do not experience the world as dominantly random or chaotic, but as more or less ordered, with changes occurring in (to a limited degree) predictable and intelligible ways. We can recognize situations or events *as* random or chaotic precisely on the field of our experience as intelligible. Were it all random or truly chaotic, we could never recognize this. The fact that change is not simply predictable but also intelligible is significant. We do not simply make predictions based on previous occurrences, but recognize that certain things must be this way rather than that. Our experience is infused with normativity and intelligibility. (David Hume's famous claim that one cannot get an "ought" from an "is" is a wonderful example of this. He, after all, makes a claim about what we *cannot* do, i.e., there is an appeal to, and recognition of, normativity even in his denial that moral normativity can arise from empirical experience.)

Stein thinks, however, that we are not simply intelligible *as* human beings but also *as* individuals. There is a normativity to us not simply as members of some species grouping but as individuals. It is this latter claim, and the particular way in which Stein spells it out, that makes her position unique. Stein does not think that our most basic formal structure is our species structure but, rather, our individual structure. Stein then marries an account of individual form to a qualified version of the Aristotelian-Thomistic claim that form is the principle in living things of growth and development. Her final position is a distinct combination of the older focus on form as a metaphysically real principle of formation with her own emphasis on individual forms as the principle of individual normativity.

Stein's concern for our individuality and her dual focus on commonality and individuality is present in nearly all of her writings, but her position is most maturely developed in *Finite and Eternal Being*. *Finite and Eternal Being* is Stein's final distinctively philosophical book. She completed it in 1936, while living in the Carmelite convent in Cologne, Germany. It draws from nearly all of her philosophical reflection: her phenomenological work on the individual, community, and state; her thought on women and education; her account of the structure of the person; her spiritual writings; her dialogues between Husserl and Thomas Aquinas; her translations of Thomas; her study of the medieval tradition—especially Augustine, Thomas Aquinas, and John Duns Scotus; her readings in contemporary science; and her practice of the spiritual disciplines of the Carmelite tradition. Although *Finite and Eternal Being* is the primary book under discussion, it is by no means the exclusive text. Stein's explicit positions on individuality are the fruit of many different avenues of reflection, and considering at least some of those will be a condition of appreciating her great opus.[3] Thus, for example, there is discussion of both Darwin and spiritual formation in chapter 2. Both are significant influences on Stein's thought on individuality.

Edith Stein and Thomism

Although my primary concern is Stein's account of individual forms, especially as articulated in *Finite and Eternal Being,* discussion of individual forms requires appreciation of Stein's distinctive account of the various types of essences and being. In clarifying Stein's positions regarding being and essence, I found it useful to compare her claims with those of Edmund Husserl, John Duns Scotus, and Thomas Aquinas. Stein herself suggests this in the foreword to *Finite and Eternal Being,* where she claims that her book is a synthesis of two philosophical worlds, the phenomenological and the Thomistic.[4] Her claim, however, should not be taken too lit-

3. For a listing of Stein's writings and the dates for their composition and publication, see the chronology put together by Marianne Sawicki on the Husserl website, www.husserlpage.com/hus_r2st.html, and available through links on the Baltimore Carmel website, www.baltimorecarmel.org.

4. *Endliches und ewiges Sein,* 1950 edition (hereafter EeS), viii–ix/*Endliches und ewiges Sein,* 2006 critical edition (hereafter ESG), 3–4/*Finite and Eternal Being* (hereafter FEB), xxvii–xxviii.

erally. There are various studies looking at Stein's "synthesis," including Mary Catherine Baseheart's dissertation, *The Encounter of Husserl's Phenomenology and the Philosophy of St. Thomas in Selected Writings of Edith Stein* (1960); Horst Seidl's more recent article, "Über Edith Steins Vermittlungsversuch zwischen Husserl und Thomas v. Aquin" (1999); and Ralph McInerny's quite complimentary article, "Edith Stein and Thomism" (1987).[5] It is not surprising that there are such studies, since two pieces by Stein have been published with the express intent of comparing Husserl and Thomas (with a decided leaning toward Thomas).[6] Further, there is Stein's translation of *De veritate*, the beginning of a translation of *De ente et essentia* (manuscript photocopy at Archivum Carmelitanum Edith Stein, Würzburg), and Stein's Habilitationsschrift (written when she tried to obtain a position at Freiburg) *Potenz und Akt*, ostensibly a Thomistic work.[7]

Thus, it seems quite natural to do studies comparing the later work of Edith Stein with Thomas Aquinas. Despite, however, McInerny's compliments to Stein's Thomism, it appears to me that

5. We could also mention Reuben Guilead's *De la Phénoménologie à la science de la croix: l'itinéraire d'Edith Stein* (Louvain: Nauwelaerts, 1974) and M.-J. Dubois's "L'itinéraire philosophique et spirituel d'Edith Stein," *Revue Thomiste* 73 (1973): 181–210.

6. In the volume honoring Husserl's seventieth birthday, Stein contributed a piece entitled "Husserls Phänomenologie und die Philosophie des hl. Thomas von Aquino." See *Jahrbuch für Philosophie und phänomenologische Forschung*, supplementary volume, Festschrift for Edmund Husserl (1929): 315–38. This was written originally as a dialogue between the two philosophers, and both versions are translated and published in Edith Stein, *Knowledge and Faith*, trans. Walter Redmond (Washington, D.C.: Institute of Carmelite Studies Publications, 2000).

7. *Potenz und Akt* was written (and rejected) in the early 1930s for the University of Freiburg. (It is published as *Potenz und Akt: Studien zu einer Philosophie des Seins*, Edith Steins Werke 18 [Freiburg: Herder, 1998].) After her entrance into the Carmelite order, Stein was asked to revise this work, and *Finite and Eternal Being* is the product of her efforts. Thus, there is a strong connection between *Finite and Eternal Being* and *Potenz und Akt*. Nonetheless, we should not read *Finite and Eternal Being* as a slightly edited version of the earlier work; Stein reworked the whole project, keeping the discussion of act and potency simply as a starting point for the study. See EeS viii–ix/ESG 3–4/FEB xxviii.

INTRODUCTION

any claim that Stein is successful at being a Thomist or a Thomistic thinker need to be approached with care. If not, it will do insufficient justice to Stein's work and result in a rather negative evaluation, as, for example, Horst Seidl has concluded. In the opening paragraph of his essay on Stein and Thomas, Seidl writes:

As is known, Edith Stein began her philosophical path from the phenomenology of her teacher, Edmund Husserl, then dedicated herself to the works of Thomas Aquinas and attempted to go beyond the phenomenological philosophy with him without opposing it to the philosophy of Thomism but rather agreeing with it. This attempt, however, as it appears to me, is not successful, neither in the great treatise *Endliches und ewiges Sein* nor in the smaller writing *Erkenntnis und Glaube*.[8]

Martin Honecker passed a similar judgment on Stein's *Potenz und Akt* by suggesting that she insufficiently understood Thomism.[9] Anton Höfliger's dissertation on the problem of universals in *Finite and Eternal Being* criticizes her at several points for failing to appreciate Thomas's position (for example, in her critique of matter as the principle of individuation).[10]

There is another way, however, to approach Stein's work, one which I think is much more consistent with her philosophical training, her explicit statements to her provincial,[11] and the content of her philosophy: Stein is not, in any strict sense, a Thomist;

8. "Über Edith Steins Vermittlungsversuch zwischen Husserl und Thomas von Aquin," *Forum Katholische Theologie* 2 (1999): 114. Seidl's article focuses on an essay in *Knowledge and Faith,* not *Finite and Eternal Being.*
9. See Hugo Ott's article "Die Randnotizen Martin Honeckers zur Habilitationsschrift Potenz und Akt," *Studien zur Philosophie von Edith Stein,* Internationales Edith-Stein-Symposium Eichstätt 1991/ Phänomenologische Forschungen, vol. 26/27, ed. Reto Luzius Fetz, Matthias Rath, and Peter Schulz (Freiburg: Alber, 1993), esp. 141 and 144. *Potenz und Akt* was written four to five years before *Finite and Eternal Being,* and Stein herself judged that the whole thing needed to be reworked. See letters 135 and 201 in *Self-Portrait in Letters, 1916–1942,* trans. Josephine Koeppel (Washington, D.C.: Institute of Carmelite Studies Publications, 1993), as well as the foreword to *Finite and Eternal Being.*
10. See also the reviews of Stein's translation of *De veritate.* Some are complimentary and some quite negative.
11. See, for example, letter 184 in *Self-Portrait in Letters.*

rather, while deeply influenced by her work on Thomas's texts, she develops slightly different metaphysical conceptions of essence and being.[12] I will argue that, in order to interpret accurately Edith Stein's position on individuality, one must first understand her more general metaphysical conceptions, which cannot, as has often been done,[13] be read simply as a Thomism which begins with consciousness.

Despite this slightly polemical beginning, it is accurate to say that Stein was greatly influenced by scholasticism and retains many concepts certainly from Thomas, but also from Augustine, Scotus, and Pseudo-Dionysius. In the following I will compare Stein's position on being and essence with Husserl's theory of essence and with Thomas and Scotus on both being and essence. In doing so, it is possible to become clearer about Stein's own metaphysical claims and thereby understand what role individual forms play in making us unique individuals.

Outline of the Text

A significant aim of this text is expository. I would like to lay out, as clearly as I can, Stein's positions regarding the differing kinds and meanings of essence, the nature of being, the relation between act and potency, and the relation of these to Stein's account of what it means to be an individual. Although the primary aim of this

12. Such a thesis gives rise to the question of why Stein herself regularly appeals to Thomas in *Finite and Eternal Being* and seems to take pains to appear as a Thomist. I will not address this question but rely on Hildegard Gosebrink's suggestion that there are many historical and contextual reasons for the style of Stein's writing (conversation, October 1999). See also her article "'Wissenschaft als Gottesdienst' Zur Bedeutung Thomas' von Aquinas für Edith Stein in ihrer Speyerer Zeit (1923–1931)," *Edith Stein Jahrbuch* 4 [*Das Christentum*, part 1] (Würzburg: Echter, 1998): 511–30.

13. Stein's work has certainly not always been so read. See, for example, reviews of *Finite and Eternal Being* by R. Allers, A. Dempf, and J. Collins: Allers in *New Scholasticism* 26 (1952): 480–85; Dempf in *Philosophisches Jahrbuch der Görresgesellschaft* 62 (1953): 201–4; and Collins in *Modern Schoolman* 29 (1952): 139–45.

text is expository, I have a secondary interest in evaluating Stein's claims. Stein is a deeply independent thinker, drawing heavily from the philosophic tradition but also articulating her own positions. In keeping with her example, we ought both to understand where she stands and to ask whether we should stand with her. Stein's questions and philosophic concerns are profound, and she posits individual forms for, I believe, very significant philosophical reasons. Further, her metaphysical stance regarding essence and being is philosophically sophisticated and relatively unique. On both essence and individuality, Stein stands close to the Scotist tradition, but her position is distinctively her own and attuned to more contemporary concerns. She incorporates individual form into her account not as a principle of *individuation* but as a principle of *individual uniqueness,* and thus individual form plays a different role in Stein's account than *haecceitas* does in Scotus's. In shifting the question from individuation to individual uniqueness, Stein offers us an important set of philosophical questions and distinctions, worthy of significant philosophical analysis. I am not aiming to provide substantive analysis of Stein's general metaphysics, but I do hope to introduce Stein's broader metaphysical claims, particularly as they are relevant to her position regarding our individuality, and to lay out a few lines for the evaluation and discussion of Stein's great work.

This manuscript is divided into ten chapters, beginning with a chapter presenting texts from throughout Stein's corpus discussing individuality and individual form. Stein consistently argues that there is an individual form or personal core for each human being. The philosophical "work," however, that Stein expects to be accomplished by individual forms is not—strictly speaking—that of individuation, and chapter 1 briefly distinguishes a number of different problems relevant to being an individual (including the questions of individuation, identity, the nature of being an individual, and two senses of uniqueness).

Chapter 2 asks why Stein posits individual forms. Stein has a number of reasons for doing so, including both elements of our experience which seem to be best accounted for by positing such an individual form and weaknesses in the classical Thomistic account. Chapter 2 looks at a number of the motivations leading Stein to posit individual forms, and focuses on (i) the intelligibility of individual personalities, (ii) the challenges evolutionary theory raises for the classic Thomistic account of form, (iii) theological reasons for emphasizing the import of each individual, (iv) the fitness of individual forms to certain spiritual models and traditions, and, finally, (v) a critique of Thomas's account of matter as the principle of individuation. Stein thinks that for each of these reasons, individual forms—in contrast to a species-form—ought to be affirmed as our most basic formal component.

Chapters 3 and 4 are dedicated to articulating Stein's broad metaphysical positions. Chapter 3 focuses on her account of essence in *Finite and Eternal Being*. Stein distinguishes a number of different types of essences, and she follows the early phenomenologist Jean Hering in positing *essentialities* [*Wesenheiten*], in contrast to essences and substantial forms. This chapter distinguishes the different types of essential structures and the relations among the various structures. Related to Stein's account of the various types of essences is her distinction among three types of *being* (actual, mental, and essential being). Chapter 4 focuses on the distinctions among these three types, and compares Stein's position to more Thomistic and Scotist positions.

Once the general metaphysical framework is clear, it is much easier to appreciate Stein's particular account of individual forms. Chapter 5 lays out that account and fills in the details of the brief sketch given in chapter 1. In short, the individual form should be distinguished from the substantial form. The substantial form is the actualization of the individual form, but the individual form has, properly, essential being which is actualized in the substantial form. It is the substantial form, in contrast to matter or the individual form, which acts as the primary principle of individuation as well as unrepeatable uniqueness. Individual forms, however, provide for our uniqueness in a weaker sense, and each person (both human and angelic) possesses a unique individual form which lays out a set of possibilities characteristic of each person as an individual and not merely as a member of her species.

The most famous thinker positing something like individual forms in the Western tradition is John Duns Scotus. Scotus's *haecceitas* is not an individual form in Stein's sense; nonetheless, there are important parallels.[14] In chapter 6 I argue that Stein's account of individual forms is more powerful than Scotus's because it can address certain recurring criticisms of Scotus's. Stein is able to do so largely because of her appropriation of Edmund Husserl's mereology. Thus, chapter 6 presents Husserl's account of parts and wholes and compares Stein's version of individual form, employing that Husserlian mereology, with Scotus's.

While she is able to respond successfully to Scotus's challenge of maintaining the distinction and relation between our genuinely common form and our individuality, Stein is nonetheless faced with other challenges, including preserving adequately the equality of all human beings. Stein can genuinely affirm that we share (structurally, not numerically) a common human form, but she cannot say that we share, at our most fundamental structural level, a common form. This presents its own set of difficulties, and there is a danger with Stein's account of creating (albeit unintentionally) a hierarchy among individual forms. Stein certainly recognized this danger and worked to show how the individual and formal differences among human beings do not lead to a hierarchy (as Thomas Aquinas thought occurred in the case of angels). Chap-

---

14. Scotus posits *haecceitas,* but not "individual forms" per se. Joshua Blander, for example, insists very clearly that *haecceitas* is not "individual form" (conversation, spring 2007). This point strikes me as quite right, and I do not want to equate Stein's individual forms with Scotus's *haecceitas;* they are certainly understood to do different philosophical tasks. But it strikes me as also correct that Scotus's positing of a formal structure of *this-ness, haecceitas,* does share something with Stein's individual forms, and that Scotus's positing of such *this-ness* had an influence on how individuality is valued. There are important philosophical differences between the positions, as should become clear in the following chapters, but they share important parallels that make comparisons valuable.

ter 7 looks at this challenge—in its various forms—and the dangers presented if not met adequately. If she fails on this point, her position on individual forms will give rise to a number of problems, including leaving us susceptible to emotional isolation, providing an inadequate support for Aristotelian virtue ethics (to which she is sympathetic), undermining the equality which provides the philosophical foundations of a political democracy, and opening Christianity to the theological challenge of a weakened support for the doctrine of the Atonement. Although I think that all of these dangers are quite serious, Stein may be able to meet these challenges, and I briefly outline either Stein's response to each point or a possible response.

In the eighth and ninth chapters, I argue that most (although not all) of what Stein wanted to account for with individual forms can be accounted for in other ways. A priori content-rich individual forms have a certain explanatory value but are not, I believe, the only or best way to account for the concerns raised in chapter 2. If an adequate, more Thomistic account of individuality could be developed, then many of the dangers raised in chapter 7 could be avoided. Although fully articulating and defending such an alternative view is beyond the scope of this study, I provide the broad outlines of such a view and point to the places in Stein's texts where she herself seems tempted to go in precisely this direction.

Stein's particular account of individual forms provides an avenue by which we may study her metaphysical account and emphasizes the philosophically rich but inadequately discussed topics of individuality and personality. Although I hesitate about certain elements in her position, her account of persons and being nonetheless presents a particularly powerful and important portrait. She herself recognized most of the challenges that I have raised, and the tensions in her account make clear that her mind was subtle and intellectually alive. The metaphysical positions she argues for in her later writings have much to offer to our contemporary discussion, even—and perhaps even especially—where we may want to disagree.

Method

As should be clear from the outline, the primary approach to this study is metaphysical. I am not convinced, however, that metaphysics ought to be our starting point in philosophical analysis. It is a critical methodological question whether we can talk directly about being and beings without first having, at minimum, a well-developed (even if implicit) account of how we are in communion with and come to know such being and beings. The philosophic adequacy of differing metaphysical accounts is surely importantly tied to the adequacy of the cognitional theory implicit or explicit in those accounts.

Unfortunately, explicit discussion of both method and cognitional theory will be strikingly absent from this study (with a few, sadly brief, exceptions in chapters 3 and 4). This is not because I think that such questions are unimportant. On the contrary, I think that they are exceedingly important, and I suspect that a full evaluation of Stein's position on individual forms as well as being and essence will be tied directly to the adequacy of her account of human understanding.

Stein's early training was in phenomenology, and she maintained a lifelong commitment to certain aspects of phenomenology. Stein was well aware of the import of methodological queries and the risks involved in jumping directly into metaphysical analyses. Her failure to develop these elements more fully in *Finite and Eternal Being* may be one of the reasons she herself describes the work as incomplete.[15] Stein writes in the preface to *Finite and Eternal Being*:

Consciousness is treated as the mode of passage to beings and as a special genus of being, but the interconnection between consciousness and

15. In several places in the preface as well as in her correspondence, Stein indicates that *Finite and Eternal Being* is a sketch that needs a great deal of filling out. For example, in the preface she indicates that the work is not intended to be a full metaphysical treatise but, rather, a ground plan of being. And in 1936 she writes to Hedwig Conrad-Martius: "You must not speak of a 'great ontology' of mine. It is only a small attempt, although at the same time it is unabashedly comprehensive" (letter 228 in *Self-Portrait in Letters*).

INTRODUCTION

the objective world will not be—in a thoroughgoing way—fundamental, and the forms of consciousness corresponding to the structure of the objective world will not be investigated.[16] The mental [*Gedankliche*] will only be adduced as its genera of being [*Seienden*] and the interconnection of beings and the conceptual grasp only occasionally will be taken into account, but they will not be comprehensively treated as a theme. This occurs because of a conscious self-limitation: what is attempted here is the fundamental structure of a doctrine of being, not a system of philosophy. *That* the doctrine of being is taken up conceptually by itself presupposes certainly an understanding of its relation to a doctrine of constituting forms of consciousness and to logic, which can be grounded only in a thoroughgoing doctrine of knowledge and science.[17]

Although she does not make it a major explicit theme, Stein is not methodologically naïve in her work. There are hints of a broadly phenomenological account of human consciousness, and in the second chapter of *Finite and Eternal Being,* in section 2, Stein explicitly embraces a phenomenological starting point for her investigation (and she does relatively regularly return the discussion to our conscious experiences).

But the precise relation of Stein's understanding of and employment of phenomenological analyses to her more metaphysical claims is both difficult and important.[18] Stein says relatively little about this relation in *Finite and Eternal Being,* although she was certainly aware that it was an important philosophic issue. Her downplaying this question in *Finite and Eternal Being,* in comparison to other questions, has been my justification for the approach in the present text. If I can introduce readers to Stein's metaphysical claims clearly enough to prompt further questions about method and cognitional theory, I will be grateful.

16. Stein footnotes Husserl's *transcendental phenomenology* here.
17. EeS x/ESG 5/FEB xxix–xxx.
18. We could add the further difficulty of her inclusion of revealed sources. Stein well recognized that we must distinguish philosophical and theological investigations, but she also has an account of the appropriate way philosophers may include theological truths. See particularly chapter 1 of *Finite and Eternal Being* as well as Karl Schudt's "Faith and Reason in the Philosophy of Edith Stein" (Ph.D. diss., Marquette University, 2001).

INTRODUCTION

Finite and Eternal Being

Although I will be drawing from a number of Stein's texts, the most significant one for this study is *Finite and Eternal Being*. Stein wrote this text in the Carmelite monastery in Cologne, and she completed it in 1936. The Carmelite order paid 3,000 marks[19] to have the type set for the printing of the book and expected Borgmeyer to put it out in two volumes. The publishing was, however, halted because of German laws against publication by non-Aryans. The book was not actually printed until 1950, eight years after Stein's death. Unfortunately, the 1950 edition was published without Stein's two substantive appendices, one on Teresa of Avila and the other on Martin Heidegger. The critical edition, however, in the *Edith Stein Gesamtausgabe* (published by Herder) corrects this oversight, and the complete text with both appendices appears as volume 11/12 of the series.

There are two English translations of the text: an unpublished translation, done by Augusta Gooch and available at the Edith Stein Center for Study and Research (run by John Wilcox and housed at Spalding University in Louisville, Kentucky), and a published translation by Kurt F. Reinhardt, appearing as volume 9 of the Collected Works of Edith Stein, published by the Institute of Carmelite Studies. Although I will use the English translations of many of Stein's writings, the translations from *Finite and Eternal Being* are my own. Because of the centrality of the book for this study and because of the significance certain terms will have for our understanding of Stein's position, I decided to use my own translations. The glossary gives an account of how I will translate certain key terms. For citations from *Finite and Eternal Being*, I will provide the page numbers from both the 1950 *Edith Steins Werke* edition (abbreviated EeS) and the more recent *Edith Stein Gesamtausgabe* edition (abbreviated ESG) as well as the English translation (abbreviated FEB). Thus, they will appear, for example, as EeS 1/ESG 9/ FEB 1.

19. This is the sum reported by Sr. Josephine Koeppel, conversation.

Glossary

Akt	act
ausgewirkt Wesen	worked-out essence
Dasein	spatio-temporal existence[1]
Einzelsein	being individual
Einzelwesen	individual essence or individual entity[2]
gedankliches Sein	mental being
Gehalt	(real or psychological) content[3]
individuelles Wesen	individual form[4]

I appreciate the advice of Karl Schudt, John Drummond, and Ryan Gable in selecting several of the translations in this glossary.

1. Since Heidegger, it is common to translate "Dasein" as "human being." Stein, however, is not using *Dasein* in this sense but, rather, following something closer to Hedwig Conrad-Martius's use of the term.

2. I will choose between these as the context dictates. See n. 4 below as well as n. 3 of chapter 1. At times *Einzelwesen* is used in a rather generic sense, comparable to *Lebewesen* (living being, animal). At such times "individual entity" is appropriate. Where Stein appears interested in something more technical, I will use "individual essence."

3. On EeS 45/ESG 50/FEB 46–47, Stein says, "The content [*Gehalt*] is essentially—if not alone—determinate for the *unity* of the structure. Joy over a good report is one such unity. . . . The experience of the content [*Gehaltes*] of 'joy' is therefore conditioned on two sides: by the *object* and by the *I*. The object—in this case, the content [*Inhalt*] of the report—does not belong as a *part* to the joy as experience-content [*Gehalt*], but belongs, however, to the *direction* toward this object (the *intention,* according to the linguistic usage of the phenomenologist)." *Inhalt* here appears to be the objective or meaning content (of the report), while *Gehalt* is the real content, following Husserl's use of meaning and real content.

4. Given my translation below of *Wesen* as essence, it appears that both *Einzelwesen* and *individuelles Wesen* should be translated as "individual essence." I have chosen to be inconsistent in order both to distinguish this term from her many other terms referring to essence and to highlight the similarities between Stein's *individuelles Wesen* and the philosophical tradition emphasizing individual forms. *Individuelles Wesen* is clearly a unique, individual form and not merely a single instance of the more universal essence. At times *Einzelwesen* appears to mean the same thing, yet at others Stein appears to mean simply a particular instance of the universal. Compare, for example, EeS 235/ESG 219/FEB 252, EeS 243/ESG 227/FEB 260–61, and EeS 463/ESG 424/FEB 506–7. See also n. 3 of chapter 1 below.

GLOSSARY

Inhalt	(objective) content
leere Form	empty form[5]
Macht	power
Möglichkeit	possibility
Potenz	potentiality
reine Form	pure form
Ruhen	abidingness
Seiende (ens)	entity, particular being (unless "being" can be used without confusion)[6]
Sein (esse)	being, existence
Träger	substrate[7]
Vermögen	ability
volle Was	full what
Washeit	quiddity[8] (literally, "whatness")
Wesen (essentia)	essence
wesen (as verb)	to be in an essential way[9]
wesenhaftes Sein	essential being[10]

5. I will not discuss Stein's use of "empty form," but it is worth noting the influence of Husserl in her choice of terms and understanding of empty form.

6. For the purposes of this text, *Seiende* will be translated either as "entity" or as "a particular being." I like "entity" for its clarity and simplicity. It avoids confusing *Seiende* with *Sein*. It does not, however, capture the connection with being and the transcendentals that Stein's German has. In *Finite and Eternal Being* V, Stein focuses on *Seiendes als solches; "*entity as such" is an insufficient translation here, and "being" is much more adequate. In a way similar to Stein's use of *Seiende* and *Sein*, we can differentiate two senses of *ens*, a nominative and a participial sense. See Augusta Gooch's *Metaphysical Ordination: Reflections on Edith Stein's "Endliches und Ewiges Sein"* (Ph.D. diss. University of Dallas, 1982), esp. chapter 2, §4.

7. I have considered several different English words for *Träger*, including "carrier" and "bearer," and I have chosen to render it "substrate" for the sake of this text (discussed in chapters 5 and especially 6 below), although I prefer "carrier" in other contexts. It is a difficult term to translate, not because the German is ambiguous, but because Stein uses *Träger* in numerous contexts. For example, in *Finite and Eternal Being* II, §6; IV, §4, 5; VII, §1; and VIII, §2, 3.

8. Stein uses *Washeiten* as the plural of *Wesenswas* because there is no plural form of "*Was*." See EeS 82/ESG 81/FEB 84. Several times Stein puts the Latin *quidditas* in brackets after using the term *Washeit*. See, for example, EeS 32/ESG 38/FEB 33 and EeS 82/ESG 81/FEB 84.

9. At EeS 8, footnote 12/ESG 16, footnote 21/FEB 547, Stein says: "The relation *esse—essentia = Sein—Wesen* is still better described in Middle High German because *wesen* then was used as a verb next to *sin (sein)*."

10. If translated from English to German, "essential being" would be *wesent-*

wesenhaftes Was	essential what[11]
Wesenheit	essentiality
Wesensform	substantial form[12] (literally, "form of the essence")
Wesenswas	essential what, quiddity (literally, "what of the essence")
Wesenszug	essential trait (literally, "trait of the essence")
Wirken	activity
wirkliches Sein	real being
Wirklichkeit	reality[13]
Wirksamkeit	efficacy

---

liches Sein rather than *wesenhaftes Sein*. (Stein used *wesentliches Sein* in translating *essentiale esse and substantile esse* in translating Thomas's *De veritate*. See Stein's "Lateinisch-Deutsches Wörterverzeichnis," in *Übersetzung: Des hl. Thomas von Aquino Untersuchungen über die Wahrheit "Quaestiones disputate de veritate,"* Edith Stein Gesantausgabe 4, ed. Andreas Speer and Francesco Valerio Tommasi (Freiburg: Herder, 2008), 888. Stein seems to be wanting something stronger than simply "essential being," but what English equivalent can capture that "something stronger" eludes me. *Wesenhaft* is not a common German word, although Stein does use it in translating *essentialiter* in Thomas's *De veritate* (see "Lateinisch-Deutsches Wörterverzeichnis," 889). *Wesenhaft* does not appear in Langenscheidt's *New College German Dictionary;* the *New Wildhagen German Dictionary* (1965), however, proposes the translations "real," "organic," "intrinsic," "essential," and "substantial." It is possible that Stein is using *wesenhaftes Sein* as a technical term picked up from Hedwig Conrad-Martius. See the text quoted by Stein (EeS 102/ESG 99–100/FEB 105) from Conrad-Martius's *Die Zeit.* Marianne Sawicki suggests that Stein's use of -*haft* and -*haftig* include "a gravitational sense . . . like 'heavy.' It pushes, it wants to go somewhere." For *wesenhaftes Sein,* Sawicki says: "I would suggest that 'wesenhaftes Sein' is: being that is beingtropic, that is, on its way to being, reaching out to being, like sunflowers reach out to face the sun, or like human being reaches out to know the world in the first lines of Aristotle's Metaphysics" (e-mail, 3/29/2000).

11. Please note that the translation for *wesenhaftes Was* and *Wesenswas* is identical. *Wesenhaftes Was* is a somewhat rarer term in Stein's work, so I trust that this overlap will be relatively innocent.

12. "Substantial form" is not a literal translation of *Wesensform.* At EeS 172/ ESG 162/FEB 180, however, she equates *substantiale Form* and *Wesensform,* and one can find uses of *Wesensform* in the sense of substantial form in Manser's article "Das Wesen des Thomismus," *Divus Thomas. Jahrbuch für Philosophie und spekulative Theologie* 2 (1925): 2–23, 196–221, and 411–13, to which Stein refers several times in *Finite and Eternal Being.*

13. Stein claims that there are three meanings of "reality" *(Wirklichkeit):* "1. that of the imperfect actuality (that is in the process of developing), 2. that of the unreached goal, 3. that of the reached goal" (EeS 212/ESG 198–99/FEB 225). These three understandings of *Wirklichkeit* are not identical with her understanding of *wirkliches Sein.* Thus, there is a bit of discontinuity in these terms. My translations, however, follow the ambiguity present in the German terms.

THINE OWN SELF

One ∾ INDIVIDUAL FORM AND RELEVANT DISTINCTIONS

Edith Stein titles the final chapter of her great philosophical opus "The Meaning and Foundation of Being Individual." She opens that chapter by saying:

> In the treatment of the being of the human person, another question is often encountered that we have touched upon in other contexts and that now must be clarified if the nature of human beings, their place in the order of the created world, and their relation to divine being is to be understood: the question of the *being individual* (of the individuality) of human beings, which can be treated only in the context of a discussion of being individual in general.[1]

Stein claims that individuality and one's position regarding the individuation of entities, especially human beings, is critical for understanding human nature, our place in the world, and our relation to God. This interest in our individuality is not, however, limited to Stein's late *Finite and Eternal Being*. It begins in her earliest works, and one can see a quite consistent position regarding our individual nature developed throughout Stein's writings. Stein argues in her dissertation, for example, that each of us has an individual structure that—in its range of possibilities—remains constant, independent of our environmental, social, or historical circumstances.[2] In *Finite and Eternal Being*, Stein explicitly rejects the Aristo-

---

1. EeS 431/ESG 395/FEB 469.
2. Stein heard Max Scheler lecture in Göttingen and his *Der Formalismus in der Ethik und die materiale Wertethik* appeared in Husserl's *Jahrbuch* as Stein was beginning her studies with Husserl. It is likely that there is some kind of relationship between Stein's theory of individuality and Scheler's, and studies comparing their accounts would, I suspect, be highly fruitful.

telian and Thomistic claim that our human form is our most basic formal structure, positing instead an individual form.[3]

In the following I would like, first, to look briefly at a number—but by no means an exhaustive collection—of Stein's comments on individual forms, making clear that she posits a unique individual form for each human being in addition to the common human form. Second, I would like to distinguish a number of different questions surrounding individuality and being an individual, and thus come to a clearer understanding of what individual forms are intended to do. In the second and following chapters, I would like to consider both why Stein posits these individual forms and how her account of individuality fits into the broader metaphysical framework of her later work, particularly *Finite and Eternal Being*.

Stein's Texts on Individual Form
In Finite and Eternal Being

In *Finite and Eternal Being*, Stein does not definitively answer the question of whether non-human animals have an individual form.[4] She does, however, very clearly posit a distinct individual form for each human being. She says, for example:

"Socrates" means *what* Socrates is, and this what—just as "human being" and "living being"—can be separated from the definition of the what of this man and grasped in [its] purity—as *essential what*.[5]

3. Stein uses both *Einzelwesen* (which I have translated as "individual essence" or "individual entity") and *individuelles Wesen* (which I have translated as "individual form"). The first, *Einzelwesen,* refers primarily (although not always) to an individual essence regardless of whether this essence is a unique (in content) instance of its kind. Thus, *Einzelwesen* is used in relation to the *allgemeines Wesen* (that is, the essence as a universal). I have chosen a rather unorthodox translation in order to emphasize the focus with *Einzelwesen* on the particularity of the essence, not in terms of content but in terms of its being an individual instance of the universal. See, for example, *Finite and Eternal Being* III, §5. The second, *individuelles Wesen,* refers to an essence that is unique and distinct in content from the common form. See, for example, EeS 79/ESG 79/FEB 81. For further explanation for my choices in the translation of these terms, see the glossary.

4. See, for example, *Finite and Eternal Being* IV, §3, 1 and 2, and VIII, §2, 9.

5. EeS 149/ESG 140/FEB 155. Stein puts a footnote here that says, "This need

⟿

Socrates goes and Socrates speaks; he chats with a craftsman or refutes a famous sophist: All of these are "expressions of his essence." Going, speaking, chatting—these all have a universal meaning that is everywhere fulfilled wherever a human being does something of the same kind. But *how* Socrates does it is like no one else. His whole doing and allowing is *such* as "he himself" is. Because of this we can also say that it is the expression of his *such being* [*Soseins*]. But *this* such being has then another meaning than that of a trait of the essence or the totality of its traits. It is something simple that is repeated in each trait, that makes the whole essence and each trait into something unique, so that the friendliness or goodness of Socrates is different from that of another human being—not only one other—although the *same* essentiality is realized here and there. The whole that is *such* unfolds itself in the individual traits and in the life of this man. It is his *individual form*.[6]

Stein posits here an individual form distinctive and unique to Socrates. Socrates is, formally, not simply human, but *Socrates*.

There are, however, a number of possible ways of understanding this claim. One might, for example, take Stein's emphasis to be on the way in which Socrates engages in common human activities. Her language of "individual form" might refer not to a form truly distinct from the common species-form, but to the *way* in which the species-form is lived out. On this reading, there would be no individual form with a metaphysical status comparable to the species-form; when an individual human being lives, chooses, values, etc., she develops habits and patterns of *how* she does these very human actions. One might come to recognize particular habits and patterns of some individual and describe them as her "individual form," but there need be nothing at least metaphysically comparable to the basic species-form.

Although I find this reading attractive in various ways, and Stein certainly does both (a) affirm a common species-form and (b) in various passages emphasize the *how* of the individual (thus

---

not mean that it also allows itself to be conceptually grasped" (EeS 149/ESG 140/ FEB 576).

6. EeS 150–51/ESG 141–42/FEB 156–57.

suggesting that the individual form offers no distinctive or exclusive content), I do not think that this interpretation fits quite as well with other passages. For example, she speaks of the individual (in her individuality) as intelligible in a comparable way to the species, and she describes the individual form as distinguishing individuals in terms of content.[7] Stein is quite explicit in the final chapter of *Finite and Eternal Being*. After giving an extensive quotation from the Thomistic commentator Josef Gredt, Stein points to her differences with the Thomistic position: for Thomas, the "individual form" would be the species-form individuated; it is an individual instance of the universal but offers no formal content different from that of the species-form. In contrast, Stein says:

> It has already become clear that we cannot agree with this conception: we see the essence of Socrates in his being-Socrates (in which the being-human is enclosed), and we observe it as not merely numerically different but, rather, different from the essence of every other human being through a special particularity.[8]

Stein finds Thomas's position, as Kurt Reinhardt translates the first sentence of this passage, "impossible to accept." We cannot be identical in content at our most basic formal level. Stein similarly contrasts her position with Aristotle's, making clear that she understands the final determination of form as the *individual form* and not the *species-form*.[9]

Both Aristotle and Thomas understand each individual human being as a substance composed of form (the species-form) and matter. Each of us has various accidents (e.g., color of skin, particular spatial location, etc.). The accidents are not "accidental" or unimportant; nonetheless, *what* we are lies at the level of substance, while our accidents are accidents *of* this substance. For both Aristotle and Thomas, our most basic formal or structural element is

---

7. See, for example, EeS 458/ESG 419/FEB 500 and EeS 365/ESG 336/FEB 395–96.
8. EeS 439/ESG 402/FEB 478.
9. See EeS 159/ESG 149/FEB 166.

our substantial form; the formal structure of *what* we are, or the kind of thing we are, is owed to our substantial form, which, according to both of them, is our species-form. We each have (or are) an individual instance of that species-form and each of us have various, different accidents, but we are formally identical at the level of our most basic substantial form.

In contrast, Stein claims that our individual form is distinct from our species-form and even more fundamental structurally than the species-form. Thus, according to Stein, it is our individual form—not our species-form—that provides the final structural determination of our substantial form.

Stein affirms an individual form for each human being, and occasionally she will describe us as having a *personal characteristic feature* or *personal characteristic*.[10] Stein affirms something unique in content about each of us; it is something deeply personal, marking our actions and our way of being in the world, relating to others, etc. We cannot have exhaustive knowledge of another's individual distinctiveness, although limited knowledge is possible, and presumably we have sufficient knowledge to be aware of the differing content of the various individual forms.

In the Earlier Phenomenological Work

Stein makes similar claims about our individuality in her earlier philosophical writings. When Stein was at the university in Breslau between 1911 and 1913, she studied psychology under William Stern. Prior to leaving Breslau for Göttingen in order to study under Edmund Husserl, in what was originally planned as a temporary visit, Stein asked Stern to propose a thesis topic and intended to write under him.[11] Stein was clearly impressed with Stern, and we can see his influence in her notion of a core which is stable throughout a person's life and contains traits and characteristics to be re-

10. Compare EeS 397/ESG 364–65/FEB 432, EeS 405/ESG 371/FEB 441, and EeS 406/ESG 372/FEB 442.
11. See *Life in a Jewish Family*, trans. Josephine Koeppel (Washington, D.C.: Institute of Carmelite Studies Publications, 1986), esp. chapter 5.

alized in life.[12] In *General Psychology from the Personalistic Standpoint,* Stern describes a shift in psychology from an emphasis on the general to a focus on the particular and individual.[13] Until the end of the nineteenth century, individual differences were treated rather unsystematically in academic psychology—a tendency Stern laments. But with the turn of the century, *personality* became a category to be studied and there was a focus on the analysis of the laws and principles of individual peculiarities.[14] There was, thus, an effort to find ways to analyze scientifically an individual person's character, not simply individual traits, but the unitary structure of the whole individual personality. Stein never proceeded in her pursuit of a doctorate in psychology beyond the initial topic and one short research trip to Berlin. After her arrival in Göttingen, she dropped psychology, turning her attention instead to phenomenology. Nonetheless, neither her interest in the individual and individual differences nor her focus on an innate core of predispositions seems to have been left behind with her psychological studies.

In her earlier writings, Stein regularly speaks of a *personal core* or *core personality (Persönlichkeitskern),* rather than an *individual form.*[15] But, as in her later work, she is committed to the notion of

12. I owe the point about the significance of Stern's work for Stein to Marianne Sawicki's introduction to Stein's *Philosophy of Psychology and the Humanities,* ed. Marianne Sawicki, trans. Mary Catharine Baseheart and Marianne Sawicki (Washington, D.C.: Institute of Carmelite Studies Publications, 2000), xiv.

13. This book was first published as *Allgemeine Psychologie auf personalistischer Grundlage* in 1935, and was translated into English as *General Psychology from the Personalistic Standpoint* (trans. Howard Davis Spoerl [New York: Macmillan, 1938]); see especially chapter 2, 1. Although this was published more than twenty years after Stein left the University of Breslau, I take these points to be nonetheless relevant.

14. Stern proposed in 1900 the name *differentielle Psychologie (differential psychology)* for this effort, which he describes: "It is not intended to be a true psychology of 'individuality' but a science of the essential differences of the functions and qualities of mind, and hence a *bridge* between general psychology and psychological comprehension of individuality" (*General Psychology from the Personalistic Standpoint,* 29).

15. As far as I can tell, however, Stein took up the term "individual form" as

a personal structure, a content distinctive in each individual and prescribing the lines of development appropriate to that individual. In her dissertation, for example, Stein describes our soul as the "bearer" *(Träger)* of persistent traits, which are expressed in our conscious life.[16] The acuteness of one's sensory perception, energy and engagement in life, strength of volitions, excitability of emotional life, etc., are understood as traits of a soul, which come to expression in the quickness with which someone may notice some feature in the landscape or the intensity of response to a moving story.

In chapter 4, §5, of her dissertation, Stein claims that the development of the traits of the soul is influenced by many things, including its incorporation with a particular physical body,[17] environmental circumstances, social influences, etc. She grants that under different circumstances an individual will develop differently, and thus there is something "empirically fortuitous" about our personalities.[18] But Stein immediately follows this claim by saying that "this variability is not unlimited." Although variation is possible, there is nonetheless also an individual form with an "unchangeable kernel" or "personal structure." Stein gives the example of Caesar:

We find not only that the categorical structure of the soul as soul must be retained, but also within its individual form [*individuellen Gestalt*] we strike an unchangeable kernel, the personal structure. I can think of Caesar in a village instead of in Rome and can think of him transferred into the twentieth century. Certainly, his historically settled individuality would then go through some changes, but just as surely he would remain Caesar. The personal structure marks off a range of possibilities

---

she shifted her account of soul toward the more Aristotelian vision of the soul as the form of the body. She thus contrasts her commitment to a fundamental individual form with Aristotle's and Thomas's to the fundamental species-form.

16. See *On the Problem of Empathy*, 3rd ed., trans. Waltraut Stein (Washington, D.C.: Institute of Carmelite Studies Publications, 1989), 39–40.

17. She says, "As the substantial unity announced in single psychic experiences, the soul is based on the living body" (*On the Problem of Empathy*, 49).

18. See ibid., 110.

of variation within which the person's real distinctiveness can be developed "ever according to the circumstances."[19]

Caesar has a structure marking what it means to *be Caesar*. One can change all kinds of things about the details of Caesar's life—as is very common in fictional renditions—but he would still remain *Caesar*, that is, the individual structure characterizing what it means to be Caesar would remain the same, even amid a myriad of changes.

Stein certainly does think that these traits must be developed. People do not enter this world with, for example, well-trained artistic sensibilities or a fully developed set of emotional responses. A child may learn to notice certain features, for example, an eagle soaring on the horizon, through experience. Perhaps a parent or adult pointed to the eagle on some memorable trip, or the child took an interest in birds and looked for them on the horizon, making herself sensitive to various features in her world. So also, our emotional faculties are not developed without training, that is, without encountering a range of stories and experiences which require that we respond in various ways and thus develop our depth and range of emotional attunements.[20] Thus, in claiming that the soul is the bearer of traits, Stein is not denying the critical import of training and habituation for the development of the faculties of soul. Nonetheless, Stein also claims that there are limits to the type of development possible for individual souls. We cannot develop—regardless of the work put in—traits outside the limits of our individual form. Just as Aristotle would claim that human beings cannot develop llama traits (although a particular individual human being can, for various reasons, fail to develop or can deform her human traits), so also Stein claims that each of our individual forms sets the limits of what we can and cannot develop. Caesar

19. Ibid.
20. See Stein's writings on education, especially "Problems of Women's Education," in *Essays on Woman*, rev. ed., trans. Freda Mary Oben (Washington, D.C.: Institute of Carmelite Studies Publications, 1996).

can become the things laid out in the form of Caesar, but he cannot become that which is articulated in the form of Brutus. So, too, each of our individual forms articulates the kinds of potencies appropriate to each of us as individuals, as well as prescribing to us what we *ought* to develop, how we ought to become ourselves *qua individual.*

∾

(Stein uses the term soul [*Seele*] in a number of different ways throughout her career. For example, in her dissertation, it is the carrier or bearer of traits. In *Potenz und Akt* and *Finite and Eternal Being,* the term is used in the more traditionally Aristotelian sense as the principle of growth and formation. In the later chapters of *Finite and Eternal Being* as well as her appendix on Teresa of Avila, *Die Seelenburg,* Stein adopts Teresa's metaphor of the soul as an interior castle, and she distinguishes the *soul* from the *spirit.* Although used slightly differently in different texts, in all of these cases, interestingly, Stein understands the soul to have an important relationship to our perception of values.[21] In the following, I will try to make clear which meaning of soul is relevant for the discussion.)

∾

Stein's dissertation focuses on our knowledge of the experiences of others, and soon after completing her dissertation Stein began working as Husserl's private assistant. She contributed three substantial essays to Husserl's phenomenological journal, *Jahrbuch für Philosophie und phänomenologische Forschung:* "Sentient Causality," "Individual and Community," and "On the State." (These are often referred to as Stein's *Beiträge* essays. The first two have been translated as *Philosophy of Psychology and the Humanities* and the

21. See Marianne Sawicki's substantial footnote on the development of Stein's account of the *soul* in Stein's *An Investigation Concerning the State,* trans. Marianne Sawicki (Washington, D.C.: Institute of Carmelite Studies Publications, 2006), 114–15. For comments contrasting Stein's early and later positions, see also *Philosophy of Psychology and the Humanities,* 200 (both Stein's text and Sawicki's footnote).

third as *An Investigation Concerning the State*.) These essays can be read as both a development of her dissertation and a contribution to Husserl's overall project.[22]

In these essays, Stein describes our experience of the world in a multilayered way, corresponding to realms or layers of the human being.[23] The most central layer is the person or the personal realm. As in the dissertation, Stein argues that the personal realm has a distinctive and individual structure. Our core thus is not simply human, but individual. As she develops her account of the personal realm, Stein places particular emphasis on that realm as the center for our perception of value. Because the personal core is central to our being, we are most at home in the world of values. It is worth emphasizing that values are not, on Stein's account, "merely subjective" but, rather, are perceived in a way analogous to our perception of color or sound. We perceive a melody, for example, through the hearing of sounds and a painting through the seeing of colors. So, too, we perceive a value through the feeling of emotions. Our emotions (in contrast to moods) are precisely our response to values.[24]

22. After writing her dissertation and three pieces for the *Jahrbuch,* Stein ceased doing strictly Husserlian phenomenology, in the sense that she no longer limited herself to phenomena given to consciousness or that which is necessary to account for what is strictly given. Insofar as Stein began incorporating revealed truths, including the Trinity, creation, etc., and insofar as she began doing what she would acknowledge as metaphysics, she can no longer be said to be doing strict phenomenology. In her later works, Stein is explicit about her shift and, in particular, her incorporation of Christian revealed truths. See, for example, her discussion of method in "Problems of Women's Education," II, B, in *Essays on Woman* and her discussion of Christian philosophy in the first chapter of *Finite and Eternal Being.* See also Karl-Heinz Lembeck's "Zwischen Wissenschaft und Glauben: die Philosophie Edith Steins," *Zeitschrift für Katholische Theologie* 112, no. 3 (1990): 271–87, and Karl Schudt's "Faith and Reason in the Philosophy of Edith Stein."

23. Once again, we might suspect Scheler's influence, as he too distinguishes levels within the individual. For particularly clear discussions of the four layers in Stein's phenomenology, see Marianne Sawicki's work, especially her *Body, Text and Science: The Literacy of Investigative Practices and the Phenomenology of Edith Stein* (Boston: Kluwer, 1997).

24. Stein makes several critical distinctions, including among different types of values—e.g., moral, aesthetic—and between the emotion itself and the *feel-*

The connection between the person and values is made in various places throughout Stein's work, but it is a particular focus in her second *Beiträge* essay. The core of each human being is our personal layer, with its distinctive, individual personal core. Thus, in each of us, "the world 'strikes a chord'" in a special way.[25] We are each particularly susceptible to differing kinds of values, and we understand who a person is "when we see which world of value she lives in, which values she is responsive to, and what achievements she may be creating, prompted by values."[26] This core is permanent. It provides an "invariable repertoire of being" that lays out the lines of development possible for each of us as individuals.[27]

Once again, in making these claims, Stein is not arguing that our core transparently expresses itself with no effort on our part. Like Aristotle and Thomas, Stein thinks that there is hard labor involved in being ourselves, and Stein agrees that we can do so to a greater or lesser extent. But, in contrast to Aristotle and Thomas, Stein argues that not only can we succeed or fail in becoming fully human, we can succeed or fail at becoming ourselves. Because we have such a personal structure which exists regardless of whether it is in fact realized, it is also possible to realize that structure to a lesser or greater degree. And unfortunately, there are numerous ways to fail to become ourselves. Stein gives various examples: a person who dies young, someone who "falls victim of a paralysis" or suffers some debilitating weakness, or someone who fails to have the experiences or meet the people who would draw out that person's individual capacities.[28]

ing of that emotion. See especially "Individual and Community," in *Philosophy of Psychology and the Humanities*, II, §3c.

25. *Philosophy of Psychology and the Humanities*, 230.

26. "Individual and Community," 227.

27. She says, "Rather her entire life is decided by the 'core personality,' by that invariable repertoire of being [also translated "essential substance"] that is not a result of development but, on the contrary, prescribes how the development proceeds" ("Sentient Causality," in *Philosophy of Psychology and the Humanities*, 92–93). I am grateful to Stephen Hampton for reminding me of this passage. See also "Individual and Community" in the same volume, p. 238.

28. *On the Problem of Empathy*, 111.

Furthermore, although the set of capacities can be unfolded to a greater or lesser extent, the capacities themselves cannot be developed or deteriorate.[29] The capacities are those that mark the lines and limits of development, and they cannot themselves be changed without some kind of divine intervention.[30] In this sense, our person can neither develop nor deteriorate. It can be "exposed," but not—in this limited sense—formed.[31] Stein is not a determinist; she clearly emphasizes our freedom and the *fiat* of the will throughout these essays. But there are limits setting the conditions for the use of our freedom, and among those is our individuality or core personality.

In Her Spiritual Writings and Lectures on Women

I would like to cite very briefly two final examples of Stein's concern for individuality. First, the concern for our individual structure and its import for our formation led Stein to caution us in our

29. There are many different senses of *development*. Stein's position in her early phenomenological writings does not disagree with the general Aristotelian-Thomistic claim that there is hard work necessary for development, but she is not—in her early work—affirming a distinctively Aristotelian-Thomistic account of development as the movement of potencies to act. Development here simply means the unfolding of essential possibilities, that is, possibilities of some essential structure.

30. See "Individual and Community," in *Philosophy of Psychology and the Humanities,* 233.

31. See *On the Problem of Empathy* IV, §5, as well as *Philosophy of Psychology and the Humanities.* She says quite strikingly in the latter text, "No development is exhibited by the core of the person or by the being of the soul that's determined by it. The living of the psyche is a developmental path in which [sentient] abilities get training. Prerequisites of this training are the powers that the person is equipped with, the external circumstances under which the living proceeds, and finally the 'original predisposition' that more or less attains deployment within the process of development. The external circumstances play a double role: they determine the waxing and waning of lifepower, and they also determine the direction of development, but to be sure, only within the latitude that the original predisposition plainly allows. If you possess no mathematical aptitude, even the most exquisite instruction won't make a mathematician out of you. But if you're gifted, the specialty to which you apply yourself can depend on the direction in which your gaze is turned through outside influences. The original predisposition undergirds the development, yet does not itself develop" (231–32).

use of role models. She ends an essay on St. Elizabeth of Hungary with commentary on the saint's life. I will quote a significant portion of the text in order to set the context, although the middle paragraph is most important for the issue of individuality:[32]

So we seem to get a conflicting picture of the saint and the formation of her life. On the one hand we have a stormy temperament that spontaneously follows the instincts of a warm, love-filled heart uninhibited by her own reflection or outside objections. On the other hand we see a forcefully grasping will constantly trying to subdue its own nature and compelling her life to conform to an externally prescribed pattern on the basis of rigid principles that consciously contradicted the inclinations of her heart.

However, there is a standpoint from which the contradictions can be understood and finally harmoniously resolved, that alone truly fulfills this longing to be natural. Those who avow an "unspoiled human nature" assume that people possess a molding power operating from the inside undisturbed by the push and pull of external influence, shaping people and their lives into harmonious, fully formed creatures. But experience does not substantiate this lovely belief. The form is indeed hidden within, but trapped in many webs that prevent its pure realization. People who abandon themselves to their nature soon find themselves driven to and fro by it and do not arrive at a clear formation or organization. And formlessness is not naturalness. Now people who take control of their own nature, curtailing rampant impulses, and seeking to give them the form that appears good to them, perhaps a ready made form from outside, can possibly now and again give the inner form room to develop freely. But it can also happen that they do violence to the inner form and that, instead of a nature freely unfolded, the unnatural and artificial appears.

Our knowledge is piecemeal. When our will and action build on it alone, they cannot achieve a perfect structure. Nor can that knowledge, because it does not have complete power over the self and often collaps-

---

32. The wording of the text is similar both to a lecture that Stein gave in Zürich on January 24, 1932, and one of her articles appearing in the *Benediktinischen Monatsschrift* 13, no. 9/10 (1931): 366–77. Thus, it was likely written just a few years before *Finite and Eternal Being*. See the editors' introduction to *The Hidden Life: Essays, Meditations, Spiritual Texts*, trans. Waltraut Stein (Washington, D.C.: Institute of Carmelite Studies Publications, 1992).

es before reaching the goal. And so this inner shaping power that is in bondage strains toward a light that will guide more surely, and a power that will free it and give it space. This is the light and the power of divine grace.[33]

Stein describes us as possessing an individual structure which longs for self-expression. We want to become ourselves. That individual structure must be unfolded, for "formlessness is not naturalness," and it needs assistance in order to do so. But the assistance cannot come as simply an imported image from without. Each of our forms is unique, and the various foreign ideas and images we import may do violence to our own distinctive individuality. Thus, we must develop ourselves *as individuals* and not merely as human beings. This is no easy task since our individuality is often deeply hidden and not easily available even to its "owner."

Second, in the late 1920s and early '30s, Stein gave a series of lectures on women and women's education. Although her primary focus in the lectures is on whether there a "feminine distinctiveness," she regularly claims that "no woman is only *woman*."[34] Although she thinks that we can talk, in some sense, about feminine and masculine souls, she does not hold a strong "essentialist" position regarding gender precisely because of the role of our individuality and individual forms.[35] She asks, for example: "Is not man like woman aware of the coexistence between individual and masculine tendencies and then eventually an opposition between

33. *The Hidden Life*, 27–28.

34. *Essays on Woman*, 49.

35. See *Essays on Woman*, 97–98, 182–83, and 201–2, as well as *Die Frau: Fragestellungen und Reflexionen* (Freiburg: Herder, 2000), 48–49. For a discussion of Stein's relation to gender essentialism, see Linda Lopez McAlister's "Edith Stein: Essential Differences," *Philosophy Today* 37 (Spring 1993): 70–77. For discussions of Stein on women, see Jane Kelley Rodeheffer's "On Spiritual Maternity: Edith Stein, Aristotle, and the Nature of Woman," *American Catholic Philosophical Quarterly* 72 [Supplement] (1998): 285–303; Maybelle Padua's *Contemplating Woman in the Philosophy of Edith Stein* (Manila, Philippines: Far Eastern University Press, 2007); and my "Edith Stein's Understanding of Woman," *International Philosophical Quarterly* 46, no. 2 (June 2006): 171–90.

them?"[36] There is such a tension precisely because we are not only gendered but also individualized. This individual form, although less explicitly discussed in her lectures on women and women's education, nonetheless significantly impacts her account of gender, our understanding of a feminine or masculine nature, and her vision of education and formation.

A Critical Qualification: Interpersonal Relations in Stein's Thought

Although individuality is a significant theme throughout Stein's works, it is worth noting that Stein also places a heavy emphasis on community.[37] She rarely talks about our individuality without also emphasizing our intersubjective and communal being.[38] Her first published comments on individuality appear in her dissertation on empathy, that is, her account of our understanding of others' experiences.[39] In her dissertation, she makes clear that our development occurs in significant part through empathy with others, in following along the experiences of others. We come to understand ourselves as beings to be encountered, beings with value, etc., through reiterated empathy, that is, through empathizing with

36. *Essays on Woman*, 57.

37. Stein ties together our individuality and our commonality as humans in her essays on women, among other places, saying, "Humanity is to be understood as one great individual; it is possible to understand salvation history only by this interpretation. Each person is a member of this whole, and the essential structure of the whole is shown in every member; but, at the same time, each has his own character as a member which he must develop if the whole is to attain development. The species *humanity* is realized perfectly only in the course of world history in which the great individual, humanity, becomes concrete. And the species *man* and *woman* are also fully realized only in the total course of historical development" (*Essays on Woman*, 189). See also *Finite and Eternal Being* VIII, §3.

38. Stein distinguishes empathic experiences—e.g., someone empathizing with *my* sadness—from communal experiences, experiences that properly belong to the community and which individuals experience not merely as *mine* or *yours*, but as *ours*.

39. Furthermore, Stein argues that empathy is more fundamental than constitution. See especially Sawicki's discussion of this point in *Body, Text and Science*.

another's empathy of us. Thus, imitation and empathy are central to Stein's account of how we come to know ourselves, recognize things as real, and constitute an objective world. The second essay that Stein published in Husserl's *Jahrbuch* is entitled "Individual and Community," and there she makes clear distinctions between individual and communal experiences and defends a substantive account of genuine communal experiences. The final chapter of *Finite and Eternal Being,* although entitled "Meaning and Foundation of Individual Being," ends with a discussion of our communion in Christ's mystical Body. Thus, while Stein puts a great emphasis on our distinct and unique individuality, she does not oppose this to our communal and relational life. My primary focus throughout this study will be on Stein's account of individuality, but it should be emphasized—and strongly emphasized—that, within Stein's broader account of the person, our communal life is as significant as our individual distinctiveness.[40]

A Set of Distinctions

Edith Stein posits individual form or an individual particularity, which is to do at least part of the work of making each of us into who we are.[41] There are, however, several problems surrounding our individuality, and in order to evaluate Stein's claims, we need to become clear about what problem or problems the individual form is supposed to address. There are at least four related, but distinct issues, including questions of *individuation, the paradigm for being an individual, identity,* and *uniqueness.*[42] I would like to look briefly at each of these.

40. There are a number of excellent studies highlighting Stein's account of community, including M. Regina Van den Berg's *Community in the Thought of Edith Stein* (Ph.D. diss., The Catholic University of America, 2000), and Antonio Calcagno's *The Philosophy of Edith Stein* (Pittsburgh, Pa.: Duquesne University Press, 2006).

41. A discussion of the following distinctions also appears as "Edith Stein and Individual Forms: A Few Distinctions regarding Being an Individual," *Yearbook of the Irish Philosophical Society* (2006): 49–69.

42. These distinctions, as well as the following discussion, owe much to

INDIVIDUAL FORM, RELEVANT DISTINCTIONS

Individuation

Individuation is the most traditional of the four issues, and Scotus's *haecceitas,* for example, was posited in order to address individuation. Individuation is simply the question of what is responsible for there being many individual instances of the same type. Initially, questions of individuation arose for those who were realists about universals. If one posits a real universal, that is, a form or structure repeated in more than one instance, then one has to posit some principle accounting for many individuals all of the same type or form. Both Plato and Aristotle understand the form as the principle of commonality and matter as the principle of individuation. Their respective accounts of form and matter differ; nonetheless, both posit matter as the primary principle responsible for there being many instances of the same form. Thomas Aquinas follows the Platonic and Aristotelian lead in declaring matter (for Thomas, designated matter) to be the principle of individuation. Matter—unlike accidents—is at the level of substance and thus could truly individuate and make a single instance of that substance, and yet it would in no way compromise the integrity of the common form. Scotus, although agreeing that a principle which could truly individuate the form and also be at the level of substance is needed, objects to matter as that principle. He thinks that positing matter as the principle of individuation denigrates what it means to be an individual. Thus he wants a principle of *this-ness* that is formal and not material and also at the level of substance and not of accident. Thus, he introduces *haecceitas,* which acts as a formal principle of individuation.

Although the most traditional of questions regarding individu-

Jorge Gracia's work. See especially *Introduction to the Problem of Individuation in the Early Middle Ages* (Washington, D.C.: The Catholic University of America Press, 1984), esp. chapter 1, and *Individuality: An Essay on the Foundations of Metaphysics* (Albany: State University of New York Press, 1988). See also Joseph Bobik's "Matter and Individuation," in *The Concept of Matter in Greek and Medieval Philosophy,* ed. Ernan McMullin (Notre Dame, Ind.: University of Notre Dame Press, 1965), 281–92.

ality, individuation is nonetheless not Stein's primary concern. She does discuss individual forms in the context of the problem of individuation,[43] but ultimately individual forms do not individuate the universal. Their primary role is not making something an individual or single instance of some type.

Paradigms for Being an Individual

Closely tied to the problem of individuation is that of the *paradigm for being an individual*. The principle of individuation is whatever element is responsible for making individuals singular instances of some type. We might ask, however, what it means to be an individual. What is the distinguishing mark of being *an* individual? Here the question is not about what makes an individual different from other individuals or even what principle "brings it about" that the thing is an individual, but simply what it means to be an individual at all. Is the paradigm for what it means to be an individual having some kind of internal unity? Is a heap then not an individual? Or ought our paradigm to be impredicability or non-repeatability? Traditionally, impredicability or non-repeatability has been seen as the mark of being an individual. Thus, both Plato and Aristotle understand matter to be the principle of individuation, for matter is that which makes a thing impredicable. Form *qua form* is always predicable; it is simply a structure that may be repeated in more than one instance. Matter (at least designated matter), in contrast, is this stuff here and cannot be repeated in more than one instance. Thus, if impredicability is the proper paradigm for being an individual, matter makes a plausible principle of individuation. If some kind of internal unity or indivisibility is necessary for being an individual, however, then it is not clear that matter makes a particularly good principle of individuation. Matter is always divisible, and if the paradigm for being an individual requires indivisibility or any kind of internal unity, then it is not clear that matter could provide this.

Stein is quite interested in the question of the nature of being

43. See *Finite and Eternal Being* VIII.

an individual and dedicates a significant part of her discussion in *Finite and Eternal Being* to precisely this issue. Although not her only concern in positing individual forms, Stein does think that the Thomistic claim that the mark of being an individual is impredicability is insufficient. She wants to raise questions about Thomas's very paradigm of what it means to be an individual. She will grant that matter makes a thing impredicable, but does it thereby make it into an individual? (I will return to Stein's critique of Thomas on this point in the next chapter.)

Identity

The question of individuation asks what is responsible for making an individual instance of some type. The question of the paradigm for being an individual asks what it means to be an individual instance. The question of identity asks not about being *an* individual but about being the *same* individual over time. Thomas Aquinas, although positing matter as the principle of individuation, claims that the substantial form is the principle of identity. It is the substantial form which is responsible for your dog being the same dog that was once a puppy and is now full grown. Once individuated, the form is that which maintains the being as the same throughout a myriad of changes (including changes in the matter).

Not only can one posit quite different principles for individuation and identity, it is not clear that problems of identity arise in all cases. Something that has no temporal span and undergoes no change—perhaps an instantaneous flash of light or a subatomic particle—would nonetheless be an individual instance of its type, and thus one could ask about the principle of individuation for that thing. It would, however, presumably have no identity over time, and thus questions of identity would be irrelevant. Thus, for there to be a need for a principle of identity, there must be something that has some kind of temporal lifespan and thus some kind of identity over that lifespan.[44]

44. For a very useful discussion of Stein's theory of identity, see Peter J. Schulz's "Toward the Subjectivity of the Human Person: Edith Stein's Contribu-

Uniqueness

Problems of uniqueness are likewise slightly different from the previous concerns. If individuation asks about what makes *this* an individual, the paradigm for being an individual asks what is meant by *this individual,* and identity asks how it is the *same* individual over time, questions of uniqueness ask how this individual can be different—and not merely numerically different—from others of its kind. Uniqueness is not a question in all cases. A factory may have a mold for some product, perhaps a chocolate wafer. As the cookie dough comes down the conveyor belt, the machine stamps its mold repeatedly, creating many individual instances of the wafer. Although each is an individual wafer, none of them is (at least in theory) different in any sense stronger than numerical. Each is the same size, with the same pattern on top, etc. Each is an individual, individuated in some way, and each maintains its identity over time. But none is unique. (By "unique" here, I do not mean impredicable or unrepeatable but, rather, *different* in some sense stronger than numerical.)

In contrast, human beings are not merely numerically different individuals, but different in some more significant way. For example, Aristotle posits that human beings all share a common human form with its human properties, such as our ability to laugh, yet it seems that every person's laughter is unique and quite different. Our laughs do not sound like a factory product, but each has its own timbre, overtones, depths from which is comes, etc. We can then ask why and how our commonality has such unique and differing instantiations.

Most responses to the question of individuation do not directly address the question of uniqueness. That which makes something a numerically individual instance need not also make that thing unique and different. Matter, for example, might be the principle

tion to the Theory of Identity," *American Catholic Philosophical Quarterly* 82, no. 1 (Winter 2008): 161–76.

of individuation, but it is not clear that it is thereby a principle of uniqueness. Each of the chocolate wafers coming out of the factory mold is an individual—and perhaps it is so because of its designated matter—but each is not therefore unique and different from the others. It seems, however, in contrast, that all human beings are, in fact, quite unique. We may all laugh, run, and climb trees, but each of us does so differently. Thus, at least for human beings, we need a principle accounting for our being unique and not simply our being individual.

Stein's primary concern in positing individual forms is not individuation (as in the case of Scotus's *haecceitas*), the paradigm for being an individual, or identity but, rather, uniqueness. I will qualify this claim slightly in the following chapters, but nonetheless—in general terms—the primary question leading her to posit individual forms is not the traditional question of individuation but a slightly more modern concern for uniqueness. She wants to give an account of how there can be many instances of the same type which differ not only numerically but also qualitatively.

Weaker and Stronger Types of Uniqueness

A further distinction, however, needs to be made between two different senses of *uniqueness*. Something may be unique in the sense that it is (a) of the same type but different (in some way more than numerical) from other beings of that type, or (b) of the same type but unrepeatably different (in some way more than numerical) from any other being of that type. Given the first sense of uniqueness, all that is required for *being unique* is that the individual has (or is) some qualitative variation on the universal feature. Thus, my great-aunt's laugh would be unique if it differed in texture or tone from my cousin's and mother's. The requirements for uniqueness here are not extremely high. All that is required is some principle accounting for qualitative differences in our common features, but we might, at least in theory, be able to find a number of people who share a quite similar and even the same texture of laugh. In contrast, the second stronger type of uniqueness (unrepeatably different) requires something more. Not only would my great-aunt's laugh need to differ in fact from a number of other people's laugh, it would also need to differ in principle from anyone else's laugh. There would need to be some feature or element, which could not be repeated, responsible for the distinctiveness of her laughter.

This stronger sense of uniqueness should be distinguished from mere impredicability. Impredicability involves non-repeatability. That which is impredicable cannot be repeated. But impredicability does not require any difference more than numerical difference. In contrast, this stronger sense of uniqueness requires a more than numerical difference that is unrepeatable.

     ~

There are thus at least five distinct questions: (1) What is the principle of individuation, i.e., the principle responsible for more than one instance of some common type? (2) What is the paradigm for being an individual, i.e., what is the mark of being an individual instance? (3) What is the principle of identity, i.e., what makes this individual the same individual through change and over time? (4) If the instances are unique, i.e., differ in any more than a numerical way, what accounts for these differences? (5) If the instances are unrepeatably unique, i.e., differ unrepeatably in any more than a numerical way, what accounts for these differences?

Individual Forms in Relation to the Various Questions

Of these problems I am most concerned with the first, second, and fourth, the problems of individuation, the paradigm for being an individual, and the weaker sense of uniqueness, all of which will need to be addressed in order to appreciate Stein's claims regarding individual forms. Stein's individual forms, however, play a role primarily in the last problem. Individual forms function primarily as a principle of the weaker kind of uniqueness.

Uniqueness in the weaker sense—that is, the differences among human beings, for example—has often been accounted for by an appeal to accidents. Thus, Thomas claims, for example, that we are at the level of substantial form identical in structure, but differ in terms of our accidents. All of us can laugh insofar as we are human beings, but the particular quality, timbre, etc. of our individual laughs is due (at least in part) to various accidental features. Thomas thus accounts for our individuation in terms of our matter, i.e., something at the level of substance and thus capable of individuating the substantial form, and our identity over time in terms of our substantial form. Our uniqueness in the weaker sense of difference, however, is not accounted for by something at the level of substance but, rather, by our accidents.[45] It is precisely this point to which Stein wants to object. Our uniqueness, she thinks, is not simply a feature of our various accidents or collection of accidents. It is, instead, at the level of substance. We are individual and unique (but not unrepeatably unique) because we each have a distinct, content-rich individual form that functions in some significant sense on the level of our substance and not simply our accidents. (This claim will be more fully developed in chapter 5.)

Individual forms, on Stein's account, are not the only elements responsible for our uniqueness, even in the weaker sense. Further, they do not function as principles of uniqueness in the stronger sense. Any form, by its very nature as a form (as a structure and principle of order and intelligibility),[46] cannot be a principle of strong uniqueness. The strong sense of uniqueness requires unrepeatability, and form by its nature is always repeatable. It is precisely because it is repeatable that it is also, to some degree, knowable. A Creator, in the Creator's great goodness, might choose not to repeat any qualitatively unique individual, but this would merely give us a situation where, in fact, all individuals of that type happen to be different. But, if the individual is qualitatively unique in virtue of a form, then it is at least possible, in principle, that that

45. See chapter 8 for a qualification of this claim.
46. Forms in both Husserl's and Thomas Aquinas's work are principles of intelligible structure. For Thomas, the substantial form is also an interior principle of growth and formation. For the moment, I am interested in form as a principle of intelligibility. Stein's distinctions, however, regarding the differing senses and types of form will be discussed in the following chapters.

form could be repeated. Thus, whatever accounts for any unrepeatable uniqueness (if present) must be a non-formal element.

Husserl accounts for unrepeatable uniqueness by pointing to the life stream and active choices of the individual—not some formal component—that makes each entity unique in the stronger sense.[47] Like Husserl, Stein does not want to account for the stronger sense of uniqueness through an individual form; individual forms are not the principle of unrepeatable uniqueness.[48] They do, however, in Stein's account *contribute* to our unrepeatable uniqueness by providing a priori conditions for our distinctive development. Because individual forms function as at least part of our principle of the weaker kind of uniqueness, they thereby set the conditions for a truly distinctive life stream (which only becomes unrepeatably unique in being lived).

Stein understands individual forms as laying out the a priori conditions or possibilities for our distinctive development, and we can only develop the possibilities sketched out within our individual form.[49] Nonetheless, these possibilities must be developed, and the actual development is what makes each of us truly unique in

47. See "Personales Ich, personale Individualität," in *Zur Phänomenologie der Intersubjektivität: Texte aus dem Nachlass Zweiter Teil: 1921–1928*, Husserliana 14 (The Hague: Martinus Nijhoff, 1973), as well as *Ideas II*, trans. Richard Rojcewicz and André Schuwer (Boston: Kluwer, 1989), esp. chapter 3, and "Natural Scientific Psychology, Human Sciences, and Metaphysics," trans. Paul Crowe, in *Issues in Husserl's Ideas II*, ed. Thomas Nenon and Lester Embree (Boston: Kluwer, 1996): 8–13. Husserl does speak of *individual forms* occasionally and claims that each person has a distinctive *Styl*. I am grateful to Tony Calcagno for pointing out this element in Husserl's thought.

48. I should qualify this claim slightly. Occasionally Stein does speak of the "unrepeatable character" (*"unwiederholbaren Eigenart,"* EeS 462/ESG 424/FEB 506), referring to the individual form. But a more comprehensive study of the text reveals that, although individual forms play a role in our uniqueness, they are not the primary element responsible for our unrepeatability.

49. She says, "Finally we conclude that the individual human being, even if he has reached *his* fullness (that is, in glory because there is before that no perfection for us), does not actualize *everything* that is marked out in the pure form of 'human being,' rather only that that is determined in *his* individual form" (EeS 213/ESG 199/FEB 226).

the sense of unrepeatable.[50] The individual form provides the possibilities for unique (in the weaker sense) development, whereas the development itself is what makes each person unique (in the stronger sense). The second part of her response allows Stein to say that uniqueness is the "product" of many factors. She claims that we differ from each other because our race, clan, generation, family, and material circumstances differ; likewise, we carry the stamp of past experiences and decisions, and our personal histories help to create our unrepeatable uniqueness.[51] The individual form, thus, does not ultimately make each person unrepeatably unique; it does, however, provide the distinctive possibilities according to which each finite personal being can develop in her own unique way.

50. See, for example, *Finite and Eternal Being* III, §9.
51. See, for example, EeS 458/ESG 419/FEB 501 and *Finite and Eternal Being* VII, §9, 4.

Two ⟿ REASONS FOR AFFIRMING INDIVIDUAL FORMS

Stein posits an individual form, which is distinct from the species-form, for each human being, and she understands this individual form as having some significant role in making individual (finite) persons[1] unique (although not in the stronger sense of unrepeatably unique). Stein does not claim that non-human corporeal entities each have an individual form.[2] She leaves this an open question, but she makes clear her commitment to individual forms for each human being (and each angelic being)—that is, finite personal beings each have a unique individual form.[3]

Full appreciation of Stein's account of individual forms and their role in our individuality requires investigation of her metaphysical claims regarding essence and being; nonetheless, several factors motivating Stein's claims regarding individuality can be considered independently. I would like to look at five of these factors, in varying degrees of thoroughness, in this chapter: (a) the intelligibility of individuals and individual personalities, (b) the

1. "Person" is used as a technical term in Stein's earlier phenomenological writings. I am not claiming here that she imports into her later writings either the technical sense of *person* or the specific account of the relation of the personal realm and individuality.

2. See n. 1 of the introduction.

3. In her 1932 essay *Der Aufbau der menschlichen Person* (Freiburg: Herder, 2004), Stein says: "First, this deeper analysis could demonstrate convincingly that here lies an essential limit between the animal and the human: that individuality comes to a new meaning with human beings that is not found in any sub-human creature" (48–49). I am grateful to Mette Lebech for pointing me to this passage in her "Edith Stein's Philosophy of Education in *The Structure of the Human Person*," *REA: Religion, Education and the Arts* 5 (2005): 63.

challenge of evolutionary theory to classic accounts of a common human nature and the need to loosen the notion of the species-form, (c) theological concerns about the value of individuality in God's eyes, (d) the pattern of development in spiritual formation, and (e) dissatisfaction with Thomas's claim that matter is the principle of individuation. Stein nowhere makes a list of the key reasons for accepting individual forms, and I have tried to discern, as best I can from what she does say, her primary intellectual motivations for affirming such forms.[4] It is not clear that all of those motivations are equally important, but Stein discusses each of them at different points and, taken as a whole, they offer a plausible case for affirming individual forms.

Intelligibility of Individual Distinctiveness

In 1933, not long after losing her post at a teaching institute in Münster due to rising anti-Semitism, Stein began working on an autobiography. She wrote it for two primary purposes: as a tribute to her mother, and as a challenge to the caricatures used in anti-Semitic propaganda.[5] In the process of pursuing those goals, Stein offers vivid descriptions of herself and many of her friends and acquaintances. Through those descriptions we can see what she has in mind when claiming that each person has a personal core.[6] She says, for example, of Max Scheler:

One's first impression of Scheler was fascination. In no other person have I ever encountered the "phenomenon of genius" as clearly. The light of the more exalted world shone from his large blue eyes.[7]

4. Variations on a few of these motivations appear in my "What Makes You You?: Edith Stein on Individual Form," in *Contemplating Edith Stein,* ed. Joyce Berkman (Notre Dame, Ind.: University of Notre Dame Press, 2006), 283–300.

5. See the foreword to *Life,* especially 23–24.

6. Stein argues in *Finite and Eternal Being* that the core of the person is not directly knowable by any but God. The traits growing out of this core might be, but the core itself is not.

7. *Life,* 259.

Of Husserl, she writes:

Neither striking nor overwhelming, his external appearance was rather of an elegant professorial type. His height was average; his bearing, dignified; his head, handsome and impressive. His speech at once betrayed his Austrian birth: he came from Moravia and had studied in Vienna. His serene amiability also had something of old Vienna about it.[8]

One can feel the contrast between the two thinkers and imagine how each would respond to a variety of situations. We can envision Scheler responding quickly to a question, filled with a transcendent vivacity, whereas Husserl would pause before beginning.

Similarly, characters in literature have a unity, and brief descriptions can tell us much about how that character will behave and develop throughout the book.[9] We often feel betrayed when an author has a character perform some action that does not fit with the personality and individual structure of that character. There are fictional characters which, Stein claims, are true, which have a "poetic truth,"[10] and those which are false. The "*genuine* poetic figures" differ from those which are "merely thought up,"[11] and we recognize the genuineness of the former by seeing how they remain "within the limits of the possibilities of the [individual] essence."[12]

Our individual personalities are not simply random or haphazard accumulations of various human traits, but have a more or less consistent internal unity and intelligibility. Although people's choices can certainly surprise us, even the choices of those very

---

8. Ibid., 249.

9. David Burrell rightly, I think, states: "We can readily discriminate great literature from trite or formulaic imitations by its singular capacity to render the individual present to us." *Knowing the Unknowable God* (Notre Dame, Ind.: University of Notre Dame Press, 1992), 21.

10. See *Finite and Eternal Being* IV, §3, 2, and *On the Problem of Empathy*, 112. See also Terrence Wright's beautiful "Artistic Truth and the True Self in Edith Stein," *American Catholic Philosophical Quarterly* 82, no. 1 (Winter 2008): 127–42.

11. EeS 152/ESG 143/FEB 158.

12. EeS 155/ESG 146/FEB 162.

close to us, in most cases those choices retain a high level of predictability. We can say, with great confidence, "Anthony will not like that," or "You hit it on the head with that gift for Zephyr. He'll love it!" Such statements are guesswork. Anthony and Zephyr have not yet responded; nevertheless, our guesses are often quite good. We can have intelligible conversations about what they would do or say, and these conversations are not just nonsense. If this is so, then there seems to be some individual structure marking certain types of behavior as fitting that individual and other types not.

Stein repeatedly uses Socrates as one of her examples, and she describes his actions as growing out of a single root or personal core. This is certainly not to deny that one can fail to be oneself or deviate to some degree from one's individual structure. But it does affirm that we do, in fact, try to make sense of people's actions, not simply in terms of what fits with human behavior in general, but what marks the core of *this* individual. We do regularly make judgments about whether Elena or Melia is developing in ways that fit each of them as individuals. And these judgments are not, Stein argues, baseless. It is precisely in relation to a personal core or individual form that we can make such judgments. (In affirming our ability to do so, Stein is not arguing that we can ever have exhaustive knowledge of another's core, but partial knowledge is possible.) The reality of our intelligibility—not simply qua human being but qua individual—and our related ability to make judgments about the appropriateness of acts for both fictional and real individuals point to an intelligible structure that is not simply human, but individual and distinctive. Human beings may be rational and have the ability to laugh, but each individual's rationality is quick and incisive, with a particular eye for the ironic, or broad, integrative, and many-layered, etc. So also, the ability to laugh may be common to all human beings, but the laughter that bubbles out of a great depth and fills a whole room distinguishes one person, whereas another may laugh with great lightness and sweetness. These individual variations on the common human traits are not simply variations, but intelligible and, more and less, articulable traits.

Thus, in part, Stein posits individual forms in order to account for this great intelligibility. If form is the principle of structure and intelligibility and we are, as it clearly seems, intelligible *as individuals* and not simply as members of our species, then there must be some kind of individual formal structure.

Evolution

Stein wants to make sense of our intelligibility as individuals and not merely as human beings.[13] She also wants to retain some version of the Aristotelian-Thomistic species-form, but one which can appreciate the developments in the contemporary sciences. It is not unimportant that Stein's earliest academic work was in psychology. Throughout her writings, Stein maintains an interest in the relation between philosophy, especially phenomenology, and the various sciences. Near the opening of chapter 5 of *Der Aufbau der menschlichen Person (The Structure of the Human Person)*, a chapter entitled "The Problem of the Origin of Species [*Arten*]—Genus, Species [*Species*], Individual," Stein writes:

Because that [i.e., grounding scientific knowledge], however, is the task of philosophy, it cannot be based on the conclusions of the positive sciences; it cannot, as is often thought, be a reservoir in which all individual knowledge is gathered in order to mark out a worldview corresponding to the "condition of science." On the other hand, it cannot overlook the present condition of science. It cannot take the physics of St. Thomas for physics or the psychology of Aristotle for psychology.[14]

Philosophy is not a natural science; its questions and methods differ from those of the natural sciences, and the philosophical perspective is broader than that of the natural scientists. Those in other disciplines begin by assuming certain definitions and funda-

---

13. A variant of this section was presented as a paper, "Edith Stein's Response to the Darwinian Challenge," at the Boston College Lonergan Workshop, June 19, 2007.
14. *Der Aufbau*, 58.

mental concepts, and they approach experience from a limited perspective. What they discover is valuable, but philosophers ought to recognize the limitations inherent in other methods and not assume the methodological perspective of the sciences.[15]

Despite the fact that the philosophical task is both different from and more foundational than the tasks of the natural sciences, philosophers must also be aware of the "present condition of the sciences." We cannot do philosophy in utter ignorance of developments and discoveries in the natural sciences, and certainly among these is the work of Charles Darwin. There has not, however, been an easy relationship between Darwinian evolutionary theory and at least certain traditional philosophical positions, chief among them Thomism. There are a number of reasons for this, including Darwin's materialist tendencies,[16] the emphasis on the purposelessness of the evolutionary mechanism and the chance involved in mutations,[17] and, most significantly, the claim that species are not static.

Although Darwin speaks of species and recognizes our ability to distinguish different groupings, he does not think that these species are in any sense permanent or immutable. A species is constantly undergoing changes through the mutations in and adaptations of individuals. Such changes, in any quite short period of

15. Importantly, Stein claims that the empirical sciences—among them, the study of evolution—look at facts, at what is the case, but they cannot provide philosophical insight into necessity and possibility. See *Der Aufbau*, 60. Presumably, whatever occurs is possible, but it need not be necessary. In contrast, philosophy involves the study of possibility and necessity.

16. Stephen Jay Gould argues that at least part of Darwin's reason for delaying publication of both *On the Origin of Species* and *The Descent of Man* had to do with his concerns about the reception of his materialist leanings. See "Darwin's Delay," in *Ever Since Darwin: Reflections in Natural History* (New York: W. W. Norton, 1977), 21–27.

17. John F. Haught makes this point particularly clearly in *Science & Religion: From Conflict to Conversation* (New York: Paulist Press, 1995), esp. 48–52. For an extremely helpful discussion of the meanings of "random" and "purposeless," see Patrick H. Byrne's "Evolution, Randomness, and Divine Purpose: A Reply to Cardinal Schönborn," *Theological Studies* 67 (2006): 653–65.

time, might be relatively minor; from a long-term point of view, we can see in these changes lines of descent connecting beings we might once have thought quite different. It is true that silver-backed gorillas are a different species from humans, but, Darwin argues, we have a common lineage. If we trace it back far enough, we can find a common ancestor as well as all the little steps that led us in such different directions. Similarly, we can understand *homo erectus* and *homo sapiens* as differing species, but there is a continuum between the two and thus only differences coming in subtle and slow degrees.[18]

In contrast, for Aristotle, although particular individuals have an origin, the species do not. The form or species is permanent, unchangeable, and each species differs in kind from all others. For a classic Thomist, the species-form is an idea in the mind of God, and each individual member of some species has an identical nature, whether that entity lives now in the twenty-first century or thousands upon thousands of years ago. If one is a human being, one's structure participates in the idea in the Mind of God and is identical in kind with all other members of the species-group. On this account, there does not seem to be any room for intermediate types or transitions from one species to another. Thus the classic Thomistic static account of form seems to be precisely what is put in question by Darwin. Even the title—*On the Origin of Species*—is a challenge to a Thomist.

18. Darwin says in *The Descent of Man,* for example, "My object in this chapter [chapter 3] is to shew that there is no fundamental difference between man and the higher mammals in their mental faculties" (*The Origin of Species by Means of Natural Selection or the Preservation of Favored Races in the Struggle for Life and The Descent of Man and Selection in Relation to Sex* [New York: The Modern Library, n.d.], 446). Darwin summarizes his claim most clearly near the end of chapter 4; he says: "Nevertheless the difference in mind between men and the higher animals, great as it is, is certainly one of degree and not of kind. The senses and intuitions, the various emotions and faculties, such as love, memory, attention, curiosity, imitation, reason, &c., of which man boasts, may be found in an incipient, or even sometimes in a well-developed condition, in the lower animals" (494–95). Benjamin Farrington collects a number of these quotations in his chapter on *The Descent of Man* in *What Darwin Really Said* (New York: Schocken Books, 1966), esp. 74–77.

Although Stein is not uninterested in the first two points of tension between Thomism and evolutionary theory,[19] her primary efforts are directed toward the final challenge: the question of the static nature of the species-form. Stein's way of addressing this challenge employs a distinctive blend of phenomenological and broadly Thomistic claims. She in interested, first, in becoming clearer about what is meant by "species" and, second, loosening the Thomistic account of the structure of the inner form. She loosens the Thomistic account in two ways: first, by emphasizing the history of designated matter and, second, by articulating an understanding of species-form with greater flexibility and leeway than is traditionally attributed to it. Stein's individual forms are tied primarily to the second aspect of her modification of the classic account of form. Although individual forms are most relevant to this final point, I would like, nonetheless, to sketch out several parts of Stein's evaluation of and response to Darwin.

Meaning of "Species"

Stein—in classic phenomenological fashion—begins by pointing to a fact of our experience: we do, in fact, recognize and distinguish many differing species.[20] We categorize entities into species-groupings, and we can describe the traits, behaviors, developmental patterns, etc. of the various species. There are thus "relatively stable forms," which do not, in any simple way, "pass from one to the other."[21] Chipmunks do not give birth to salamanders, or whales to naked mole rats. The traditional explanation for this stability has

19. See especially her comments in *Der Aufbau* V, II, §10. Stein is not a materialist, and thus the points where she agrees with Darwin will be limited. Similarly, Stein does not think that the development of biological species occurs by chance, at least from an ultimate perspective.

20. She writes: "That things are and that there is a qualitative manifold of things are the first facts of experience from which all knowledge opens up" (*Der Aufbau,* 61).

21. She says, "The question assumes that there are species, that is, a series of relatively stable forms that at present do not objectively pass over from one to the other. The philosopher attempts to determine what is to be understood by these species" (*Der Aufbau,* 60).

been that the species lines are permanent and that little chipmunks have always descended from other chipmunks. Stein refers to this theory as the "descendent theory" *(Deszendenztheorie).* But this explanation is not, Stein points out, the only explanation for our experience; the manifold nature of our experience with its richness of differing species need not be accounted for by a permanence of members of each species-type or by the isolation of each species line. She finds it quite intelligible that members of differing species could have originated from each other and from some common original source. But from this, it need not follow that *species,* in all senses of the term, have an origin.

We can distinguish at least three different meanings of the term "species." First, "species" may refer simply to a grouping of beings. All individuals are part of a common species if they can reproduce and have viable offspring. Thus, Arabian horses and Tennessee Walkers are both breeds of the species horse because they can reproduce and have offspring capable of further reproduction, whereas mules—that is, offspring of donkeys crossed with horses—are usually sterile. And thus donkeys and horses are differing biological species. This understanding of the term "species" is our most common use of the term and is likely what Darwin had in mind in the title of his famous work.

We can contrast this biological meaning of "species" with a second metaphysical meaning: the Thomistic "species" or "species-form." "Species" in this sense refers not to a number of individuals categorized together because of their reproductive potential, but to an inner form, the principle of growth and development. The species-form is not first an external grouping but an individual inner principle of formation.

Thomas Aquinas is commonly understood to claim both (a) that each individual entity is a unity of species-form, in this sense, and matter, and (b) that our most basic formal structure will line up with species in the first sense. It is in virtue of the structure of the inner species-form that each entity is appropriately recognized to be a member of its biological species grouping.

Both of these senses of "species" can be distinguished from a third, more phenomenological understanding. "Species," for the phenomenologist, may refer to permanent eidetic and ideal structures. Husserl contrasts essences or species with facts. Facts are contingent, what happens to be the case. The essence, species, or form, in contrast, refers to what *must* be the case. Whether there is, in fact, a triangle in some room, triangles of necessity must have three interior angles adding up to 180 degrees. Thus, "species" here refers to essential and necessary structures. In this sense, "living thing," "four-legged," "dog," and "Labrador retriever" may all be distinct *species*.

Stein's simple response to Darwin is that, although species in the first sense may have an origin, species in the third sense—that is, as ideal structures, unities, and relations—do not, and cannot, have a material origin. Particular material conditions may present more fitting conditions for the expression of certain species in contrast to others, but the species themselves, as the conditions for the possibility of any beings at all, do not have an origin.[22] In the concluding section of chapter 5 of *Der Aufbau*, Stein says:

The being of a qualitative manifold is not understandable without a manifold of formal principles. The relationship of these formal principles to one another and, all the more so, the temporal order of the origin of the created world exist on this ontological foundation of various possibilities.[23]

Stein understands the *species* first and primarily as permanent essential possibilities. She further claims that there is a layered realm of forms with greater and lesser generality. For example, "color" and "shape" are more general species than "red" or "square." The more general forms may make possible or justify certain possibilities—e.g., squareness and triangularity are both possibilities for "shape," whereas "sweet-toned" is not—but these more specific pos-

22. See particularly Stein's discussion in chapters 2 and 3 of *Finite and Eternal Being* for an account of the relation of the actual to the essential.
23. *Der Aufbau*, 73.

sibilities may, or may not, appear in some individual shape. Thus, the more general species can present possibilities but may not require any one of them.[24] Both the more general and the more specific forms are, however, ontologically permanent ideal structures, and these forms with the various possibilities laid out in them are the foundation for the differing regions of being in the real world. Thus, Stein distinguishes the permanence of phenomenological species from the relative impermanence of biological species, and she grounds the intelligibility of the latter in the former.

The Historical Character of Designated Matter

This has not yet, however, addressed the challenge evolutionary theory presents to the classic Thomistic account of form. Thomas understands individual corporeal beings as a unity of two principles: *form* and *matter*.[25] The form is the primary internal principle of growth and development for each entity; forms are qualitatively distinct and structurally (but not numerically) identical, except in terms of their accidents, among all members of the species. Our different matter individuates the form, and our matter is significant for whether we are male or female, for which among the human capacities are easier to develop, and for whether full human formation is, by any natural means, possible. But matter most properly is the potency to be formed, whereas form is the principle of formation and structure. Neither form nor matter exists independently. Form (at least of corporeal things in this life) cannot exist without something which it informs; matter as potency for formation does not exist independent of form.[26] Our most significant formal component is the species-form, i.e., that in virtue of which we are members of our biological species.

24. Stein uses the example of a rose. The final color of a rose is not a certain shade of red because it is a rose. The particular shade of red is a possibility of the essence rose, but that red is not required by the fact that it is a rose. See *Der Aufbau* V, II, §7.

25. Sometimes it is said that Thomas understands us as a unity of three principles: form, matter (which together make the essence), and act of existence.

26. Thus, the Thomistic and phenomenological accounts agree that manifold differing types of entities must be due to differing forms, not differing matter.

Stein wants to preserve this general account, and in particular the general distinction between *form* and *matter,* while also loosening up the Thomistic account of form. She does so in at least two ways. The first is not obviously at odds with Thomas's explicit positions, although the second is.

Stein's first move in loosening up Thomistic forms is to emphasize the previous formations involved in our designated matter. Thomas understands matter as the principle of individuation of the form. The form provides the structural component and *qua structure* is always repeatable. Matter is what is this, here, now; it is unrepeatable and makes the form into an impredicable individual entity. Pure matter does not and cannot exist independent of formation. Matter as the principle of individuation for Thomas is not, however, pure matter but, rather, designated matter, i.e., matter with quantitative dimensions.[27]

Stein takes the claim that *designated matter,* in contrast to pure matter, is the principle of individuation to have significance for the issue of evolution. Designated matter—matter that is this, here, and now—came to be this, here, and now. It has a history and has been involved in previous formations. As such, it carries the imprint of those previous formations. Thus, the matter involved in the individuation of the form need not be utterly formless. It would have to be capable of being further formed in ways fit to the requirements of the form involved, but it need not be utterly formless. She says: "It is wholly thinkable that a material change becomes the condition for the taking up of a new form and thereby the new individual as exemplar of a new species."[28] Presumably, by this, she has in mind the way in which a certain cell arrangement or a mutation in that arrangement may provide the condition for a new structural type, or perhaps the way in which the structure of *homo erectus* could provide conditions useful for the arrival of *homo sapiens,* etc.

Thus, Stein thinks that each individual is a unity of a number

27. See Stein's summary of Thomas on individuation in chapter 8 of *Finite and Eternal Being.*
28. *Der Aufbau* 67.

of formal components: first, those involved in its primary principle of development and, second, those relevant to the history of the material involved. These two sets of formal components should be distinguished according to higher and lower in the thing,[29] and, Stein affirms, there would be a single substantial form. Thus, Stein's first way of fitting an evolutionary account of the origin of species to Thomism is to emphasize the history of the designated matter involved in individuals and to argue for a multitude of formal elements within each individual, even if she also insists on a principle form guiding development and formation and providing a center of identity.

Greater Flexibility within the Species-form

Although Stein's emphasis on the history of our matter may help address the evolutionary challenge, it does not yet address the key issue. For Thomas, the species-form—that is, the structural element making us members of our biological species—provides the final determination of form. The *species* as biological category is structurally identical with the fundamental lawfulness of our inner form. There does not appear to be much room here for intermediate evolutionary stages or gradual change from one species to another.

Although Stein does not explicitly criticize Thomas on this point in *Der Aufbau,* she clearly recognizes the problems that the classic position presents, and she articulates, in contrast, an account of form with flexibility and leeway. She says, for example:

The type of appearance and the inner form do not coincide. They stand indeed in an internal relationship in which nothing in the appearance type can come to be that is not delimited in the form as *possible.* But not everything delimited in the form is *necessary;* the form allows leeway [literally, "rooms to play"].[30]

29. See *Der Aufbau* V, II, §5. By *higher* and *lower* here Stein is not referring to a form's place on the Great Chain of Being but to which form is the dominant principle of growth and development providing an internal unity to the entity as a whole (the *higher form*) in contrast to those subsumed under the overarching forming power (the *lower forms*).

30. *Der Aufbau,* 68. This passage, however, is not conclusive since there are a number of things that "room to play" could mean.

In another passage, she contrasts two possible positions, including (a) the Thomistic vision of individuals as structurally identical and common exemplars of the category of biological species, and (b) the non-Thomistic claim that each individual is a qualitatively unique presentation of the biological species and thus an individual's fundamental structure may differ from other members of its biological species. The latter position is, Stein notes, Thomas's position regarding the angels.[31]

Although Stein does not explicitly endorse the second of these positions in this section of *Der Aufbau,* she undeniably does so in *Finite and Eternal Being.*[32] She says—using quite strong language—that she does not think that, for human beings at least, the final designation of form is the species-form but, rather, an individual form that differs in content for each and every human being.[33] The most basic formal structure of our inner form, according to Stein, is not our species-form, but our individual form. Individual forms, however, are not opposed to the species-form but, rather, specifications of the more general form. If, for example, the ability to laugh is part of the human form, the particular type of laugh—deep rolling guffaws, or joyous light snickers—is marked out in the individual form. The human form sets out a general set of human potencies; our particular individual forms specify these potencies and reveal variations within that set of potencies.

With the introduction of a more flexible species-form and specifications of those forms in our individual forms, Stein can affirm that we are all members of a common species and are so in vir-

31. She cites *Summa theologica* I, q. 50, and *De veritate,* q. 8/9.

32. Stein does not make evolution a major theme in *Finite and Eternal Being,* and, as far as I can tell, Darwin is not mentioned by name. The terms "evolution" and "evolving," however, show up quite regularly in the published English translation of *Finite and Eternal Being.* This is misleading. Generally, they are used to translate the terms *"Entwicklung"* or *"entwickeln,"* and not to address any scientific theory. Nonetheless, a number of Stein's comments are significant and probably refer to Darwin's theory of evolution. See especially *Finite and Eternal Being* IV, §4, 13, and VIII, §2, 5, §2, 9, and §3, 2.

33. Kurt Reinhardt translates Stein's comments about Thomas's position: "I pointed out before that I find it impossible to accept this point of view" (FEB 478). For a different translation, see my version in chapter 1.

tue of a common species-form, but she has also accounted for the structural differences among members of the species. We are not, in our most basic formal structure, identical (even if we are so in our general formal structure), and there can thus be quite a bit of structural variation among members of the same species. With the introduction of this structural variation, Stein has also opened the door for variations that may lead to transitions from one biological species to another.

I should emphasize that Stein is not convinced that what is properly meant by "individual form" will be present in non-personal beings in the way in which it is present in persons (both human and angelic). It might be fair to summarize Stein's claim in *Finite and Eternal Being* by saying that each finite person has a distinct individual form. Because of our individual forms, the species must be understood in a somewhat looser manner than the traditional Thomistic account. Non-personal individuals may not have an individual form per se, but their species-form should likewise be understood to have more variability and leeway than the classic account of form.

Attractiveness of Darwin

Darwin is committed to a multiplication of species and the gradual transition of one species into another; he understands the differences between species to be a matter of degree and not kind. Stein finds these descriptions plausible, although she would claim that they are only relevant to species in the biological sense and not in all other senses. Species as ideal structures do not evolve; as ideal structures, they do differ in kind and not merely degree. But individuals may come to exemplify these species through a biologically evolutionary process.

Not only does Stein think Darwinian evolution quite plausible, she also finds it philosophically attractive because of the way in which it, first, emphasizes the import of each individual, and, second, emphasizes the interdependence and unity of all organic life. Stein claims that individuals are the site not only for the propagation and preservation of the species, but also its transformation, and she thinks that this role of transformation emphasizes the import of each individual in a way that the classic Thomistic position does not. Each individual, on the classic model, is a greater or lesser actualization of the form. There is a single structure which counts as the human form, and various individuals reveal that to a greater or lesser extent. On Stein's account, in contrast, each individual reveals a distinctive face and specification of a more general form. She says:

> Each individual has, however, also a heightening significant *for* the whole of the species. The individual entities *embody* the species and *preserve* it through procreation; in the individuals, the species also experiences, moreover, a gradual *reshaping.* It separates into *varieties* [*Spielarten*], in which it can be seen more meaningfully that the material structures are, from the standpoint of the distinctiveness of species, not merely *accidental,* more or less full actualizations that according to the favor or disfavor of external conditions (that is also the case); they express the distinctiveness of the species in several ways and directions and may therefore be regarded as *end structures* that are intentionally pre-designed in and with the particular species.[34]

There can thus be different possible expressions of a species. Such expressions are structurally different, yet nonetheless all are properly part of a common species.

Stein does not understand this transformation and evolution as an accident of our material condition, but a quite purposeful event. This evolution may appear non-purposive from a purely material point of view, but this does not in any way mean that it is truly non-purposive.

We are *qua individuals* exceedingly valuable. We are also, however, deeply tied to our species community and the community of all organic life. Stein writes in *Der Aufbau:*

> It is not, however, the only possibility that the living breath of God means the origin of a new life. Perhaps it is generally wrong to look at

---

34. The final phrases here follow Reinhardt's translation, since it is particularly clear and illuminating. EeS 456/ESG 418/FEB 499.

an organic structure in isolation, loosed from the process of generation in which it stands. Perhaps the living form, which is effective in the first organism of a particular species, is from the very beginning not to be grasped simply as the form of this one organism, but rather as the form of the whole species (understood as the totality of all individuals of the species); and the process of life, in which their existence is, as one, aimed from the very beginning, through the individual, and worked out up to the last, is perhaps that to which uniquely "the species strives." (Thus the undoubted humankind of the Holy Scriptures is comprehensible as the whole created in Adam.)[35]

Each new individual is a relatively independent and self-standing entity, but it is nonetheless deeply tied to the history in which it stands. She makes a similar point in *Finite and Eternal Being*:

Although each individual entity is an independent actual thing (πρώτη οὐσία or substance), we must still see the totality of all individual things standing in a relation of common descent as an actual whole with its own laws of life (certainly not as independent, because it is actual only *in* the individuals, and therefore it is not a *substance*). The individual thing is therefore a carrier of the distinctiveness of the species and its development.[36]

Stein does not deny that the *proto ousia* is the individual substance. But she also wants to emphasize that the individual carries in her and carries forward the history of the species and, thus, the members of the biological species compose a kind of whole, even if not the unity of a substance.

In summary, Stein thinks that, although species in the biological sense might evolve, species in the phenomenological sense do not. The meaning of *being human* does not change, even if there come to be instances of such human beings only through an evolutionary process. Further, within the intelligible structure of human being, for example, quite a bit of variation and differing specifications are possible, and thus there are many different and unique

35. *Der Aufbau*, 64.
36. EeS 457/ESG 418/FEB 499.

human individual forms. Finally, these differences, although tied to our material situation, are also the work of Providence. None of us, in all of our individuality and personality, Stein claims, are an accident of fate. Each of us has significance both as individuals revealing a new and distinctive face of our species and as members of a common biological history and species life.[37]

Theological Concerns

Individual forms account for our intelligibility as individuals, and they fit into Stein's modification of the Thomistic species-form in light of evolutionary theory. Stein likewise raises theological concerns in support of individual forms. Human beings, according to Stein's understanding of Christian doctrine, have immortal souls. Surely God would want a great variety of unique and distinctive human beings present before the throne. We live in hope of a future life, and our place in that life is not simply a generic human one, but an individual, personal one. If we were simply human in our structure and not also individual, then each of us would be a greater or lesser actualization of the human form. In contrast, Stein claims that each of us carries "our own unrepeatable mirror of God in his soul."[38] We are not merely numerically different examples of the human form but, rather, are each a distinct individual form. Stein describes the varieties of unique souls as a "garland" [Kranz] adding to the beauty and variety of creation.

Further, Stein does not think that our uniqueness is merely a contingency of our particular conditions. Each individual's uniqueness is not unrelated to her historical, social, and cultural conditions; as Stein puts it, "the individual soul blooms in the place prepared for it—made ready through the historical development of its

37. It should probably also be emphasized that Stein understands us as more than merely biological entities. Although there might be a biological foundation for both our human and individual development, neither can be reduced to our purely biological features and capacities.

38. EeS 473/ESG 433/FEB 517.

people, its narrower homeland, its family."[39] But these conditions do not merely lead to a greater or lesser development of the common human form and thus differences based in differing degrees and kinds of incompleteness but, rather, we are valuable in our structural uniqueness. Each of us "reproduces the divine image in a 'wholly personal way.'"[40] Each soul is a particular and unique mirror of God and reflects his glory in a unique way:

When, however, the earthly life ends and everything falls away that was temporary, then each soul knows itself "as it is known" [1 Cor 13:12], i.e., as it is before God: as what and according to which God has created it, wholly personally, and what it is in the order of nature and grace—and that which belongs to it essentially: the power of its free decisions.[41]

We are created "wholly personally," and she suggests that in each soul, God creates a unique dwelling place. We do not live simply to propagate the species, sending the human form on to another generation. She says, "God wanted to create in each human soul a 'proper' dwelling so that the fullness of divine love would find through the manifold of different varieties of soul a wider scope for its participation."[42] Thus, to be a member of the body of Christ is to have a unique place in it, and "already from nature none is identical with the others."[43]

Spiritual Development

Stein appended two essays to *Finite and Eternal Being:* one concerning Martin Heidegger's pre-1936 essays and the other entitled *Die Seelenburg,* "The Castle of the Soul."[44] The latter essay begins

---

39. EeS 464/ESG 425/FEB 508.   40. EeS 461/ESG 422/FEB 504.
41. EeS 462/ESG 423/FEB 505.   42. EeS 462/ESG 423/FEB 506.
43. EeS 481/ESG 440/FEB 526.

44. These were removed from the 1950 edition of *Finite and Eternal Being* but have since been published in volume 6 of the Edith Steins Werke, *Welt und Person: Beitrag zum christlichen Wahrheitsstreben* (Louvain: E. Nauwelaerts and Freiburg: Herder, 1962), 39–68 and 69–135. See also pages 445–525 in the critical edition of *Endliches und ewiges Sein* in the Edith Stein Gesamtausgabe.

with a presentation of Teresa of Avila's image of the soul as a castle with many rooms. In her exposition, Stein quotes extensively, although not exclusively, from Teresa's *The Interior Castle* and focuses on the seven "rooms," beginning with the outer wall of the castle (our relation to the external world), through the kinds of prayer that are the doors into progressively deeper rooms, until one finally reaches the innermost room, marriage with God.

We can see in chapter 7 of *Finite and Eternal Being* and in her appendix on Teresa's mystical thought a reminder of what Stein thinks is at stake in any metaphysical description: if it cannot account for all our experiences, including religious ones, and if it fails to take into account the richness of the interior life, then it will be inadequate.[45]

Stein describes human beings as having a "double life" in the sense that, like plants and animals, we take in matter and form it into ourselves, but we also have a spiritual life, which includes the capacity to be aware of ourselves and to take a stance in relation to ourselves as well as other things.[46] As spiritual, we are self-aware and free. We are not obligated to follow any particular desire or impulse, but choose (to a greater and lesser extent) who and how to become. We are not, however, simply spiritual beings but, rather, spiritual beings whose consciousness and freedom "climb out of" a depth, and we must come to know ourselves.

Stein distinguishes two types of realms we must come to understand: the external world or context in which we live, and the inner world.[47] The latter is not simply our stream of conscious experience, but "what is not immediately conscious out of which the conscious life climbs."[48] She provides a number of examples in-

45. She says, "Thus, we believe it is allowable, on the basis of interior self-consciousness and the conception gathered from that of the universal form of being-a-person, to accept the uniqueness of the interior of each human soul and with that of the whole person insofar as it is formed from the interior" (EeS 460/ ESG 422/FEB 504).

46. See, for example, EeS 458/ESG 419–20/FEB 501.

47. See *Finite and Eternal Being* VII, §3, 1 and 2.

48. EeS 337/ESG 311/FEB 365.

cluding experiences of struggling to understand some problem or situation. Some days it is hard "to get it." We have trouble understanding something and feel quite dumb. That "dumbness" is not directly perceived. I do not see it, nor am I immediately aware of it. I am immediately aware of trying to think through the problem and the frustration of failing, but I do not directly experience the dumbness in the way I might a rash or headache. Through my frustrated attempt to solve the problem, I ascribe to myself a trait that expresses itself in this experience but is understood to be more than this present experience.

Behaviorists (e.g., B. F. Skinner or John Watson) deny the existence of traits outside of the actions themselves. There might be the experience of frustration, but no underlying feature of my being that is called "dumbness." In contrast, Stein thinks that our experiences reveal a set of abilities and traits, some of which are permanent and some temporary. We have a cheerfulness or a tendency to despondency, a sharp judgment or a quick recognition of connections. These abilities and traits explain the predictability and intelligibility of at least much of our experience, and they make up the "dark depth" out of which consciousness works. Part of our development, including especially our spiritual development, is coming to understand these depths, that is, coming to know who we are.[49]

When Stein distinguishes the spirituality of human beings from that of angels, it is in precisely this element of having a soul with traits which need to be discovered that she finds the difference.[50] For angels there are no hidden depths out of which their spirituality arises and with which they must acquaint themselves. Non-human animals, on the other hand, lack freedom over their souls and thus the abilities to search out, know themselves, and take a position in regard to both themselves and the exterior world. Animals are subject to instinct; human beings are not.[51] What is

---

49. See, for example, *Finite and Eternal Being* VII, §3, 2 and 4, VII, §9, 2, and VIII, §2, 10.

50. See EeS 342–43/ESG 316/FEB 371.

51. See *Finite and Eternal Being* VII, §8.

called our spiritual life begins when one has this personal forming power, that is, when the I is awake and conscious of itself.[52] But
in the case of human beings, this spiritual life confronts not only a
body but also an already formed soul.[53]

Stein introduces Teresa's image of the soul as a castle in *Finite and Eternal Being*, chapter 7, §3, 3, describing the soul (or the
Seelische) as a "'room' in the middle of the bodily-psychological
[*seelisch*]-spiritual whole."[54] In the soul there are many apartments
"in which the I can freely move."[55] Rather significantly, she claims
that this interior castle is not an empty space but, rather, has some
character. She returns to the analogy with the body: the body takes
in nutrients from outside itself and thus is receptive. But it can be
receptive precisely because it has in itself some structure, and when
the body receives nutrients it does so in a way particular to and
characteristic of itself. In the same way, the soul is receptive, but
this is not simply a filling of an empty container but a reception appropriate to the character of the soul and in a way particular to the
uniqueness of each soul.[56]

Stein claims that our experience is one of coming to recognize
a personal structure existing in some sense prior to our conscious
experience of it.[57] It is this personal core that is developed or unfolded in one's interior life, and this is part of the inner world in relation to which the I takes a stance. Thus, at least part of what spir-

52. See *Finite and Eternal Being* VII, §9, 1.

53. She says, "The soul must 'come to itself' in a double sense: *knowing* itself
and *becoming* what it should be. In both, its freedom has a part" (EeS 395/ESG
362/FEB 430). We could compare this with the great emphasis she puts on freedom in the appendix *Die Seelenburg.*

54. EeS 344/ESG 317/FEB 373.

55. EeS 344–45/ESG 318/FEB 373.

56. Stein concludes *Finite and Eternal Being* VII, §3, 3, by claiming that "this
essence with its unique character gives to the body, as to all personal, spiritual
action, its characteristic imprint and moreover radiates out of him in uncon-
scious and involuntary ways" (EeS 345/ESG 318/FEB 374).

57. Stein's account of education is distinctive and tied to her commitment
to essential being. Education involves a significant degree of "unfolding" something that is in some sense. This claim will be filled out in more detail as we look
at Stein's account of essential being.

itual development consists of is a deeper recognition of our own individual nature.

Critique of Thomas on Individuation

Stein was asked by her superiors, when she was in the Carmel in Cologne, to revise her 1931 Habilitationsschrift *Potenz und Akt*.[58] Stein began these revisions, and there are several manuscript copies marked with her corrections.[59] During the process, Stein became deeply dissatisfied with her original work; she says in a letter to her baptismal sponsor, Hedwig Conrad-Martius, that she now (in 1935) finds the work "completely inadequate."[60] Throughout the first hundred or so pages, Stein revised and corrected a number of things. As the manuscript proceeds, however, the number of changes drops off, and it is likely, as she says to Conrad-Martius, that there were so many changes she wanted to make that she opted to begin anew rather than revise the old. *Finite and Eternal Being* is the result of this beginning anew.

One of the interesting changes that appears in the edited manuscript copies of *Potenz und Akt* is the explicit removal of comments about matter as the principle of individuation. Stein at one point was fairly sympathetic to Thomas's position on individuation, but by the mid-1930s, she had changed her mind and explicitly rejected that claim.[61] In the final chapter of *Finite and Eternal Being*, Stein makes her case against Thomas on individuation more fully.

58. Some of the themes discussed here are also addressed in my "Edith Stein and Individual Forms: A Few Distinctions regarding Being an Individual," *Yearbook of the Irish Philosophical Society* (2006): 49–69. *Potenz und Akt* has been published with Stein's corrections as volume 18 of Edith Steins Werke (Freiburg: Herder, 1998).

59. See the manuscripts at the Archivum Carmelitanum Edith Stein in Würzburg and the Edith-Stein-Karmel in Tübingen. The latter has far fewer corrections.

60. *Self-Portrait in Letters*, no. 205.

61. See, for example, page 59 of the manuscript copy, where she deletes the sentence: "Therefore, it is here well justified that we see matter as the individualizing principle." ("Demnach ist es hier wohl berechtigt, den Stoff als das indi-

REASONS FOR INDIVIDUAL FORMS

Stein's individual forms are not her primary alternative to Thomas's account of individuation, but they do play some role in our individuation, and thus consideration of her rejection of Thomas's position is relevant to a study of individual forms. It is rather curious that Stein saves her critique of Thomas on this point for the final chapter. Only after utilizing the notion of individual form in her phenomenological descriptions in chapter 2, her more metaphysical analyses in chapters 3 and 4, and her descriptions of spiritual phenomena and development in chapter 7, does Stein offer explicit arguments against alternative positions. This ordering suggests that Stein's central arguments against and objections to matter as the principle of individuation are not contained here but, rather, are found in the previous descriptions and in the alternative metaphysical framework she sketches. With that qualification, the explicit arguments should still be considered.

Stein relies on J. Gredt's commentaries on Thomas, and she takes his position to be that designated matter, that is, matter with quantitative dimensions, is the principle of individuation for all finite, corporeal things. Form is responsible for our membership in a species, while matter is responsible for our being individual members of that species. Matter seems to be an adequate principle of individuation because it (a) is at the level of substance rather than accident, (b) makes a thing to be impredicable or, as Stein states it, incommunicable, which is Thomas's paradigm for being an individual, and (c) does not compromise the commonality of the species-form. Feature (a) is critical. Whatever individuates a being must individuate *the being;* accidents are accidents of some substance, and a thing may undergo numerous accidental changes without losing its nature as an individual substance of this type. Thus, the principle of individuation, if it is truly to individuate the substance, must be at the level of substance rather than accident. Stein argues that Thomas cannot mean *solid* matter when he talks

viduierende Prinzip anzusehen," copy at Archivum Carmelitanum Edith Stein, Würzburg.) The removed sentence would have been on page 43 of the Edith Steins Werke published version. See also pages 61 and 63 of the manuscript copy.

of matter as the principle of individuation because solidity is an accident. Whatever it means to be designated matter, it must mean something involved in more than accidental traits (e.g., solidity).[62] Thus, the matter which individuates is neither prime matter nor matter characterized by its accidents but, rather, she claims, "concerns much more the relation of matter to a not-yet-determined extension *(quantitas indeterminate)*."[63]

Thomas understands such designated matter as the principle of individuation,[64] but not as the principle of identity or uniqueness. Designated matter is responsible for the individuation of a corporeal being, but it does not account for identity over time or more than numerical difference. The form, however, once individuated by matter, remains so individuated, even if separated from the body. Designated matter, if thought of without any form, would be simply something *here* rather than *there*.[65] (Properly speaking, it can be thought of without form, but it can be neither imagined without form nor known without form. Without form, neither imagination nor knowledge are possible.) As a here rather than a there, matter is unrepeatable and impredicable. What is predicable can be said of many things. Here (rather than there) cannot. Thus, designated matter seems capable of making some form to be unrepeatable and impredicable.

Stein broadly grants these points, but then she questions whether impredicability is the proper paradigm for being an individual. First, while it is true that matter cannot be in more than one place at one time and thus matter would make one thing distinguishable (in spatial terms) from another, is this sufficient for being an indi-

62. See EeS 434/ESG 398/FEB 473.

63. EeS 434/ESG 398/FEB 473. I am not interested at this point in asking whether Stein's account of Thomas is accurate.

64. Thomas makes a threefold distinction among: *prime matter, determinate* or *designated matter* (which is the principle of individuation), and *matter of indeterminate quantity* (which is the matter relevant to definitions of corporeal beings). I am grateful to Fr. Joseph Koterski for pointing out this distinction. As far as I know, Stein does not explicitly repeat this threefold division.

65. I appreciate Fr. Norris Clarke's willingness to discuss this point in Thomas with me.

vidual?[66] She raises the question of whether recognizability to us as distinct is the same thing as being an individual. Second, matter, in order to be matter, surely must have some formation. Thomas does not claim that prime matter, or pure potency, is the principle of individuation but, rather, designated matter, space-filling matter. Even if we understand it as ordered to some indeterminate quantity or extension, it is not completely indeterminate.[67] As such, must there not be some form involved in making it determinate *as matter*? Matter can already be contrasted with spirit. Matter is that which is space-filling, divisible, and extended, and it can be contrasted with the genus of spirit, which is not space-filling, divisible, or extended. Matter differs in some intelligible and articulable way from other genera, and presumably it does so in virtue of some formal element.[68] If so, then designated matter simply cannot be so sharply distinguished (at least in the way Thomas needs) from form.[69]

Stein thinks that there are two fundamental problems with Thomas's account of individuation. First, Thomas's paradigm for being an individual is insufficient (and thus his requirements for what could individuate the form are likewise insufficient). Stein takes being an individual to require both (a) incommunicability, or impredicability, which is a requirement which designated matter would seem to fulfill, and (b) indivisibility, which, in principle, matter could not fulfill. Heaps are not individuals, whereas each grasshopper is. What makes a heap non-individual is its divisibility; one can divide it in half and still have a couple of heaps. In contrast, you cannot divide a grasshopper in half and end up with a couple of grasshoppers.[70] Stein understands indivisibility as having

66. See *Finite and Eternal Being* VIII, §2, 4.

67. See EeS 441/ESG 404/FEB 480–81.

68. See *Finite and Eternal Being* IV, §3, 20, where she lays out the contrast of these two genera.

69. See, for example, EeS 441/ESG 404/FEB 481 and EeS 442/ESG 405–6/FEB 482.

70. One could, however, do this with a worm, which raises some questions about Stein's criteria of *indivisibility*.

a character such that the thing cannot be divided without losing its identity. Stein does not, by this, mean that the thing must be incapable of any kind of division. We can remove a leg or two from the grasshopper and still have a single grasshopper. But it is indivisible in the sense that it cannot be divided into further things of its kind. Stein further develops her account of the paradigm for being an individual by describing individuals as entities which are "species determined and closed as a unity of form."[71] A bar of gold is impredicable, but it is not, Stein thinks, an individual. It may be an impredicable whole of a sort, but it is not an individual.[72] In contrast, a blue finch is an individual. It is "closed" or unified as a single instance of this species-determination, and it is indivisible into further instances of its kind.

Second, Thomas needs to account for how the form which causes matter to be matter (in contrast to something else) relates to the other forms, including especially the form which the matter is supposed to be individuating. If matter individuates form, then what individuates the form causing matter to be matter (and thus capable of individuating anything at all)?

Stein raises a further curiosity with matter as the principle of individuation. There are cases where numerous individuals all share in the same material.[73] Consider the case of your individual cells, which come to make up a single kidney, which is then the kidney of one individual human being. Each of these—each cell, the kidney, and the human being—would be individuals, and yet they share in the *same* matter. If we can have many individuals all of the same matter, surely matter alone cannot be the principle of making something an individual.

～

In the previous chapter, I distinguished five problems concerning individuality (individuation, the paradigm for being an individual, identity, and two questions of uniqueness). The first, the

---

71. EeS 441/ESG 405/FEB 481.   72. EeS 441/ESG 405/FEB 481.
73. See EeS 442/ESG 405/FEB 481.

problem of individuation, concerns the principle by which there are several individuals all of one type. But intimately tied to this is the second question of what it means to be *an individual*. It is clear that the paradigm Thomas prefers (in the context of his discussions of matter as a principle of individuation) is that of impredicability or incommunicability. A thing is individual if it cannot be predicated of any other. Thus, the form cannot be the principle of individuation because a form can, by its very nature, be repeated. In contrast, matter is the final and ultimate incommunicable substratum.[74] Thus, matter seems to be that which makes a thing nonpredicable and therefore individual.

If being an individual involves indivisibility and not simply impredicability, then some formal element might be a contender for the principle of individuation. Form provides the kind of unity relevant to being unified as a species; it is in virtue of some formal component that grasshoppers are indivisible in contrast to heaps of gold. Matter, by its nature, is divisible, and thus if being an individual involves being indivisible, then matter would not make a particularly effective principle of individuation. Thus, Stein claims that matter "is not that which grounds the being-individual, but rather that which is claimed through the form."[75] On the other hand, form does not seem to be a particularly good candidate for the criterion of impredicability. Form, as the principle of intelligibility and structure, is precisely that which can be repeated. Stein, however, distinguishes a number of different kinds of form, as will be discussed in particular in chapter 5 below, and puts forward at least one kind of form that may succeed in providing impredicability.

Thomas was loath to attribute individuation to the form, especially our substantial form, the species-form, because that is the basis of our similarity, what makes all human beings human. Thus, it seems a bit undesirable to attribute individuality to something

---

74. See EeS 440/ESG 403–4/FEB 480 where Stein quotes from Gredt's *Die aristotelisch-thomistische Philosophie* II, 244–46.

75. EeS 445/ESG 408/FEB 486.

that performs a different—even opposite—task. Stein avoids this difficulty without giving up her claim that individuality is due to the form by claiming that the "substantial form" is not the species-form but, rather, an individual form.[76] Insofar as she sides with Scotus in holding that the appropriate paradigm includes indivisibility, Stein has reason to look toward the formal construction of the thing if an adequate principle of individuation can be found there.

Conclusion

Stein clearly and consciously posits individual forms for finite personal beings in clear contrast to the Aristotelian-Thomistic tradition. It seems to me that there are several motivations for this. First, our experience of ourselves and others as well as fictional characters reveals that there is an intelligibility to our individuality. We are intelligible not simply as members of the human race but also *as individuals.* Second, evolution presents distinctive challenges to the traditional Aristotelian-Thomist understanding of species-form, and the affirmation of individual forms as well as a loosening of the concept of species-form enables Stein to affirm both some account of a common species-form and the possibility of the evolution of biological species. Third, the theological significance of each individual as a unique member of the mystical Body of Christ fits well with an account of individual forms. Fourth, Stein's understanding of spiritual formation, influenced by the writings of St. John of the Cross and Teresa of Avila (as well as, very likely, her own experience as a contemplative nun), suggested experiences she wanted to account for and incorporate into her philosophical treatises. Among the images most significant for her is Teresa's interior castle of the soul, which Stein interprets as an individually characterized "castle." Finally, philosophical dissatisfaction with

76. I have put *substantial form* in scare quotes because the identity of the individual form with the substantial form is not as simple as I have implied here. I will return to this issue in chapter 5.

the Thomistic answer leads her to consider another option. If one accepts (as Stein, for the most part, appears to do) the classic Aristotelian-Thomistic claim that there are two primary metaphysical principles in all corporeal things, matter and form, then there are only two options for the principle of individuation: either the matter or the form. (See the nuances of this claim in the following chapters.) If Stein rejects matter, which she does in rejecting Thomas's position, she needs to turn to form. The common form cannot individuate itself; therefore, she needs another formal principle to do so.

Three ⁓ TYPES OF ESSENTIAL STRUCTURES

Stein posits *individual form* as a metaphysically real principle distinct in content for each finite personal being. In the following three chapters I would like to look more carefully at the kind of principle the individual form is intended to be and therefore the role it plays in making each of us individual. In order to do so, it is necessary to look at Stein's general theory of essence and essential structures (chapter 3), her account of being (chapter 4), and the way in which individual forms in particular fit into Stein's account of both and thus act as a principle of individuality (chapter 5). My primary interest in this chapter will be (a) to contrast briefly the two major traditions Stein is drawing from in *Finite and Eternal Being* on the question of essence, (b) to distinguish Stein's differing types of essential structures, including essences and essentialities, and (c) to articulate briefly how the differing structures are nonetheless related. (The first and second sections will be important for appreciating Stein's position regarding individual forms; the third clarifies a number of claims but is not necessary for the broader analysis.) Although the theme of this chapter is Stein's differing types of essential structures, I will save discussion of one further structural component—substantial form [*Wesensform*]—for chapter 5.

The Scholastic and Phenomenological Traditions
Part of Stein's aim is to find a common language for medieval and contemporary philosophy,[1] and her project is clearly one of synthesis.

---

1. See EeS 7/ESG 15/FEB 6–7. The dominant medieval figures Stein has in mind are Augustine, Thomas Aquinas, and John Duns Scotus.

In the foreword to *Finite and Eternal Being,* she claims that this text represents a "coming-together" of phenomenology and Thomism.[2] This should not be understood as an attempt to remain true to the fundamental tenets of either phenomenology or Thomism but, rather, in a creative venue, as Stein's own metaphysical positions, which draw heavily from both traditions and attempt to reconcile them to the degree and in the ways that fit with her own projects.

It is worth noting that "scholasticism" is by no means identical with Thomism or any particular philosophical position. "Scholasticism" refers to a way of doing philosophy rather than any set of claims. Nonetheless, the prominence of Platonic and Aristotelian ideas in the scholastic debates is significant. When phenomenology first appeared, some people hailed it as (or accused it of being) a return to scholasticism.[3] Strong strains in philosophy since Kant have argued that our concepts, personal and social histories, experiences, and language so shape our understanding of the world that we cannot know the world as it truly is or as it is in itself, but rather only as it appears to us. Phenomenology, certainly in the early phenomenological schools, did not accept this Kantian position.[4]

2. See EeS viii/ESG 3/FEB xxiii. *Finite and Eternal Being* is Stein's third attempt to bring these two philosophical worlds together. Her first was her article written for Husserl's *Festschrift* (written twice, both of which are published in *Knowledge and Faith*) and the second was her Habilitationsschrift *Potenz und Akt.*

3. In her dissertation, Mary Catharine Baseheart says, "In Husserl's early works some of the critics of his phenomenology and of Scholastic philosophy saw a retrogression to medieval concepts and theories" (preface, *Encounter,* ii), and Husserl is quoted as saying that phenomenology "converges toward Thomism and prolongs Thomism" (see Elisabeth de Miribel's *Edith Stein: 1891–1942* [Paris: Éditions du Seuil, 1956], 73, and Jude Dougherty's "Edith Stein's Conversion: How a Jewish Philosopher Became a Catholic Saint," *Crisis* 10, no. 11 [December 1992]: 41). See also Husserl's comments comparing his approach to scholasticism in "Philosophy as Rigorous Science" in *Husserl: Shorter Works,* ed. Peter McCormick and Frederick Elliston (Notre Dame, Ind.: University of Notre Dame Press, 1982), 175 and 176.

4. Kant's claims also put in question the traditional metaphysical project of articulating the nature of reality. Although the early phenomenologists rejected Kant's phenomena-noumena distinction and subsequent denial that we have access to the real, phenomenologists have tended to be hesitant about the move to traditional metaphysics. Husserl, for example, describes phenomenology as first philosophy (and not metaphysics), sharply distinguishing the two, and he is

Phenomenology began as an unabashedly realist movement, that is, claiming that we are always already in contact with the real. The question is not *whether* we understand the real, but *how* we do so.[5] A further point of important compatibility is in the phenomenological and medieval focus on essences. Stein says:

> The turn toward the objective essentialities [*Wesenheiten*] allowed phenomenology to appear to contemporaries as a renewal of scholastic tendencies.[6]

The strongest commonality between phenomenology and Thomism appears to me to lie in the objective analysis of essences [*Wesensanalyse*]. The method of eidetic reduction that looks away from the factual Dasein and all accidents in order to make visible the essence [*Essenz*] appears to me—Thomistically considered—justified through the distinction[7] of essence [*Essenz*] and existence in all created things.[8]

---

quite hesitant to move to any metaphysical claims. One of the striking qualities of *Finite and Eternal Being* is Stein's explicit attempt to move from phenomenology to metaphysics.

5. It is not clear that Husserl remained committed to this position in his later writings. He increasingly sounds more Kantian, beginning with *Ideas I*. I think that Husserl can be read as largely a realist throughout all of his work, but it is true that his positions become more nuanced as one moves into the later writings. See Richard Cobb-Stevens, Dan Zahavi, Robert Sokolowski, and John Drummond for examples and defense of this type of reading of Husserl.

6. "La Phénoménologie" (hereafter Juvisy), in *Journées d'Études de la Société Thomiste* (September 12, 1932): 102. In *Life in a Jewish Family*, Stein writes: "The *Logische Untersuchungen* had caused a sensation primarily because it appeared to be a radical departure from critical idealism which had a Kantian and neo-Kantian stamp. It was considered a 'new scholasticism' because it turned attention away from the 'subject' and toward 'things' themselves. Perception again appeared as reception, deriving its laws from objects not, as criticism has it, from determination which imposes its laws on the objects. All the young phenomenologists were confirmed realists. However, the *Ideas* included some expressions which sounded very much as though their Master wished to return to idealism" (250).

7. *Trennung* is commonly translated as "separation" or "division." Stein, however, translates *distinctio* (in Thomas's *De veritate*) with *Trennung*; thus, it seems appropriate to use "distinction" in this case. See Stein's "Lateinisch-Deutsches Wörterverzeichnis."

8. Juvisy, 109. Stein's use of *"Essenz"* here is noteworthy: Stein rarely—if ever—uses *Essenz* in *Finite and Eternal Being*.

Both the Aristotelian-Thomistic and the phenomenological traditions are committed to the reality (in some sense) of intelligibility
or essential structures. Both affirm that experience is never the experience of "bare particulars."

Edmund Husserl defined himself, in part, by arguing against
the British empiricist tradition, and one example of this can be
seen in his understanding of essence. He claims, against Locke and
Hume, that what is universal is not a generalized image but rather
an idealized content; the "universal," rather than a word or image
representing all particular things with comparable traits and qualities, is an essence common to many things.[9] In *An Essay concerning Human Understanding* Locke argues that the only things which
exist are particulars and that ideas, thus, become general when we
separate "from them the circumstances of Time, and Place, and
any other *Ideas,* that may determine them to this or that particular Existence."[10] In so making the idea *general,* it can represent
more than one individual, "each of which, having in it a confor-
mity to that abstract *Idea,* is (as we call it) of that sort."[11] Abstract
ideas or universals are particular ideas in the mind which are sufficiently general as to represent all sensible objects of a certain degree of similarity. Likewise, Hume accounts for the "universal" by
claiming:

When we have found a resemblance among several objects, that often
occur to us, we apply the same name to all of them, whatever differences
we may observe in the degrees of their quantity and quality, and whatever other differences may appear among them. After we have acquired
a custom of this kind, the hearing of that name revives the idea of one of
these objects, and makes the imagination conceive it with all its particular circumstances and proportions.[12]

9. See, for example, Husserl's *Logical Investigations,* Investigation 2, chapter 2, section 10. I am grateful to Terry Wright for reminding me of this particular section.

10. John Locke, *An Essay Concerning Human Understanding,* ed. Peter H.
Nidditch (New York: Oxford University Press, 1975), 411.

11. Ibid.

12. David Hume, *A Treatise of Human Nature,* ed. L. A. Selby-Bigge, 2nd ed.
revised by P. H. Nidditch (New York: Oxford University Press, 1978), 20.

TYPES OF ESSENTIAL STRUCTURES

According to Hume's *Treatise,* the universal is simply a word that has the power to revive for us the image of many particulars that are similar or sufficiently alike.[13]

For both Locke and Hume, there is no universal (and, therefore, one need not individuate it). There are only individuals. Some words or ideas, those we call "universal" or "general," may be applied to many things. They offer a shorthand way of referring to Joe, Jane, and Tony without actually holding before us the image of Joe, Jane, and Tony. They are not, however, "universal" in any sense stronger than that. The word or idea is itself a particular with the power to bring to mind other particulars.

In contrast, Husserl accepts a "universal" content. It is not merely a generalized image representing many things that could (more or less) be classed together but is, rather, a content common to all things of that "type." In the First Investigation of the *Logical Investigations,* Husserl makes a distinction among the object intended, the act of intending, and the ideal content in terms of which it is intended.[14] The first is *that which* we perceive, imagine, or remember (e.g., a table); the second is the particular act itself (e.g., perceiving, imagining, or remembering); and the third is the ideal content in terms of which we perceive, imagine, or remember (e.g., *as a table* or *as brown*). To use one of Husserl's examples, we might contrast Napoleon as an object considered from the ideal content "victor of Jena." We can think of Napoleon *as* the "victor of Jena" or *as* the "vanquished of Waterloo." These ideal structures or content remain the same, even if someone is mistaken about the object. One might, for example, quite mistakenly think that Hegel is the "victor of Jena." The ideal content—"victor of Jena"—re-

13. He claims that after we have become accustomed to using one word to refer to several things (for example, "human being" for Jane, Joe, and John), when we hear the word we revive the idea of only one thing, but the habit of applying that same word to other things makes us feel as if we can use it with wider generality. See p. 20 of the *Treatise.*

14. *Logical Investigations,* trans. J. N. Findlay (New York: Humanities Press, 1970), 290; I, §14.

mains the same, but the object understood in terms of that content does not.

Husserl claims that such ideal content or essential structures are present in all conscious acts. Consciousness is intentional; essences provide the *intention* or meaning in terms of which we experience.[15] For Husserl, essences are not and cannot be particular words or ideas with broad reference. Such a view presumes that we first experience particulars *as* particulars and then develop such general concepts or names. In contrast, Husserl argues that experience does not support such an account of itself. We do, in fact, always already experience in terms of certain intelligible and "universal" categories, and thus intelligibility and universality are, although distinct from, nonetheless inseparable from the experience of "particulars." "Prior" to perceiving the white, furry mess *as a cat,* I must have the ideal intention of "cat." This priority need not be a temporal priority; insofar, however, as it is *other* than the sensible or empirical experience, it is a genuine but non-particular aspect of our experience. Thus, in contrast to Locke and Hume, Husserl posits a universal that is more than a particular word or image capable of "standing in" for many things; rather, he posits a content that transcends many particulars and may be fulfilled in more than one instance.

Like Aristotle, Husserl affirms that, although we may point to particulars, we know in terms of universals, and thus Husserl aligns himself with the broad realist tradition in the debate regarding universals.[16] Despite, however, this quite significant similarity,

15. I have intentionally left the phrasing somewhat ambiguous here. Husserl certainly wants to affirm that constitution is active and not merely passive reception, but he does not claim that we *construct* the world. Husserl is certainly not a Kantian idealist in *Logical Investigations* (nor, do I think, in any of his works), but he does want to affirm both that our experience of the world is orderly and meaningful and that this is to be explained through structures of meaning and meaning-constituting acts.

16. Stein divides the positions in this debate in a quite distinctive manner. See her discussion in *Finite and Eternal Being* III, §10, as well as chapter 4 of this volume.

Husserl's account of universals differs from that of Thomas Aquinas in at least two related respects. First, for Thomas, there can only be essences of things which exist. In chapter 1 of *De ente et essentia,* Thomas points to the two ways of understanding the Aristotelian categories—as categories of *assertion* and categories of *being*—and argues that the notion of *essence* is derived from being, not from categories of assertion.[17]

In contrast, phenomenological essences are stable contents which give the possibilities for how a world may be described. They are the essential structures within an object, making it *that kind of thing* under any possible circumstances, and the phenomenological focus is on necessary structures regardless of whether the object does, in fact, exist.[18] Stein describes Husserl's position, saying that *essences* show "how a world and various possible worlds can be constructed for a consciousness."[19] Positive sciences investigate the factual conditions of the actual world; in contrast, phenomenology considers the conditions for knowledge such that a scientific investigation is even possible. Thus, the focus in phenomenology is not primarily on the being of an essence as a real thing, but on the necessity within essences and essential structures.[20] Phenomeno-

17. Thomas distinguishes being as divided through the ten genera and being as the truth of propositions. He claims that essence has being (that is, is a being) in the first way; essence is "that through which and in which a being has the act of existing" ("On Being and Essence" in *Selected Writings of St. Thomas Aquinas,* trans. Robert P. Goodwin [Indianapolis: Bobbs-Merrill, 1965], 36).

18. This distinction between phenomenological and Thomistic understandings of essence needs to be qualified. In a very real sense Thomistic essences also provide the possibilities for how a thing can unfold, but they are possibilities (or potentialities) of an already existing thing. For more on this distinction, see my "Edith Stein and Thomas Aquinas on Being and Essence," *American Catholic Philosophical Quarterly* 82, no. 1 (Winter 2008): 87–103.

19. "Husserl's Phenomenology and the Philosophy of St. Thomas Aquinas: Attempt at a Comparison," trans. Mary Catharine Baseheart, in her *Person in the World: Introduction to the Philosophy of Edith Stein* (Boston: Kluwer, 1997), 144. The reference to "possible worlds" is Stein's way of explaining phenomenology and need not imply that Husserl ever used (or would have liked) the language of possible worlds.

20. In her article on phenomenology, Stein says: "With the systematic devel-

logical essences may be said to be transcendent in the sense that they are valid for any possible world; were a Martian, for example, to experience joy (joy is one of Stein's favorite examples), it would go through the same basic structure that every joyful human being, animal, or divine entity goes through in experiencing joy. Essences thus can be said to provide the possibilities of being, not in the sense of a necessary condition for activity in a real being—as a healthy dog has the possibility (potentiality) to bark—but in a sense analogous to logical being. Real things can come into existence only according to what is possible. Essences are thus transcendent insofar as they are different from real things and prior to, or other than, real things. Husserl's distinction between *facts* and *essences* usefully makes this point. *Facts* are and are contingent in the sense that they might not have been or could be otherwise. *Essences* are necessary and could not be other than they are. If something is, for example, joy, it must have such and such a structure. Husserl's language of a priori ought to be understood in this sense. Husserl is not claiming that essences are a priori in the Kantian sense that they are utterly independent of empirical experience, but that they are in some sense different from empirical experience even if only encountered within our factual life.

A second way to contrast the Thomistic and phenomenological essences is in the number of essential structures. Thomas's paradigm and his recurrent examples are natural entities—acorns and oak trees, human beings, birds, etc. Thomas follows Aristotle's focus on a biological model, and because essence is that through

---

opment and application of intuitive knowledge and with its theoretical emphasis, phenomenology distances itself from Kantian philosophy and, at the same time, from the Aristotelian-Thomistic tradition. Certain points of concern find themselves near Plato and in the neo-Platonic, Augustinian-Franciscan direction within the ecclesial philosophy and theology of the Middle Ages" ("Was ist Phänomenologie?," *Theologie und Philosophie* 66 [1991]: 572. Reprinted from *Wissenschaft/Volksbildung—Wissenschaftliche Beilage zur Neuen Pfälzischen Landes-Zeitung* 5 [May 15, 1924]). See also Philibert Secretan's discussion in *Erkenntnis und Aufstieg: Einführung in die Philosophie von Edith Stein* (Innsbruck: Tyrolia-Verlag, 1992), esp. 128–30.

which something has being, essence can be said most properly of substances and only in a secondary way of accidents.[21] In contrast, the phenomenologist's primary concern is the realm of consciousness—what is accessible to the conscious subject—and anything with a structure available to consciousness is a legitimate concern of phenomenology. We can, thus, analyze the essence of red, pear-shaped, consciousness, time, two, etc. Not surprisingly, phenomenology has many more essential structures than it appears a Thomistic system would allow.

Stein is clearly committed, like both Husserl and Thomas Aquinas, to some form of realism regarding intelligible structures.[22] Like Husserl and Thomas, she argues that essential structures are intimately related to all conscious experience. She sides with Husserl in affirming a myriad of essences and essential structures, but she then distinguishes different *types* of essential structures as well as differing types of being such structures may have. In doing so, Stein acknowledges that living entities "carry" their essence in a different way than non-living things do, and thus she acknowledges Thomas's claim that actuality is not unimportant for our account of essence. Even if there is a real distinction between essence and existence, existence is nonetheless relevant to our account of essence. Thus, although Stein's account of essences in *Finite and Eternal Being* owes much to Husserl's phenomenology, Stein has adapted her account in certain ways that acknowledge some of the emphases of a more Thomistic position.

21. He says in the first chapter of *De ente et essentia* that "essence is truly and properly in substances, but is in accidents only in a certain way and in a qualified sense"(*Selected Writings of St. Thomas Aquinas,* trans. Robert P. Goodwin [Indianapolis: Bobbs-Merrill, 1965], 36).

22. "Realism" has been used in a number of senses thus far. Stein is a realist both in the epistemological sense (i.e., she thinks we can have knowledge—true but not exhaustive knowledge—of the world as it is in itself, in contrast to Kant's claim in *Critique of Pure Reason*) and in the debate regarding universals (i.e., she thinks that universals, in some sense of the term, are real).

Stein's Distinctions among the Essential Structures

As noted in the glossary, Stein uses numerous words to describe various aspects of and kinds of essences. Part of her challenge is certainly figuring out what terms to use as she negotiates the differing traditions, and she dedicates a section of *Finite and Eternal Being* (chapter 1, §3) to the dangers and difficulties of words. In the following discussion, I will use the unfortunate English word "essentiality" for Stein's *Wesenheit*, while reserving "essence" for *Wesen*. Although I am hesitant to subject anyone to the word "essentiality," one advantage of doing so is that a certain degree of consistency can be preserved in translating *Wesenswas* as "essential what" and *wesenhaftes Sein* as "essential being." Further, "essentiality" is Dorian Cairns's choice for translating *Wesenheit* in Husserl's works, while "essence" is reserved for *Wesen*.[23] In following Cairns's choices here, the clear phenomenological overtones are preserved.

Keeping these phenomenological overtones is important for appreciating Stein's overall project. Early in *Finite and Eternal Being*, Stein embarks on a discussion of essential structures, and she consciously chooses phenomenological terms[24] rather than *Essenz*, which she used in translating Thomas Aquinas's *De veritate*. Further, Stein begins *Finite and Eternal Being* with phenomenological

23. *Guide for Translating Husserl* (Martinus Nijhoff, 1973), 136. Stein does, however, use *Wesenheit* once in translating *De veritate* (at I 1c). See her "Lateinisch-Deutsches Wörterverzeichnis," 888.

24. In chapter 3, she says, "We do not want to use the much disputed and ambiguous name of *Idea* for these structures but, rather, the phenomenological expression *Wesenheit*" (EeS 62/ESG 63–64/FEB 63). *Wesenheit* is not Husserl's most common term for referring to essences (he more frequently chooses *Wesen*), but he does use it on occasion. Although Husserl rarely used *Wesenheit*, many phenomenologists following him preferred the word (see, for example, Jean Hering's essay "Bemerkungen über das Wesen, die Wesenheit, und die Idee," *Jahrbuch für Philosophie und phänomenologische Forschung* 4 [1921]: 495–543). Stein herself regularly used the word *Wesenheit* when discussing Husserl's position. See, for example, her comments at Juvisy from 1932 and her 1924 article on phenomenology.

analyses, and she consistently speaks of experiences of the *I*. The second chapter of *Finite and Eternal Being* begins an analysis of *being*, starting with a phenomenological approach, and Stein initially limits herself to the realm of the *pure I* and its experiences. Although not stating that she is doing transcendental philosophy in this chapter, it is clear that her focus shares a concern for "the sphere of constituting acts."[25] While attempting to develop a model that includes biological examples, her first paradigms are phenomenological: the experiences of a conscious ego (even if not a *pure I* in precisely Husserl's sense).[26]

Prior to discussing essence in relation to real things, Stein puts forward essentialities [*Wesenheiten*] as necessary for understanding; she makes the strong claim that without such essentialities and without our experience of them, nothing could be understood.[27] On the surface, this appears simply to be the general phenomenological claim that experience is always in terms of certain intelligible structures. For example, without some kind of experience of the necessary structure of joy, we could not recognize another, different moment as also an experience of joy. There is a content [*Gehalt*][28] or structure to joy, consistent in one person's joy over an upcoming wedding and another's at a beautiful sunny day. Each experience has a different object, subject, length, and intensity, but each is an experience of joy because its structure is that of *joy*. Our ability to understand anything presumes that there are essential elements making a thing to be what it is and distinguishing it from another, and thus making each experience intelligible as such and such a (kind of) thing.

25. I have taken the phrase from Stein's comments about transcendental phenomenology and the transcendental reduction. See Juvisy, 110. In the final section of chapter 2, she asks: "Can we say something about the relation to pure being still within this restriction [i.e., the reduction]?" (EeS 53/ESG 57/FEB 55).

26. See *Finite and Eternal Being* II, §6. I am grateful to Terry Wright for reminding me of this section.

27. See, for example, *Finite and Eternal Being* III, §2–5.

28. She says, "The unity of an experience and its delimitation against others (not alone, but still essentially) is conditioned through its *content* [*Gehalt*]" (EeS 61/ESG 63/FEB 62).

Stein, however, makes a further distinction between *essence* and *essentiality*, which figures prominently in her account of essence. It is likely that Stein owes this distinction to the work of Jean Hering (although perhaps not exclusively so). In 1917 Stein sent a letter to a fellow phenomenologist, Roman Ingarden, discussing Jean Hering's work on essence,[29] and Hering's article published in the 1921 *Jahrbuch* ("Bemerkungen über das Wesen, die Wesenheit, und die Idee") clearly impressed her. She quotes extensively from it in *Finite and Eternal Being*, drawing particularly on his distinction between essence and essentiality. Hering denotes the essence [*Wesen*] as "the *character constituting* the object." An essence is a structure *of* some object. As such, however, the essence is dependent on something else (namely, its object). In contrast, essentialities are independent. Each essentiality is that "which is fully free in itself from a relation to objects, something which 'is what it is.'"[30] My joy

29. She makes several interesting comments regarding Hering's article in a letter to Roman Ingarden: "Because of the history of essence [*Wesen*], you should get in contact with Hering (via Miss Ortmann). I heard again in Göttingen that he will study regular theology. One must, thus, place before him now the choice: either he does it or you. It is not good that these things eternally remain unworked out because he once began them. Besides, I wanted to come to agreement with you over several [things] that I have found in the work, or rather, did not find. Hering's μορφαι (ποιον and τὶ) are indeed essence [*Wesen*] in concrete (I would not say 'real essence [*Wesen*]' because the objects are not limited to real), they make the object what it is. The corresponding pure essentialities [*Wesenheiten*] would be εἶδος and ideal object. The distinction between ποιον and εἶδος, on one hand, τὶ and ideal object, on the other, appears to me to be formal-ontological: namely, that between "object" in a narrow sense (to which in the apophantic sphere the nominal meaning corresponds) and attribute (predicate, determination or how you want to name it). What his 'idea' is, that is, I believe, really not clear in the work. In places it is without doubt 'meaning,' that is not, however, held consistently throughout. Hopefully, [it] becomes clear to you out of these sparse comments what I mean. I would have sent to you happily our further illustrations to the theory of essence; that seems, I believe, however, too mysterious for a censor not schooled in phenomenology" (*Briefe an Roman Ingarden 1917–1938* [Freiburg: Herder, 1991], 37–38). The letter was written in 1917 to Roman Ingarden in Poland; it would have gone through censors in order to reach him—thus, the last line.

30. Hering, "Bemerkungen über das Wesen, die Wesenheit, und die Idee," 496–98 and 510.

at an upcoming event differs from joy itself. My particular joy has the essence of joy, whereas Joy itself is an essentiality.

Stein follows Hering in his distinction between essence and essentiality, and she argues for the latter by claiming that in order to explain and account for contingent, real, "developing" things—things with both actuality and potentiality—there must be something "withdrawn" from time, i.e., not experiencing the gradual unfolding over a period of time. All experienced joy begins with some initiating event—be it a lovely flower, a full night's sleep, or a piece of good news. The joy then more or less gradually fills us, developing in various ways—perhaps bubbling up, giving us greater energy, or filling us with a sense of peace and well-being. Finally, it will slowly diminish as the joy is replaced with other emotions. Our joy is not simply one moment, a single snapshot, but the whole unfolding experience. It unfolds, however, according to certain prescriptions making that experience one of *joy* rather than *discontent, melancholy,* or *ecstasy,* and distinguishing the joy we are now experiencing from our hunger, the content of what we are now remembering, etc. If we can so distinguish between the temporal, unfolding event that is our experience of joy and the prescription according to which that temporal event unfolds, then we cannot simply identify the essence with the essentiality. One is temporal and particular; the other is atemporal, prescribing the "route" of all temporal events of this type. Thus, Stein concludes in chapter 2 of *Finite and Eternal Being* that (contra Heidegger),[31] although beings with both actuality and potentiality are temporal, not all being is temporal.[32]

31. In this, we can see one critique of Heidegger's focus on the temporality of being. One of the aims of *Being and Time* is to show "*time* as the possible horizon for any understanding whatsoever of Being" (trans. John Macquarrie and Edward Robinson [San Francisco: HarperSanFrancisco, 1962], 1). Insofar as this is understood as the claim that we must understand things through time, Stein would agree. Insofar as this is the claim that all things are, therefore, temporal, Stein would not. Stein insists that our understanding requires non-temporal wholes which are understood from within the flow of time.

32. See *Finite and Eternal Being* III, §1, and the discussion in the following chapter.

~

Stein distinguishes the essence of joy as it is in my joy or any-one else's from *Joy itself*, the essentiality. She argues that in our ex-periences

we discover as well something different that arises in our flowing and transitory being, what we can comprehend and hold tight after it has arisen as a whole, as a limited structure. Although arising in the flux of time, it appears now as released from this flux, as timeless. The tem-poral flux, the experience in which the unity arises *in me* and *for me*, stands under laws that determine its course and are not themselves fur-ther flowing and transitory, but rather fixed and resting.[33]

Stein distinguishes the essence (as the structure of some particular experience and subject to temporal unfolding) from that structure as an atemporal essentiality. My experience of joy at a beautiful day has its own essence—the essence of my joy at this day—and this essence is distinct from the essence of Erika's joy at her upcom-ing wedding. Both, however, are rooted in the essentiality of Joy it-self. We refer to both as experiences of *joy*, and when so referring we mean neither precisely this experience nor that one but, rather, that which is common to both, i.e., that which makes both to be of this type.

Stein describes these essentialities as a kingdom of meanings (ultimately rooted in God), which supply the archetypes for the real world. She says that "*meaning* demonstrates itself as the intrin-sic law, dominating this flux."[34] In chapter 3, §11 of *Finite and Eter-nal Being*, Stein argues that nothing temporal is possible without a foundation removed from time, without a timeless form or struc-ture "that regulates the characteristic course of each temporal hap-pening."[35]

Further, Stein argues that no *knowledge* of real, temporal things would be possible without there also being a realm of timeless mean-ings, and only through these meanings is knowledge in general pos-

33. EeS 101/ESG 99/FEB 105.   34. EeS 102/ESG 100/FEB 106.
35. EeS 99/ESG 97/FEB 102.

sible. We understand things in terms of structures, types, and categories, and we understand necessity and possibility in light of these categories. Likewise, we measure and judge existing things in light of these meanings. We might say, for example, that "her joy was cut short." But "cut short" in comparison to what? A single, instantaneous flash of light would not be "cut short"; it is not the kind of thing meant to have an extensive temporal duration. In contrast, joy may be cut short. Such judgments are possible because "joy" has a particular structure, and we can thus recognize a particular example as a case of joy and can recognize when particular cases fail to develop that structure fully.

Stein claims that essentialities as atemporal essential structures differ from temporally unfolding essences, that essences are dependent upon such essentialities, and that our knowledge is similarly dependent on them. Thus, like Husserl, Stein focuses on the content and essential structures available to consciousness; in contrast, however, she distinguishes two kinds of essential structures: those part of and belonging to objects (named essences [*Wesen*]) and those independent of objects and atemporal (named essentialities [*Wesenheiten*]).[36]

Stein's distinction between essences and essentialities is significant. On the one hand, it allows her position to lean slightly in more Thomistic directions by distinguishing those intelligible structures which are significantly related to actual being (essences) from those which are not (essentialities). And thus *being* on Stein's account is not unrelated to her understanding of essence. (This claim will be fine-tuned in the next chapter.) On the other hand, however, this distinction also pushes Stein's position in a more Platonic direction. In *Finite and Eternal Being* III, §1, for example, she explicitly compares essentialities with the Platonic

36. She says, "The essence is distinguished from the essentiality in that it [the essence] belongs to the object while the essentiality is something independent in relation to the object. We speak of the 'essentiality Joy,' but of the 'essence of *the* joy'" (EeS 71/ESG 72/FEB 73).

Ideas, although named *Wesenheiten*—a phenomenological term—rather than *Ideen* (ideas). In an article discussing Husserl's a priori, John Drummond gives a nice characterization of one difference between Socrates and Plato:

> The difference between attending to the similarity of like things and attending to that identical feature by virtue of which they are similar is one way to understand the difference between Socrates and Plato. Socrates in his search for definitions sought the common, the similar characteristics in terms of which we could justify calling many objects by the same name. Plato, on the other hand, recognized that to call things by the same name entailed that there existed some *one* thing, some one form, by virtue of which the objects called by the same name had similar properties.[37]

He continues by noting that what distinguishes Husserl's and Plato's positions "is that Plato thought these ideal, universal objects existed independently of the particulars which shared the property in question. Husserl, on the other hand, recognizes that such objects are present to us only when we turn our attention from the multiplicity of similar things to that which is the same and grounds the similarity [*Erfahrung und Urteil*, 397]."[38] Stein and Hering appear to follow Plato rather than Husserl on this latter distinction (although Stein's position cannot be seen as simply Platonic, as will be seen with her notion of essential being, discussed in chapter 4). Insofar as essentialities are not simply essences but, rather, possess an atemporality that essences lack, Stein understands the essentialities to exist in some sense independently of essences. Further, insofar as the essentialities ground and prescribe the unfolding of the essences, the essentialities are more basic than the essences.

Thus, I do not think that we can read essentialities as simply abstractions from the essences. We might recognize essentialities through our acquaintance with various joyful experiences and thus various essences of joy, but the essentialities are more than simply an abstraction from differing joyful experiences. It is, I think, a significant question whether Stein ought to have followed Plato rather than Socrates and Husserl on this point. Doing so, however, fits extremely well with her particular account of being and fits smoothly with her account of individual forms. My primary aim in this chapter is expository, but full evaluation of her account of essences and essentialities is, I think, important, and doing so will require investigating not simply her account of essences and essentialities but also her account of human understanding. The distinction made between essences and essentialities is not unrelated to an account of *how* we come to understand intelligible and atemporal structures. The following section attempts to outline briefly Stein's account of the relation of these intelligible structures to our understanding and to develop her account of both essences and essentialities a bit more fully. I have not, however, engaged in the more difficult task of evaluation here. There are a few—very few— evaluative comments on Stein's account of human cognition and thus the adequacy of her distinctions in the final chapter.

Relations among the Essential Structures

The relations among essences, essentialities, and our knowledge ought to be articulated a bit more fully. First, the relation of necessary structures met in the flow of consciousness (essences) and atemporal "entities" which appear to ground this knowledge (essentialities) can be sketched as shown in figure 1. A person intends the essence of some thing *as* an instance of some essentiality. For example, I recognize this experience as joy. This experience is not *joy itself,* but, in the experience, the essentiality Joy is, in some sense, realized.[39]

The longest discussions of essentialities appear in chapter 3 of *Finite and Eternal Being,* and in §2 of that chapter, Stein raises the question of whether the essentiality Joy would exist if no one ex-

39. See *Finite and Eternal Being* III, §2 and §3.

Figure 1. Relation of Consciousness and Necessary Structures

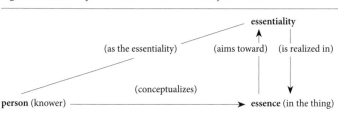

perienced joy. Her answer is twofold. First, she notes that the essentiality Joy "is" not in the same way that an experience of joy is. The essentiality has no power and is unable to make any particular experience of joy come about. It is, therefore, unreal in the sense that it is unefficacious.[40] But, secondly, she argues that there could not be an experience of joy if the essentiality Joy had not been previously in some way because the essentiality "is that which makes possible all experienced joy."[41] "Previously" here does not mean "preceding in time." The essentialities are not in time; rather, they are, as she puts it, "the final *conditions of the possibility of objects.*"[42] Likewise, she says that essentialities are "the condition of

---

40. In chapter 2, §5, Stein denies the real existence of "universal joy," that is, an essentiality Joy "running about." All "universals" are dependent on a spiritual nature that have that experience. Thus, the essentialities have their being most properly in God. Insofar as we are oriented toward intelligibility and search for rational patterns and structures of things, we are also oriented toward (and ascending toward) the divine as we come to know the natures "ruling" the unfolding of real being. All search for meaning is also implicitly a search for God. Mary Catharine Baseheart describes the project of *Finite and Eternal Being* as an attempt to begin with the *pure I* and arrive at Eternal Being. There are several ways Stein attempts this in *Finite and Eternal Being;* we can see one of these in Stein's description of knowledge and its bases. See *Person in the World,* 112.

41. EeS 62/ESG 64/FEB 64.

42. EeS 63/ESG 64/FEB 64. Here Stein is quoting from Jean Hering's essay, 510. She has left out, between the two sentences, the lines: "Nur weil es sie gibt, sind Morphen möglich, welche dem Gegenstand den Inhalt ihres τì und, wie wir noch hören werden, auch sein Wesen überhaupt in seiner ganzen Fülle vorschreiben."

the possibility of real being and its first steps, of the actual and the potential."[43]

Essentialities are the conditions for real beings, but they do not themselves "come into being": "The realization of an essentiality does not mean that *it* becomes actual but, rather, that *something* becomes actual which corresponds to it."[44] Stein claims that the essentialities are not themselves real (in the sense of efficacious, although they have some level of being), but they are nonetheless necessary. The role she attributes to them is that of giving order. Essentialities give to the life of the I order and intelligibility, and without them the I-life would be chaos with no differentiation.[45] Essentialities appear to be the essential content of an experience (but as a static, independent meaning—not as experienced) such that it is an experience of joy rather than sadness or giddiness. We experience an essence, an individual instantiation that imitates the transcendent essentiality, but it is through the essentiality that the essence has its identity as being of this type rather than that. Thus, it is ultimately in virtue of the essentiality that we can recognize this essence as an instance of the universal.

Stein consistently uses the language of structure [*Gebilde*] when discussing essentialities, for example, *Joy as such*[46]—that which is common to all experiences of joy—and suggests that these are wholes, although our experience of them can never "stand still."[47] Someone may first feel a sort of explosion of spirit, a desire to dance and clap her hands, she may look about for someone else to share the news with, and gradually the explosiveness of the

43. EeS 66/ESG 68/FEB 68.

44. EeS 66/ESG 68/FEB 68. She says, "Wherever and whenever joy is experienced, the essentiality Joy is *realized*" (EeS 62/ESG 64/FEB 63). Interestingly, Hering uses the language of *realisieren* rather than *verwirklichen*. Essentialities are met only via essences, but, she argues, they are, nonetheless, necessary in order to make sense of essences.

45. See EeS 64/ESG 65/FEB 65 and *Finite and Eternal Being* III §2.

46. See, for example, EeS 61/ESG 63/FEB 63.

47. See *Finite and Eternal Being* III, §1. Please note that here she speaks of "unities of experience." These will be connected with (although distinguished from) essentialities in III, §2.

feeling decreases. She smiles and may have a lift of spirit, but she returns to her work, perhaps with renewed energy but with a lessening of the emotion that originally pulled her away. The joy as experienced goes through phases and has a temporal beginning, increase, waning, and disappearance. But, Stein insists, it is—in content—a whole and as such can be distinguished from the event motivating the joy, the contemporaneous feelings of hunger, the work to which one returns, etc.[48]

When Stein insists that essentialities are necessary in order to make sense of anything and intimates that they are that which we intend experienced objects as, she also makes clear her stance that understanding requires experience. The essentiality is realized in the essence, and we experience essentialities only through coming to know essences. In chapter 3, §3 of *Finite and Eternal Being*, Stein clarifies the role of essentialities as principles of meaning as well as the relationship of essence and essentiality by returning to the example of joy. She gives the example of Thomas Aquinas's definition of joy as "a *passion of the ability of desire,*" which is distinguished from negative passions by its object.[49] After quoting and developing in more detail Thomas's definition of joy, Stein claims that, while all his comments are "certainly correct, clear and plain observations," they do not capture Joy as such.[50] In order to understand these remarks, one must first already know what joy is. Such a definition may clarify our concept of joy, but only by providing a kind of indicator pointing toward Joy; if one has not experienced joy, no definition will ever enable us to understand it.[51]

In chapter 2, §2, she asks:

"I," "life," "joy"—who can understand what the words mean if he has not experienced it in itself? But if he has experienced it in itself, then he

48. See *Finite and Eternal Being* III, §2.
49. EeS 67/ESG 68/FEB 68. She cites *De veritate* q. 26 a. 4. Stein gives extensive attention to Thomas's definition of joy; I have, however, only briefly quoted here her opening comments.
50. EeS 68/ESG 69/FEB 69.
51. See EeS 65/ESG 67/FEB 66.

knows not only *his* I, *his* life, and *his* joy, but rather he also understands what I, life, joy are *generally*, and only because he understands that can he know and grasp *his* I, *his* life, *his* joy as *I, life, joy.*[52]

I take it that we should understand essentialities as eidetically necessary structures which we can recognize as necessary—that is, the structure that any experience which is joy must have—when we meet them through particular essences. *(I, life,* and *joy* are among the simple essentialities, which cannot be defined because they are the units of meaning which cannot be broken down further. The simple essentialities may combine into more complex meaning-units, for example, *bittersweet.)*[53] If one has not encountered some joyful experience, one simply cannot know the essentiality Joy.[54] Thus, Stein concludes her discussion of Thomas's definition of joy: if we had not experienced that content, no definition would make clear exactly *what* is being defined.[55]

Although Stein claims that essentialities are fundamental for knowledge, we do not access them directly nor are we often explicitly aware of them. Essentialities—although related—differ fundamentally from both concepts and essences. In an interesting passage, Stein claims:

Actually, we speak in everyday life very seldom of essentialities. Objects, principally graspable things, are those with which we deal in life and

52. EeS 65/ESG 67/FEB 66.
53. See EeS 64/ESG 66/FEB 66.
54. She says, "What is now common, that we name with the word 'joy.' It suggests to thought that it could be the *essentiality* Joy. Of the essentialities it was said earlier that they present the final meaning and are the properly intelligible. Thus, they must also be that which gives, ultimately, to words their meaning. Indeed, that is what is the last ground of all intelligibility, what makes possible linguistic understanding and verbal communication. *That which brings to expression names properly and finally are essentialities.* If we, however, want to bring to expression linguistically nothing else, then our language would consist only of *proper names*" (EeS 76/ESG 77/FEB 78–79).
55. She says, "It was said: essentialities cannot be defined. No one can make intelligible to me what joy is if I myself have not experienced joy. If I have, however, experienced joy, then I understand also what 'joy generally' is" (EeS 67/ESG 68/FEB 68).

of which we speak. Only the contemplative thinker discovers in ways that are far removed from the attitude of daily life that there is generally something like essentialities, and then he needs great effort to make what he means intelligible to others. And yet the purely practical person also could not speak of the things with which he deals if there were no essentialities.[56]

In life we deal with objects, yet through our everyday experiences we can—she claims—gain insight into essentialities. Following Thomas, she argues that our knowledge comes "purely through the observation of finite beings, which we meet in the naturally experiencible world."[57] Our knowledge of essentialities comes through meeting an instantiation in an essence. And, because of this, gaining knowledge is a difficult process; the meaning-structures do not appear at once in all their clarity and distinctness but, rather, only veiled and blurred, and we must work to gain clear knowledge of them.[58] Nonetheless, there is something different from objects and their essences: essentialities.

A final distinction is in order. Stein has distinguished essentialities (which are in some sense independent of objects) and essences (which belong to objects). She has, however, two understandings of "object." An object can be understood as that "which stands *against* or *opposite* a knowing spirit."[59] "Experience," "joy," "essence," and "essentiality" are objects in this sense; they are each a *subiectum logicum*.[60] (She calls this description "the wider sense of object.") Or, an object can be understood as a free-standing thing *(substantia subsistens)*.[61] In this sense, "experience," "joy," "essence," and "es-

56. EeS 76–77/ESG 77/FEB 79.

57. EeS 227/ESG 212/FEB 243.

58. See EeS 280–81/ESG 260–61/FEB 301–2. Stein suggests that this is one effect of the Fall on our knowledge. Knowledge is possible in a post-lapsarian world, but it is difficult. Like tilling the land, we do not distrust that land or suspect that plants will not grow, but both involve hard work.

59. EeS 69/ESG 70/FEB 71.

60. See EeS 70/ESG 71/FEB 71.

61. She describes such an object as "what has its existence in itself, a being in itself" (EeS 70/ESG 71/FEB 71).

sentiality" are not objects. When Stein insists that every object has an essence, she is referring to objects in the first sense. She claims that we can speak of "the essence of an essence";[62] this claim would not make sense if we understood essence solely in relation to freestanding things. Rather, all objects, that is, all things "about which we can form a logical judgment," have an essence.[63] Essence as such names the structural element of a thing which we may come to know (and which, in contrast to a concept, is not subject to the will).[64] The essence is the structure *of* an object and, in that sense, belongs to the object.

Everything, including qualities and quantities, have an essence, i.e., "an enduring definiteness of its what."[65] The essence is precisely what makes a thing what it is, and nothing can be anything without an essence—"an essence-less object is unthinkable."[66] In order to be intelligible, all beings must have an essence or structure. Essences, however, are not objects (in the narrower sense). Everything has an essence, but the essence needs something else in order to exist or to have real being. All essences are the essence *of*

62. She says, "If it is said in the 'first principle of essence' that every object has an essence, then not only would objects in the narrower sense of the word be meant. Also qualities and experiences have an essence, yes, we must also speak of the essence of an essence" (EeS 70/ESG 71/FEB 71).

63. Augusta Gooch in her dissertation on *Endliches und ewiges Sein* describes objects in the wider sense "as being *(Seiendes)* about which we can form a logical judgment" ("Metaphysical Ordination: Reflections on Edith Stein's 'Endliches und Ewiges Sein'" [Ph.D. diss., University of Dallas, 1982], 181).

64. For more on her account of the *concept,* see EeS 71/ESG 72/FEB 72–73.

65. EeS 131/ESG 125/FEB 136. Stein insists that each thing including universals have their own essence; she says: "We can and must also speak of the essence *of the* human being [in contrast to the essence of *this* human being]. To the essence of man it belongs that he has a body and soul, is endowed with reason and is free" (EeS 70/ESG 71/FEB 72). Near the beginning of *Finite and Eternal Being* III, §4, she claims that the essence of *this my* joy is different from the essence *of* joy; it is a different object and, thus, a different essence.

66. She says, "That it is *essence of something,* quality *of an object,* points to it as something *dependent.* It is that through which the *what of the object is determinate* (τὸ τί ἦν εἶναι). Because of that an 'essence-less' object is unthinkable. It would no longer be an object, but rather only the empty form of such a one" (EeS 69/ESG 70/FEB 70–71).

something; the essence is simply the graspable content and structure of a thing. In this sense, essence is not the internal principle of being, but a stable and graspable aspect of the thing (so long as it is that thing).[67]

Stein claims that the essence belongs to the thing and stands over against the knower, but she does *not* say it is independent of the knower. Rather, we can see it as precisely that *which* is intended by the knower but not as the intention itself. In *Finite and Eternal Being* III, §5, she contrasts three statements: 1) "joy has made me healthy," 2) "in his life, the joy has outweighed the pain," and 3) "joy is a movement of spirit." These three all relate to joy and share in a common essentiality (that of Joy). But they point to different objects: the first, "joy has made me healthy," refers to this particular joy which has given the speaker health. The second, "in his life, the joy has outweighed the pain," refers to his joyful experiences throughout his whole life. And the third, "joy is a spiritual movement," refers to all joys, both real and possible, experiencible by persons. The objects of each statement make up quite a range, beginning with a very particular joyful experience in the first statement to all possible joyful experiences in the third. They are all about joy, and thus each description intends the same essentiality, but the objects—the joyful experiences in question—differ.

Thus, Stein distinguishes essentialities and essences by removing essentialities from any direct connection to things or any particular instantiation. The essentialities provide structure both to objects and to knowing. (They are not, however, self-predicable; Stein declares that the essentialities do not have the attributes they exemplify.[68] The essentiality Joy is no real joy; it is not cheery; and

---

67. Stein quotes Jean Hering's "Fundamental Principle of Essence" [*Hauptsatz vom Wesen*]: "*Every object* (which may be also its way of being) *has one and only one essence which makes up the fullness of the traits constituting it as its essence*" (EeS 69/ESG 70/FEB 70, quoting Hering, 497). "Object" here refers to objects in the wide sense. The essence is "the constituting characteristic of an object" (quoting Hering, 496, EeS 69/ESG 70/FEB 70) and "its existence in essential predicables" (quoting Husserl's *Ideas I* §2, p. 9, EeS 69/ESG 70/FEB 70).

68. "The essentiality Joy is no psychological state; it has no grade, does not

it does not arrive, build, and wane in certain ways. It is, presumably, the necessary structure of joy but is not itself an instance of joy, which requires time in which to be realized.)

Conclusion

Stein thus distinguishes several senses of the term "object" and several types of intelligible structures, including both essences and essentialities (both of which are distinguished from "concepts," although that is not discussed here). She describes the relation of essences and essentialities to our knowledge in differing ways, although claiming that both are necessary for knowledge. Stein does not explicitly state that each individual form is an essence rather than an essentiality, but presumably—because each of us *has* an individual form—individual form is first and foremost an essence, and not an essentiality (or concept). But, like all essences, our individual form would ultimately be rooted in some way in essentialities and thus the timeless realm of meaning.

---

make itself known in bodily expressions and does not strive toward words and actions" (EeS 68/ESG 69/FEB 69).

Four ～ TYPES OF BEING

Stein's account of the types of and relations among the essential structures is relatively complex. What allows her to make the distinctions that she does is her concept of essential being.[1] Stein does not think that being is identical with actuality. Rather, she thinks that "being" can be said in at least three ways. In the following, I would like to lay out her view of three kinds of being, focusing particularly on *essential being (wesenhaftes Sein),*[2] and show how her

Some of these ideas have appeared in other forms: in chapter 6 of Sarah Borden, *Edith Stein* (New York: Continuum, 2003); and in Sarah Borden Sharkey, "Edith Stein and Thomas Aquinas on Being and Essence," *American Catholic Philosophical Quarterly* 82, no. 1 (Winter 2008): 87–103.

1. Tony Calcagno suggested that Stein's discussion of the differing types of being might be usefully compared to the lively debate in her time among various Neoscholastics, especially the Neo-Thomists. Stein was certainly in conversation with Neoscholasticism of the day, working closely with Erich Przywara on her translation work, publishing the first German translation of Thomas's *De veritate* (with its possible import for reception of Thomas's thought), cultivating a personal friendship with Jacques Maritain and his wife, attending and being a lively participant in at least one major conference on Thomism and phenomenology in France, and writing several works aimed at bringing together the phenomenological method and scholastic thought. It is surely the case that contemporary Thomistic debates on being were part of the background of Stein's thought. Exactly how, however, her account of essential being would fit into those discussions is, sadly, beyond my expertise.

2. Augusta Gooch translates *wesenhaftes Sein* as "substantial being." This is a good way to translate it insofar as Stein sees essentialities, the paradigmatic things with *wesenhaftes Sein,* as a kind of *proto ousia.* Therefore, what has *wesenhaftes Sein* is a kind of first substance. See Gooch's draft translation of *Finite and Eternal Being* (copy at the Edith Stein Center for Study and Research, Spalding University). But I find that it is difficult for me not to associate the language of "substance" and "substantial being" with a substantial form. Stein does not associate *wesenhaftes Sein* primarily (if at all) with a Thomistic substantial form, and I think that it confuses her metaphysical claims to import such language. Trans-

understanding of essential being leads her to a Scotist rather than a Thomistic position regarding universals. For Stein, as for Scotus, there is something importantly different about nature or essence that allows it to maintain its identity, whether it is in a mind or in a thing. Stein focuses on the distinct *being* of essence, rather than its *unity,* but there are important similarities in the two positions. Finally, I would like to sketch out Stein's development of this position, looking at her brief arguments for essential being and her use of this category to articulate an account of potentiality.[3]

Actual Being, Mental Being, and Essential Being

In *De ente et essentia* III, Thomas Aquinas distinguishes three ways of considering essence: according to its act of existence, which can be (1) as it exists in things or (2) as it exists in the mind, or according to its character, what he calls (3) "an absolute consideration of the nature."[4] These three ways of considering essence parallel Stein's distinction among three types of being, what she calls real being *(wirkliches Sein),* mental being *(gedankliches Sein),* and essential being *(wesenhaftes Sein).*[5] Stein's divisions among the three sorts of being appear on the surface like Thomas's distinctions. *Real being* is active and efficacious in the world. We might think of kittens now pouncing and chewing on ears and tails. *Mental being* is being as thought (the kittens as remembered, anticipated, or imagined). Finally, *essential being* encompasses the "what-ness" of things, the kitten-ness. It is the being of intelligibilities and is

---

lating *wesenhaftes Sein* as "essential being" has the further advantage of preserving the consistency of my other translations (for example, *Wesen* as "essence," *Wesenswas* as "essential what," etc.). See the glossary for a more thorough listing of my translations for these terms.

3. For a very interesting discussion of Stein's account of being and non-being in *Potenz und Akt,* see Walter Redmond's "A Nothing That Is: Edith Stein on Being Without Essence," *American Catholic Philosophical Quarterly* 82, no. 1 (Winter 2008): 71–86.

4. See "On Being and Essence," 47.

5. See, for example, *Finite and Eternal Being* III, §6, §11, §12, and IV, §2, 11.

that which is common to both the kittens and my thought of them, making my thought a thought *of* kittens.

For Thomas, there is a real distinction between the being of a thing and its essence (except in the case of God, whose essence is His existence); existence is not a part of the essence of created things.[6] Therefore, the same nature has the ability to be *either* in the kitten or in the mind; because the type of existence is not a part of the essence, the two kinds of existence (mental or real) can be predicated of the same essence.[7] But nature or essence is in either things or minds—we do not meet a nature floating about in an absolute state. Nature considered absolutely is merely a way of considering nature that prescinds from any act of existence. When considered absolutely, one considers only the things proper to the essence; for example, for a human being, that it is rational and animal, but not that it lives in Paris or Boise.[8] An essence has being only in things or in minds. When Thomas refers to an absolute consideration of essence, he is not discussing how an essence may *be*, but the way it may be considered, prescinding from questions of being. Thus, the real distinction between essence and existence appears to mean that essence as the genuine and authentic structure may be in various things (of the same type) or in minds. To speak of the *same* essence is to speak of an essential structure of identical content.

6. There is certainly debate about how we should understand Thomas's distinction between essence and existence. At the beginning of the text, I, §2, Stein simply says of Thomas's position: "Within the *being* [*Seienden*] *(ens)*, being [*Sein*] *(esse)* and *essence* [*Wesen*] *(essentia)* are distinguished. The equation of ὄν and οὐσία, originating with Aristotle, survives only for the *first Being*. With this division, *being* [*Sein*] *as such* is first grasped—separated from *what* is" (EeS 4/ESG 12/FEB 4, the second sentence is not in the ESG edition).

7. He says, "If the question arises whether the nature so considered can be said to be one or many, neither should be conceded, because each is extrinsic to the notion of humanity, and either can happen to it" ("On Being and Essence," 47).

8. Thomas says, "The nature of man considered absolutely abstracts from every act of existing, but in such a way, however, that no act of existing is excluded by way of precision. Now it is this nature so considered which is predicated of all individuals" ("On Being and Essence," 48).

Stein holds to a real distinction between the essence of a thing and its existence. She takes a step beyond Thomas, however, in claiming that the essence—in order to be truly distinct from real existence—must also have a being distinct from real being. If it *is* distinct, it must be in some way. She calls the being of essence (belonging to essence in contrast to real being): essential being.[9]

The Debate Regarding Universals

In *Finite and Eternal Being* III, §10, Stein makes clear that her position goes beyond the moderate realism attributed to Thomas. In order to do so, she begins by distinguishing nominalist, conceptualist, and realist positions: the *nominalists* accept only universal names but no universal (that is, identical in content) concepts or things;[10] the *conceptualists* recognize a universality of concepts, but claim that there is nothing in reality which corresponds to these universal concepts;[11] finally, the *realists* believe that there are in reality natures which correspond to the universal names and concepts. Stein clearly falls into the realist camp; she claims that "'being real' and 'being known' are different ways of being in which what is realized *in rerum natura* [and] what *in intellectu* becomes an *actu intelligibile* is *the same essential what [Wesenswas]*."[12] Stein holds to the reality of the intelligible structure; there is, indeed, some structure that is (structurally) identical in all instances of one type.

Stein further distinguishes, however, three perspectives within the realist camp. First, an *exaggerated realism,* which she identifies with the common interpretation of Plato, claims that there are universals existing somewhere outside of minds and the things of our everyday life. Secondly, she points to a line of thought *(extreme realism)* identified with John Duns Scotus, who taught "a being of

---

9. She claims that "it is in any case clear that essential being is distinguished from and independent of the real being of the thing" (EeS 91/ESG 90/FEB 95).
10. Compare with the discussion of Hume in chapter 3 above.
11. Compare with the discussion of Locke in chapter 3.
12. EeS 97/ESG 95/FEB 100.

the universal in things."[13] Finally, there is a *moderate realism* associated with Aristotle, Boethius, Anselm, and Aquinas. This group distinguishes the matter contained in, or the content of, the universal concept, and the form of universality.[14] The same content may have being in an individual thing or in the mind, but the form of universality can exist only in a mind. Thus, "universal" comes to mean "predicable of many things," although as a content (in either things or in an individual thought) the universal is always individual precisely because it is invariably this universal or that one.[15]

Stein's Scotist realism

Stein identifies herself with the second, the Scotist perspective. While Stein agrees with the distinction of the moderate realists between matter and form, she asks how we should understand this *form of universality* that can have being only in a spirit. What does it mean to have mental being? Stein claims that an absolute consideration of an essence is different, in some significant way, from other mental considerations. For a rather mundane example, we might think of square circles and four-sided triangles, and then round circles and three-sided triangles. All four thoughts would seem to have mental being, and yet the second set has something different from the first set. Stein wants to describe the difference in terms of the possession of an additional kind of being. Although all four thoughts have mental being, only the last two have essential being as well. Thus, Stein rejects the moderate realism of Thomas because it does not strongly enough distinguish various *ways* of being in a mind.

Both the moderate realists and those in the Scotist tradition agree that essence can exist in different ways and can be grasped absolutely when one prescinds from the thing's real or mental be-

13. EeS 94/ESG 92/FEB 97.
14. Here matter and form should not be understood as two principles of a corporeal substance but, rather, as analogous terms useful for discussing the content and structure of universals.
15. See EeS 94/ESG 93/FEB 97–98.

ing. Stein, however, wants to make clear what one grasps in coming to consider an essence absolutely: in knowing an essence, the mind grasps and possesses the intelligibility as something beyond itself. The *act* of knowledge is all mine, but *what* I know (not only the object of knowledge but also *as* it becomes known) can be known by another.[16] She says:

> In the act, that which is grasped by the spirit and that which it finds in a real essence as its what are the same. It [the what] maintains a characteristic unscathed-ness and virginity over against its *realization* as its *intellectualization*. It is what it is whether it is realized or not and whether it is known or not.[17]

The content of essence has a unity and character which it maintains regardless of its "state." And because the *essential what* which is found in many things is the same, we can give to it the meaning of universality.[18] Thus, in insisting on the "unscathed-ness and virginity" which characterizes the universal in the mind (in contrast to other mental or conscious experiences), Stein claims that her conception of the universal goes beyond moderate realism, although not as far as exaggerated realism.

Considerations in Favor of Essential Being

Scotus on the Unity of the Common Nature

Scotus argued against both nominalism (using an argument equally applicable to conceptualism) and exaggerated realism, claiming that neither could adequately account for universals. The nominalist argues that the only things which exist are the singular, particular things. If this were the case, there would be no universal (outside of the mind). But then our knowledge, which is univer-

---

16. See EeS 97/ESG 95/FEB 100. I am not sure what the qualification "*as* it becomes known" adds. Stein insists on this, but I am a bit confused by that insistence.
17. EeS 97/ESG 95–96/FEB 100–101.
18. See EeS 98/ESG 96/FEB 101.

sal, could not be true of things. We would be unable to say with any accuracy that Peter, Jane, and Herbert are all human beings or to predicate humanity of any of them.[19] On the other hand, exaggerated realism, which claims that the universal exists somewhere outside of the things, is likewise problematic. On what grounds is the universal accurately predicated of a plurality of things? If the universal exists *in* the things, then it may be predicated truthfully of the things. If the universal, however, is not in the things but, rather, the predication of the universal to a plurality of things is performed by the intellect, then why should the universal be predicated of some things and not others? Thus, the problems with exaggerated realism and nominalism end up being quite similar: in both cases, we need to ask how universals can be predicated truthfully of things. If the universal is separated from things by existing either merely in the intellect or in a separated realm, it cannot be predicated with accuracy of anything else.[20]

Scotus tries to avoid these problems by claiming that what we call a universal or common nature *(natura communis)* is neither universal nor singular but, rather, is indifferent to both universality and singularity.[21] The common nature in itself is not universal, but when it has existence in the mind, it is a universal, that is, predicable of many things.[22] When it has existence in things, it is

19. He says that if the common nature were simply a logical being, then "we would know nothing about reality, but only about our concepts, and our opinion would not change from the true to the false with the change in the existence of a thing" (*Quaestiones subtilissimae in metaphysicam Aristotelis* VII, q. 18, n. 10; VII, 459; quoted and translated in Maurice Grajewski, *The Formal Distinction of Duns Scotus: A Study in Metaphysics* [Washington, D.C.: The Catholic University of America Press, 1944], 144).

20. See Efrem Bettoni's discussion in *Duns Scotus: The Basic Principles of his Philosophy*, trans. and ed. Bernardine Bonansea (Washington, D.C.: The Catholic University of America Press, 1961), esp. 53–58.

21. Strictly speaking, the common nature would be indifferent; the universal, however, would not be. Scotus distinguishes three "universals," calling the nature in the thing the *physical universal*, the universal in the mind as intended of things the *metaphysical universal*, and the universal as a concept capable of being predicated of many the *logical universal*.

22. He says, "But not only is the nature itself indifferent of itself to being in

singular. But because it is, in itself, indifferent to both universality and individuality, being made universal (in the mind) or singular (in things) does not affect the integrity of the common nature, and we may thus truly know what is truly in the thing.[23]

Scotus further claims that the common nature *as such* has some kind of unity.[24] It is a unity less than that of numerical unity, and, thus, it does not exclude the possibility of being in a multitude of entities. Nonetheless, the common nature itself has its own characteristic unity. He says, "Even without any operation of the intellect there is some real unity in a thing, less than numerical unity—that is, less than the proper unity of a singular. This lesser unity belongs to the nature by itself."[25] If the common nature as such has an integrity and unity of its own prior to its existence in either the mind or in things, then there must be some principle sufficient to make it either universal in the mind or singular in things. Thus, we can see why Scotus claims that there is some *positive* principle of individu-

---

the intellect and to being in a particular—and therefore also to being universal and to being particular or singular. It does not primarily of itself have universality even when it does have being in the intellect. For even though it is understood under universality (as under the mode of understanding it), nevertheless universality is not a part of its primary concept, since it is not a part of the metaphysical concept, but of the logical concept" (*Ordinatio* II, d. 3, p. 1, q. 1, n. 33, in *Five Texts on the Mediaeval Problem of Universals: Porphyry, Boethius, Abelard, Duns Scotus, Ockham,* trans. and ed. Paul Vincent Spade [Indianapolis: Hackett, 1994]).

23. He says, "A material substance from its nature is *not* of itself a 'this.' For in that case, as the first argument deduces, the intellect could not understand it under the opposite aspect unless it understood its object under an intelligible aspect incompatible with the notion of such an object" (*Ordinatio* II, d. 3, p. 1, q. 1, n. 29).

24. He says, "Just as unity in common follows *per se* on entity in common, so too does any unity follow *per se* on some entity or other. Therefore, absolute unity (like the unity of an individual frequently described above—that is, a unity with which division into several subjective parts is incompatible and with which not being a designed 'this' is incompatible), if it is found in beings (as every theory assumes), follows *per se* on some *per se* entity. But it does not follow *per se* on the entity of the nature, because that has a certain *per se* real unity of its own" (*Ordinatio* II, d. 3, p. 1, q. 6, n. 169).

25. *Ordinatio* II, d. 3, p. 1, q. 1, n. 30.

ation; there must be something sufficient to make the common nature (which in itself is indifferent to either universality or individuality but, nonetheless, has its own unity) individual in things and universal in the mind.[26]

Scotus posits a formal unity to the common nature prior to any act of intellection, and he holds that the formal unity acts as a guarantor of the truth of our knowledge of nature. While Thomas appears to claim a similar result in *De ente et essentia* in distinguishing nature as it exists in things, nature as it exists in the mind, and nature considered absolutely, Thomas's position is, nonetheless, rather different. His idea of nature considered absolutely is still a nature *considered*. For Thomas, nature in an individual has the unity and being proper to an individual thing, i.e., it is individual. Nature in the intellect has the unity and being proper to the intellect, i.e., it is universal (or, more properly, the content is individual while the form is universal, that is, applicable to many things). And nature absolutely considered has neither unity nor being; it is simply a way of considering nature in relative separation from any act of existence. Thus, we can say that there is a real distinction between nature in the mind and nature in things, while there is a conceptual distinction between nature considered absolutely and nature in the mind.

Stein on the Essential Being of Essence

Stein appears to have many of the same concerns about universals as Scotus, and in many ways her response echoes Scotus's: she claims that the common nature is indifferent in itself to either universality or individuality, and she goes beyond the moderate realism of Thomas Aquinas in insisting that there is some integrity to the common nature prior to either its intellectualization or its instantiation in things.[27] She differs from Scotus, however, in how

26. See Bettoni, *Duns Scotus,* esp. 58–65.

27. She says, "The universal essence is indeed, although it 'occurs' many times, *one*. It is *the same* which is realized or can be realized here and there and in all individual essences [*Einzelwesen*] belonging to it, while the individual es-

89

she explains the unity of nature. Rather than claiming that there is a unity to the common nature less than numerical unity, she attributes to nature a different kind of being than that which either real things or thoughts have. Essence or nature has essential being and maintains its integrity despite its becoming universal in the mind or its becoming individual in things by retaining (in both intellectualization and instantiation) its proper mode of being: essential being. Furthermore, essential being is not a kind of being in contrast to and excluding either real or mental being, and thus nature can take on either variety of being without losing or compromising its essential structure.

Both the moderate realists and those in the Scotist tradition agree that essence can exist in different ways and can be grasped absolutely when one prescinds from the thing's real or mental being. Earlier it was noted that an absolute consideration of essence for Thomas is a matter of considering essence without considering any act of existence. Thus, one might look at the essential structure of human nature, looking away from the accidents accompanying any existing human being (for example, a particular skin tone). Stein, however, wants a more thorough account of why some aspects of human nature turn out to be essential whereas others are accidental. In order to justify an absolute consideration of essence, Stein posits an essential nature to essence independent of our consideration of it. It is not the human mind which is entitled to make some aspects essential and others not; rather, we need to recognize the essential character as such. Such recognition is grounded in the genuinely essential nature of the universal.

Further, Stein claims that if nature has some essential structure, it must also have some kind of being. What is must be in some way. She writes, "What is for another the condition of being must itself have a being."[28] Because the possibility of real being is grounded in entities with essential being,[29] we cannot call them

---

sence [*Einzelwesen*] is possible and real only in one—in *its*—object. It can have 'its equal,' but it cannot have 'multiple occurrences'" (EeS 79/ESG 79/FEB 82).

28. EeS 66/ESG 68/FEB 68.

29. She claims that the possibilities [*Möglichkeiten*] of the real world lie in

Figure 2. Entities and Types of Being

Ὄν = being [*Seiendes*]

I. Οὐσία = existing being
  1. πρώτη οὐσία = τόδε τί (individual thing)
  2. δευτέρα οὐσία = determination of the essence as determination of the what (genus- and species-determination up to the final determination) = τί εἶναι
  2a. δευτέρα οὐσία (πῶς) = determination of the essence as determination of the such= ποιὸν εἶναι

II. Λόγος νοητός = mental being [*Seiendes*]

III. Ὄντως ὄν = εἶδος (essential being as the ground of being and ground of the essence for I and II)
  1. Essentialities = elements of being [*Sein*]
  2. Quiddities (essential what [*Wesenswas*]) = composite meaning-structures
     Πρῶτον ὄν = Πρώτη οὐσία = Λόγος
     First being [*Seiendes*] = essence — being [*Sein*] = meaning

---

Source: EeS 147/ESG 138–39/FEB 152–53.

nothing. In order to have an essential structure, independent of the realization of the nature in things or minds, nature must first have some kind of being, what Stein calls essential being.

Relations among the Types of Being

In *Finite and Eternal Being* IV, §2, 11, Stein draws up an outline linking the three kinds of things with the three types of being (figure 2).[30] Each category describes not the type of being [*Sein*] but the type of entity [*Seiende*] with that being. Thus, things with real being in category I include (1) individual real things, (2) essences (that is, essence as instantiated), and (2a) traits of essence, including its

---

these structures, and she distinguishes a double sense of possibility: (1) a "possibility of essence" [*Wesensmöglichkeit*] which makes possible the real being with its deeper potentialities, and (2) the potentialities themselves. See EeS 102/ESG 99/FEB 105 & 565.

30. Her discussion in chapter 3 focuses on essential being [*Sein*], whereas here she charts out the distinctions between different beings [*Seienden*].

such (that is, how it is). The second group includes mental beings (thoughts), and the third encompasses essentialities and the essences of things in their structure.

The third category, *essential being,* is the proper "home" for essentialities.[31] It is, however, not a "home" for essentialities in the sense of a *realm* of being—as if essential being were in some place as mental beings are "in" a head or real beings are currently living things.[32] Eva-Marie Knoche aptly says that, for Stein

> essential being is no special kind of being but rather "an indestructible meaning-part of all being." Essential being is an enduring, ruling being that survives all changing relations. It is timeless unfolding of pure structures of meaning beyond act and potency.[33]

Essential being refers to the intelligibility of being and is "present" in all things (insofar as they can be known), in thoughts, ideas, chairs, rhinoceroses, and God. (Essential being would not, however, be present in the unintelligibility of a thought of square circles, even if the thought of square and circle each have essential being.) If something has essential being, then it is intelligible, and if it has no share in essential being, it is nothing, nonsense, or contradicto-

31. She says, "For the essentialities, as we have learned about them thus far, essential being is the only being. For the essences, in contrast, being real in their object is possible, and the relation to objects whose what they determine lies already in their characteristic way of being. This double being corresponds to the mediate place of essences between essentialities and the 'real world'" (EeS 81/ ESG 81/FEB 84). The "transcendent" essentialities exist, according to Stein, but not in the same way as either concepts (with mental being) or essences (with real being, although they also have essential being). Essentialities have primarily essential being.

32. Even in the case of mental and real being, these divisions into "realms" fail to work. Thoughts are also real, and what is real could also be what is thought (particularly for Stein, who follows Thomas in seeing real things as created by the thought of God).

33. "Philosopisch[*sic*]-theologische Anthropologie bei Edith Stein mit dem Schwerpunkt auf 'Endliches und ewiges Sein—Versuch eines Aufstiegs zum Sinn des Seins-'" (Diplomarbeit, Eberhard-Karls-Universität Tübingen, 1988/89), 32–33, translation mine, quoting EeS 303/ESG 280–81/FEB 326. Copy at Edith-Stein-Karmel, Tübingen.

ry. Thus, what is thought, for example, must have both mental being and essential being insofar as it is thought clearly.[34]

Stein describes the "world" of essential being—that is, the kind of being structures and intelligibility entities have[35]—as a layered realm [*Stufenreich*][36] filled with manifold "unities of meaning distinguished and delimited from one another through content."[37] Within this realm, there are: (a) the essentialities, (b) "the essential traits of composite structures which we name *essential what* [*Wesenswas*],"[38] and (c) essences and quiddities with greater and lesser generality. The second two entities "in" the realm of essential being may also gain real being in things, that is, their essential being and necessary structure may unfold in time and through various kinds of matter. In contrast, the being of essentialities is solely changeless and timeless.

Essential being as a kind of being in contrast to real or mental being is described as having a kind of repose or abiding in itself that is neither currently living nor an initial step toward real being (that is, it is neither act nor potency); it is "no *becoming* and *passing away*," yet it "stands in *opposition to real being*."[39] Thus, in addition to the contrast between act and potency, she adds a second contrast between act and *wesenhaftig*. With Stein's claim regarding essential being—even when seen as a part of other beings—being cannot be simply identified with *act*.

In *Finite and Eternal Being* III, §8, she says:

The being of the essentiality and the quiddity is abidingness [*Ruhen*] *in itself.*[40] Because of that it would be described in German most concisely and appropriately with *wesen*.[41] Therein is expressed still more impres-

34. See also *Finite and Eternal Being* VIII, §2, 6.

35. We should ask to whom something must be intelligible for it to have essential being.

36. See EeS 81/ESG 81/FEB 84.

37. EeS 101/ESG 99/FEB 105.

38. EeS 81–82/ESG 81/FEB 86.

39. EeS 88/ESG 87/FEB 91.

40. While the quiddity may unfold temporally, most properly its being is essential.

41. That is, "being in an essential way." This is *Wesen* (essence) used as a verb and thus not capitalized.

sively than in the Latin [words] *essentia—esse* the close association of being and essence. Becoming and passing away, on one side, *wesen,* on the other, stand opposite each other as being in motion and being at rest [*bewegtes und ruhendes Sein*]. Both are being [*Sein*]. If, however, one objectively precedes the other, it is *wesen.* Because, as movement aims at rest, so all becoming has a *wesen* as [its] goal. Thereby, *essence* [*Wesen*] and *wesen* are necessary to be *something* and to be able *to be* something. Because of the close connection of essence [*Wesen*] and existence [*Sein*] it is understandable that there have been such great difficulties and that one has come so late to distinguish a particular being [*Seiende*] and being [existence, *Sein*] or to distinguish essence and existence [being] within the particular being [*Seienden*], so far as this was nothing real. Even so, it is understandable that some—apparently contradictorily—described nearly existence itself [and] nearly the essence, as *act.*[42]

She claims that to be *something* (that is, to have an essence giving the thing structure rather than chaos), a thing must be able *to be* something (that is, it must have essential being, limiting and "channeling" the possibilities for real being). Being is not just act but also rest; it includes both the striving toward a *telos* and that *telos* itself, complete and quiet. Or, we could say that the being of any particular entity includes not only what it now is, but also what it can and could be, that is, the essential possibilities of the being.

Stein turns to one of Aristotle's expressions for nature, τὸ τί ἦν εἶναι (approximately, "that which was to be"), and suggests that it is in the notion of essential being that this phrase finds true expression.[43] Only that "what is essential *is* unchangeably that which it *was.*"[44] Only things with essential being (that is, the possibilities and essential structure of a thing) are unchangeably what they always were.

Essentialities, while paradigmatic of things with essential being, are not the only things that have this being. Essences, while able to gain real being, always retain their essential being. In a rather long passage in III, §8 (which I will interrupt for commentary), she says:

---

42. EeS 90/ESG 89/FEB 93. 43. See EeS 89/ESG 88/FEB 93.
44. EeS 90/ESG 88/FEB 93.

Our designation of *being in an essential way* [*wesens*] as the abidingness [*Ruhen*] of essentiality or quiddity in itself, as opposed to becoming and passing away, appears to exclude a transition of essentiality or quiddity from non-being to being—as found in the expression *reception of being.*

If essentialities and quiddities [*Washeiten*] have essential being, then they have a being of repose and completeness. If something is *at* the goal, it cannot still be in transition *to* the goal. Thus, the expression "reception of being" (the Thomistic reception of real being by the essence) is rather problematic. She continues:

We could indeed speak of a reception of being if we think of the *realization of the essence,* but the essential being appears to allow no beginning, the essential what [*Wesenswas*] no separation from its essential being.

Stein reinterprets "reception of being," thus, to mean the reception of real being or of the realization in real being of an essential structure which exists "already" insofar as it has essential being.[45] She then compares her position with Thomas's:

Is it in contradiction to this if St. Thomas says: "Of the quiddity it is said that it is created; for before it has a being, it is nothing outside of the spirit of the creator, and there it is not as creature but rather as creative essentiality"?[46] [*De potentia* q. 3 a. 5 ad 2] . . . If we search to make clear the meaning of this sentence and think of what Thomas understands with *quiddity,* then he shows rather a confirmation of the conception developed here. The *quiddity* is that *for which* a thing is formed, that *what* it is, "a part of the composite whole" [*De veritate* q. 3 a. 1c]. It is also named *form.* From that Thomas distinguished the *idea* in the sense which he named "creative essentiality" in the previously cited place; "because this name *idea* appears to mean a form separated from that whose form it is." "It is that, according to which it is formed; and this is the exemplary form to whose image something is formed."

45. She says, "If the talk of reception of being is to have a meaning, then that *which* receives the being must have a kind of being already before the reception of real being" (EeS 91/ESG 90/FEB 94). See also Andreas Müller's *Grundzüge der Religionsphilosophie Edith Steins* (Freiburg: Alber, 1993), esp. 237.

46. "Essentiality" is used here to refer to the divine ideas, and it is not necessarily used in a way identical with Stein's understanding of "essentiality."

Thomas claims that an essence does not have being prior to its existence in a thing. Thus, "reception of being" for Thomas does not mean that essence, which already was, receives being (analogous to a glass which is filled with water). Rather, a created essence, which is distinct from its existence, exists only in a unity with being. Nonetheless, Thomas does distinguish the quiddity or essence from the divine idea, or as Stein calls it, the "creative essentiality." Stein exploits this distinction in order to present her own position. Of the Thomistic notion of the divine ideas, she says:

These exemplary forms have, according to the Augustinian understanding of the Platonic doctrine of ideas which Thomas here follows, their being in the divine spirit. From these are distinguished the *created forms* which have their being in the things. Under the created forms we must evidently understand the essence *realized* in things. The being that they receive is the *real* being that they have in things. The "becoming created" is nearer to what we have understood under *reception of being*. But if the discussion of reception of being should have a meaning, so must that *which* receives the being already have a kind of being before the reception of real being. Thomas could admit that only in the sense in which he grants a being to the archetypal [*urbildlichen*] ideas: as being in the divine spirit. In the meaning, however, he must concede it. For if one supposes that the image remains behind the archetype, so that the what of the thing does not coincide in its content with the creative idea, then it is indeed unthinkable that the creator could not have already known the image as it is in the way that it has fallen short of the archetype.[47]

Following Augustine, Thomas affirms that the exemplars for real things are the divine ideas, and he distinguishes between a human being and the archetype Human Being in a way roughly analogous to a copy (made individual in matter) and its original. The copy or created essence receives being in the act of creation, but this does not mean that the created essence was anything or existed in any way prior to "receiving" real being. Before the created essence received being in the act of creation, only the exemplar existed. In

47. EeS 90–91/ESG 89–90/FEB 93–94.

contrast, Stein has given essence more than just real being; essence itself also has essential being. Thus, for Stein, *reception of being* can have a meaning beyond that given to the phrase by Thomas: an essence with essential being may receive real being.

She further argues that we can move toward a goal precisely because we "carry" our goal along with us. Our essence or quiddity, with its essential being, is the goal (for example, the full humanity) toward which a human being aims. The quiddity has, and cannot be separate from, its essential being, although a human being *realizes* or *unfolds* that essential being only in real being. In III, §12, she says:

> Every finite thing *receives* its being (we must, according to our interpretation, say its *real* being) as something added to its essence. With that, a *real* separability between essence and real being is expressed. The essential being appears to us as not really, but only mentally, separable from the essential what [*Wesenswas*].[48]

There is, for Stein, a real distinction between essence and its real being, but only a mental one between essential being and essence. Essence, thus, always has essential being and may gain real being.

Essential Being and Potentialities

Stein uses this model in order to answer questions regarding the ontological status of potentiality:[49] what is actual (as opposed to potential) exists in the realm of real being. What is potential (as well as what is possible) rests on essential being. Various levels of possibility and relations among potentialities are explained through relations in the realm of essential being. What is potential is what is not fully real, but it is not nothing. Likewise, Stein insists that we cannot identify essence in a simple way either with what is

---

48. EeS 105/ESG 102–3/FEB 109.

49. Stein states that part of her project is to understand "act and potency as levels or ways of being" (EeS 34/ESG 40/FEB 35). I have interpreted this as a question of ontological status.

currently living and "real" or with non-being. The levels of an entity do not all exist in the same way. If we identify the essence of the thing simply with real being, then we cannot distinguish act and potency. For the potential is what is really possible yet is not actual.

The thing is its whole essence—past, present, and future—not simply what is now realized. Stein's image seems to be something like an electric current running through a wire: essence is the full wire; it is that which determines what course the current must take and in which it "comes alive"; what is real (existent) is the current itself, where and how it is at the present moment. But the whole wire is not "unreal" insofar as it directs what is possible for the current; it holds the course according to which the current can unfold. Likewise, essence would include the potentialities of the being, through which real being "flows." The wire image is limited in numerous ways. For living things, there is rarely just *one* way in which the being can unfold (as with a well-constructed wire); there are often many and various possibilities and potentialities. Nonetheless, all that is possible must be "written" on essence. (The wire analogy is also deeply problematic insofar as neither essential being nor essences are properly spatial, but I hope that this image may be useful even if severely limited.)

Stein describes the essence of Socrates as "being-Socrates," not "Socrates." That is, she describes his essence with an emphasis on the being distinctive to it. She writes:

Is being-Socrates, not "Socrates," the essence of this man? And if it is thus—is then "Socrates" still something other than this man and being-Socrates something other than the spatio-temporal existence [Dasein], the real being of this man? Otherwise it would come out that in the individual human being spatio-temporal existence [Dasein] and essence coincide: they would coincide in the "real essence," the πρώτη οὐσία. . . . That would, however, be the abolition of all that has been said up to now about essence and being: the *principle of essence*—that every object *has* its essence and that each essence is the essence of *an object*—would collapse if essence and object were the same. It would not be possible to understand with St. Thomas the essence as possibility, potency, the existence as act. The possibility of not existing is lost for the individual: the opposition of finite and eternal being would be abolished. The beginning, therefore, cannot be right. "Socrates" as the name of the final determination of the essence means something different than the human being Socrates himself, and the being-Socrates of this human being must be something different than his spatio-temporal existence [Dasein].[50]

In the last line she says that the final determination of "Socrates" is something different from the human being himself and that *being-Socrates* means something different from this existing being. The final determination of "Socrates" is, I take it, the form of "Socrates." The man Socrates differs from his formal structure; he is not merely that structure but a living, unfolding being. I read the second claim here, her claim that this particular existing being differs from *being-Socrates,* to mean that the essence differs from the real living being. *Being-Socrates* is the essence *of* the object, in contrast to the existence of the man Socrates himself.

Socrates's essence is, according to Stein, *being-Socrates.*[51] His nature is to be *in* the form of "Socrates" (as well as all the other determinations relevant to essence), not merely to "be" that form. The essence (the *being-Socrates*) prescribes the lawfulness according to which Socrates's development should unfold: e.g., that he should begin as a small child, grow and mature, developing his skills. It is rooted in his nature, his *being-Socrates,* that he should develop in certain ways, but what actually occurs may not fulfill the form of Socrates or its prescriptions on how he should *be* Socrates. Perhaps in his nature was the potential for great empathetic understanding that was never developed. Thus, the actual being, Socrates as he lived in 440 B.C., need not fulfill all possibilities of the essence, the *being-Socrates,* which Socrates has.

50. EeS 148–49/ESG 140/FEB 154.
51. We can see the influence of Jean Hering here. He talks of "being-red" as a certain moment in the object (see "Bemerkungen" II, §1). The color in an object is the object's "being-red," not simply "red" or "red-ness." These latter terms refer, rather, to the color as an ideal content and not specified or belonging in any object.

Presumably, however, we carry these "laws" of our essence within us. (In using the language of "law" here, I do not mean to imply that there is a single prescription for development.) They are a part of our form. We can thus make sense of her language: Stein continually says *entfalten* (to unfold) and *Entfaltung* (unfolding) rather than *werden* (to become). Something that unfolds uncovers what is already there, whereas *becoming* need not have that implication. We could use the image of a seed unfolding or developing according to the prescriptions of the DNA which were present at the conception of the seed (with, of course, the caveat that there may be a wide range of possibilities available in the essence). The seed need not sprout, shoot up a stalk, develop leaves, flowers, and fruit; there may be a drought one year or a late frost may kill the new growth; but if the plant ever grows, it may only grow according to what is already there in the DNA. Likewise, Stein suggests that human beings (including in their psychic and spiritual unfolding) may develop only what was already present and "prescribed" in their essence.

Thus, Stein makes a threefold distinction; she distinguishes, first, the real being of temporally unfolding things, secondly, their essential structure or essence, which both makes them *what* (the kind of thing) they are and functions as the goal of their development, and, finally, the thing in this moment of time, where it is on the way to its goal. Thus, she says:

It is "the same" what was in "original reality" from eternity in God and what becomes real in time in the things. In things the separation of the what and the essence from its realization, of essential from real being, is now possible. In God, however, this proves impossible.[52]

God's essential being and real being are one, as His essence and existence are one. In created beings, however, neither our essence and existence are to be identified nor are the essential being of our essence and the present state of the essence, its present point in the unfolding process.[53]

52. EeS 111/ESG 108/FEB 114.
53. One question this claim raises is: how are we to understand her claims

Conclusion

Essence is characterized as having essential being, and I take it that her categorization "essential being" is, in part, a way of giving logical categories and essential structures a basis or ontological grounding without following the Kantian move of making them structures of the mind or consciousness. Kant avoids the Humean conclusion that there is no necessity (but only habits of association) by placing necessity within an a priori of consciousness. Stein, following Husserl, makes the same move by placing necessity not within consciousness but within essential structures (for Stein, this is articulated in terms of the kind of being that these structures have, rather than within their forms themselves). Facts may always be contingent, but essences have an eidetic necessity which is independent of any particular fact (although perhaps known only through facts). Thus, the ontological grounding for logic, mathematics, and all essences is similar and lies in the kind of being these things have. Contra Kant, Stein does not think that the necessity of each lies in consciousness, and her claim regarding the essential being of various essential structures can be seen as part and parcel of her general rejection of idealism.[54]

In positing a kind of being distinct from real or mental being and, further, in claiming that certain things, i.e., essentialities, have essential being but cannot gain real being in things (in contrast to essences and traits of the essence), Stein makes a claim that looks strikingly Platonic: there would be truly existing things (albeit with essential being, not real being) running around somewhere out there distinct from all entities we actually experience or

---

that essential being is incomplete in itself? I take it that the response is that it too is striving toward and united in real being; God is the source of that actualization for the "separated" essential beings (i.e., essentialities).

54. It is not clear to me that Husserl is an idealist, but Stein was concerned about this issue, and throughout *Finite and Eternal Being* Stein makes clear her realistic stance; she says, for example, "We have conducted the whole consideration with the silent assumption that corresponds to natural experience: that there is a multitude of objects" (EeS 309/ESG 286/FEB 333).

can experience. Stein avoids making such a claim by identifying essential being ultimately with the divine ideas.[55] Things with essential being are always either in real things (and thus have real existence in the things) or in the mind of God[56] (and thus have mental being in addition to essential being). Essences thus have essential being and may gain actual being as the essence of some entity unfolding in time; essentialities, in contrast, never gain *temporal* being, but they do have mental being in the mind of God in addition to their essential being. Thus, essential being becomes—like the unity Scotus ascribes to the common nature—a being less than other types of being insofar as it must always accompany another kind of being.

In conclusion, in following Scotus rather than Thomas on the nature of universals, Stein insists that there is some necessity, unity, and being to essential structures independent of and in some sense prior to its instantiation in things. She articulates this claim through the concept of essential being, which is a kind of being distinct from real being (although always accompanying real being), giving integrity to the *telos* of finite, developing beings and providing a theoretical framework for discussing potency, potentiality, possibility, and necessity. The category of essential being likewise plays a role in her understanding of individual forms, individuality, and individuation, as will be seen in the next chapter.[57]

55. She says, "The being of essentialities and quiddities is not to be thought of as an independent next to the eternal. It is the eternal itself that shapes in itself the eternal forms—not in a temporal happening—according to which it creates the world in time and with time" (EeS 103/ESG 100/FEB 106). Likewise, she also says, "Thus the being of unities of meaning also cannot be independent of God" (EeS 102/ESG 100/FEB 106). See also *Finite and Eternal Being* IV, §3.

56. Stein dedicates II, §12 to a discussion of the inner life of the Trinity and the relations of real and essential being in the divine persons.

57. In this chapter I have been concerned primarily with exposition, but there are nonetheless several things which are puzzling to me in the notion of *essential being*. Given her different types of being, it is unclear to me what *being* means and, therefore, what each of these types has in common. Being can mean, in the case of *real being*, act and dynamic, efficacious activity. In the case of *essential being*, it means rest and stability. Thus, not all being is dynamic. Some being is—in the case of *essential being*—static. An analogical concept of being

is certainly common in the Thomistic tradition, but Stein's concept of "being" is not merely analogical, but—it initially appears—equivocal. There is no one thing which it means *to be*. Rather, being in the case of real being means activity, whereas being in the case of essential being means static stability. I do not yet know how Stein would address this problem. She might, as Nicholas Madden suggested (correspondence, March 2007), claim that being is not a *what*, and thus one cannot expect a conceptual articulation comparable to that given regarding essences. I do not know if this would work or whether Stein would agree and will not pursue it in the following. But I would like to note it as a question that needs to be addressed if Stein's metaphysical claims are to be defensible.

Five ◠ PRINCIPLES OF INDIVIDUALITY

I would like to turn to Stein's theory of individuation and individuality in light of the claims laid out in the previous two chapters regarding essentialities, essences, and essential being. As seen there, Stein distinguishes essences, which are capable of temporal unfolding and which are the essence *of* something, from essentialities, which are atemporal and (in some sense) ground the essences. Stein further claims that both essences and essentialities have a distinctive being as essential structures. This essential being can be contrasted with actual being, even if it is not independent of such actual being. In chapter 4 of *Finite and Eternal Being*, Stein makes a further distinction between the essence *(Wesen)* (or more specifically, the pure what of the essence)[1] and its *Wesensform*, which I will render as *substantial form*.[2] Given this distinction, we need a

1. In the following I will take *essence* to be approximately identical with *pure what*, that is, the what or nature independent of its real being (and thus taken purely in its essential being). At times, however, the essence refers to the nature of the thing; if and when the thing really exists, the essence may refer to the real being as well as to the essential being. In her thesis on *Finite and Eternal Being*, Eva-Marie Knoche points to this in saying that within the essence, Stein distinguishes the *pure what (rein Was)* and the *being of the what (Was-sein)*. See *Philosopisch-theologische Anthropologie*, 39–40. For the sake of the following, however, when I refer to *essence*, I am concerned primarily with it in its essential being.

2. *Substantial form* is not at all close to the German *Wesensform*, which would be more appropriately translated as "form of the essence" or even "essential form." "Form of the essence" strikes me as an awkward and cumbersome English phrase, and "essential form" rings too much like "essential being" (or the form with essential being) to be helpful. *Wesensform* should be understood *in contrast to* essential being and sharply distinguished from the *essential what* (with its essential being). The term best able to capture what she means by *Wesensform* is "substantial form." See also the explanation in the glossary and

clarification of her claim that the basis of individuality is formal.[3] In this chapter, I would like, first, to present her distinction between substantial form and essence; second, to sketch out briefly Stein's claims regarding the principle of individuation and the principle of uniqueness for each human being; and, finally, to consider what role (if any) individual forms play in this.

Essence *(Wesen)* and Substantial Form *(Wesensform)*

Essentialities and essences are distinguished, at least in part, because essences can experience a temporal unfolding of their meaning, whereas essentialities cannot. Both essences and essentialities have essential being, and insofar as their being is essential rather than real, they are atemporal and, thus, properly static. Essential being is defined in contrast to temporal movement, and in their essential being, essences do not change, become, or develop. (Essences may, however, receive real being.[4] When this happens, what is static in essential being unfolds in time. It is in this sense that an essence may experience temporal unfolding and may "develop.") Thus, Stein's essence cannot be understood simply as *form* in either Aristotle's or Thomas's sense. For Aristotle, form is the principle of *act* as well as the principle of intelligibility. While the essence with essential being is the principle of intelligibility for Stein, it cannot also be a principle of act without compromising its non-real (that is, essential) nature. In order to avoid this difficulty, Stein posits a

---

EeS 236/ESG 221/FEB 253, where Stein equates *Wesensform* with *forma substantialis*.

3. See, for example, *Finite and Eternal Being* VIII, §2, 5, and the discussion in chapter 2 above.

4. Stein distinguishes essences and essentialities in this way (see the discussion and cited passages in the previous chapter). The distinction here, however, needs a bit more fine-tuning. Nothing exists purely in essential being—including essentialities—therefore, both essences *and* essentialities should have some kind of real being. Thus, the distinction between the two should *not* be that essences can receive real being in addition to essential being whereas essentialities have solely essential being. Rather, essences can receive a temporal unfolding of their meaning, whereas essentialities cannot.

second notion of form which supplies the principle of real being for the thing: the substantial form *(Wesensform)*.[5]

Stein develops this distinction between *Wesen* and *Wesensform* through an analysis in IV, §4 of Aristotle's uses of *form* and *ousia*. Aristotle claims that it is "not the matter and not the form which become but, rather, the composite of both."[6] Stein comments on this:

> That which becomes is the new human being to whom being-human is proper. There is a sense in which one can say that the "being-human" does not become. On the other hand, however, each human being has *his* being-human that is distinguished from that of all others and is not before he himself is. If it is *form* that is discussed in both cases and if the two sentences should not contradict each other, then evidently the meaning is different in each.[7]

On the one hand, *being-human*—that is, what it means to be a full human being—does not become. This is, rather, the goal which is realized in the life of a human being. On the other hand, the particular human being herself does become. Thus, *form* as the goal and *form* as the being herself cannot be identical.

Stein argues that if *ousia* is intended to designate that which has a priority in being, then the goal should be called *ousia;* it is that which is the fullness of development. As the goal of an entity which is now in the process of developing, it cannot—while the thing is in process—yet be fully realized.[8] Thus, if understood as *ousia,* the goal is precisely what is not-yet-real. Aristotle further claims, however, that the goal is the *cause* of the movement, that for the sake of which there is something. In order to be a cause, it must be real in some sense.[9]

Stein concludes that the answer to these difficulties must be found in a distinction between *eidos* and *morphe (μορφή),* or, using

5. See, for example, EeS 304/ESG 282/FEB 327–28.
6. EeS 208/ESG 195/FEB 220. Stein footnotes Aristotle's *Metaphysics* Z 8, 1033b.
7. EeS 208–9/ESG 195/FEB 220–21.
8. See EeS 212/ESG 198/FEB 224–25.
9. See *Finite and Eternal Being* IV, §4, 4.

her terms, between *pure form* and *substantial form (Wesensform)*.[10] (This distinction is not identical with that between essence [*Wesen*] and substantial form, as will be seen in the following section.) She articulates the difference between these by claiming that the *pure form* does not become or pass away (as such, it has essential being), but it does prescribe *how* the object is realized and toward what end. It is, she says, "at the same time the goal and the way to the goal."[11] Stein states that the pure form both gives the goal to the entity, acting as a final cause, and stipulates how the being should reach that goal. She describes the latter as a "temporal shape," providing, for example, the laws according to which a human being must develop in order to be a human being.[12] One reaches the goal contained in the pure form by realizing and "unfolding" according to the laws of that form. The nature of any particular (finite) being is precisely to unfold *according to* such and such a form. Thus, she focuses on acquiring *(gelangen zu)*, being-in *(sein in)*, and unfolding *(entfalten)*, rather than developing *(entwickeln)* or growing *(wachsen)*.[13] So long as we are *in* the form of human being, that is, developing according to the laws laid out in the pure form, we *are* in fact a human being.[14]

10. See EeS 213/ESG 199/FEB 225–26.   11. EeS 213/ESG 199/FEB 226.
12. See EeS 232/ESG 217/FEB 249.

13. See also the discussion in chapter 3. In an article on Stein's philosophy, James Collins notes that "there are some indications that Edith Stein was in the process of subordinating all of the key metaphysical concepts in Aristotle and Aquinas to a theory of being that is much closer to Heidegger. In a brief note, she agrees with the latter thinker that temporality is the distinguishing mark of finite being as such, rather than the composition of essence and existence. That is perhaps why she views finite being chiefly in terms of the unfolding and the being-unfolded of meanings" ("Edith Stein as a Phenomenologist," in *Three Paths in Philosophy* [Chicago: Henry Regnery, 1962], 104). Here we can see one example of such a Heideggerian turn. Her concern is not with the "part" of the person per se that makes her human, but with the kind of *activity* which does so, and it is precisely this activity of "unfolding" according to a certain kind of lawfulness that makes one a human being.

14. At the beginning of *Finite and Eternal Being* IV, §3, 2, Stein raises the question: what does it mean to "be in this form"? In speaking of Socrates, one refers to—as Stein puts it—the *what (Was)*, what is *wesenhaft-ig* and structural. She says,

Like Aristotle, Stein sees the form as that which the thing becomes, but Stein insists on separating the pure form and the substantial form.[15] Rather than positing one form which acts as both the formal and final cause, she posits two forms. The first, the pure form, acts as the final cause. It is the goal of the thing's development, that which it is aiming to become (including the ideal path for becoming). The second, the substantial form, is the formal cause *in* the entity. Stein claims that this distinction allows us to understand how a thing can be said to be *incomplete* or *deficient*. Such *incompleteness* or *deficiency* lies in the relation or gap between the thing and its goal. The pure form exists prior to the thing or the thing's realization of the goal, and thus it may act as a final cause. In contrast, the form within the thing (the substantial form) is not prior to the thing but exists as soon as the new being exists.[16] As such it acts as a principle of (real) being; she says, "The substantial form [*forma substantialis*] is that through which something has independence and its own being [*esse substantiale*]."[17] This form acts

---

"'Socrates' signifies *what* Socrates is, and this what allows itself to be released—just as 'human being' and 'living creature' [do]—from the what-determinateness of this human being and grasped in its purity—as *essential what [wesenhaftes Was]*" (EeS 149/ESG 140/FEB 155). Stein claims that what we come to know is the essential what in which the entity unfolds.

15. In EeS 213/ESG 199/FEB 226, Stein suggests that we make a threefold distinction: first, there is the pure form that does not become or pass away; secondly, there is the form in the thing, the principle of being and development; and finally, there is the pure form *as it is in the thing,* that is, as the laws written upon the substantial form. I will develop this threefold distinction in the following section.

16. See *Finite and Eternal Being* IV, §3, 19, and §4, 3. At EeS 307/ESG 284–85/FEB 331, she says: *"Finite being is the unfolding of meaning; essential being is timeless unfolding beyond the opposition of potency and act; real being is the unfolding out of a substantial form, from potency to act in time and space."* (The italics are Stein's.) We might ask whether Stein has needlessly multiplied the number of forms. Might not all of these be accounted for by a single kind of form and, as seen under different aspects, performing different roles?

17. EeS 236/ESG 221/FEB 253. The German *selbsteigenes Sein* is not equivalent to the Latin *esse substantiale*, despite Stein's placing of the Latin in the parenthetical phrase. Her equation of the two is understandable, however, if we remember her distinction between two meanings of "object" (see the discussion in chapter 3 above). That which has its own being is "self-standing," or "freestanding."

as "ground of its efficacy and ability to be efficacious" and is that which moves the entity toward its end and goal.[18]

Stein's Account in Contrast to Thomas Aquinas's

Stein dedicates *Finite and Eternal Being* IV, §4, 3 to the distinction of pure form and substantial form, and her discussion sounds much like Thomas's position. Thomas distinguishes the form in a thing from its archetype, or the divine idea according to which it is created.[19] Likewise, Stein distinguishes the form in the thing (the substantial form) from the archetype (the pure form).[20] Stein's pure forms are ultimately the divine ideas, which God uses in creating the world. The forms in things, the substantial forms, are reflections of the archetypes. Thus, Stein appears to follow Thomas in his synthesis of Plato and Aristotle, positing both forms separate from this world and forms within things.

Nonetheless, Stein's position differs slightly from Thomas's. As seen in the previous chapter, she posits essential being as a kind of being which both mental and real entities may have but which is not reducible to either mental or real being. Essential being is distinct from temporal becoming, and things with essential being do not *become* or *develop*. An entity with essential being may be *unfolded* in time, but its essential structure does not thereby *become*, i.e., move from potency to act. Stein has further claimed that essences have essential being and that objects have essences.

We thus need to distinguish the pure form from the object, the

18. EeS 214/ESG 200/FEB 228.
19. See, for example, *De veritate* q. 3, a. 1.
20. In *Finite and Eternal Being* IV, §4, 3, she says: "If the things appear as *images* [*Abbilder*] of the pure forms and these [the pure forms] appear as *archetypes* [*Urbilder*] toward whose realizations the substantial forms work, then it is not possible to think of an 'accidental' agreement of two fully separated worlds. Both point according to their origin to the same causality, which makes intelligible their connection. The pure forms are incorporated into the unity of the divine Logos as the archetypes of things in the divine spirit, who sets the things into spatio-temporal being [*Dasein*] with their inscribed temporal shape" (EeS 217/ESG 202–3/FEB 231).

essence of the object, and the object's substantial form. The pure form, as the archetype, and the essence, as the image[21] or reflection of the pure form, both have essential being. Even as "written upon" a substantial form, the essence retains its own kind of being. Stein understands, however, the principle of growth and development to be the substantial form—and not the essence—of the object. The "set of instructions" written into the substantial form, in contrast, is the essence of the object. And the object or entity develops, unfolding (more or less) that structure.[22] Thus, Stein distinguishes not only the pure form from the substantial form (and thus the final cause from the formal cause), she also distinguishes the essence and the substantial form, at least insofar as the essence in its essential being differs from the real being of the substantial form.

Thus, the man Socrates, for example, would have a pure form as an archetype or idea in the mind of God, acting as the final cause of his development. He would have an essence—being-Socrates—which has both essential being *qua essence* and real being in its temporal unfolding between circa 470 and 399 B.C., and which acts as the principle of intelligibility. Finally, he would have a substantial form which acts not as a principle of intelligibility, but as a principle of growth and development. The substantial form has primarily real or actual being, although it has "written upon it" the instructions for growth and development from the essence.

Essence, Substantial Form, and the Aristotelian Categories

We can see Stein's second distinction between the essence and substantial form at work in her discussion of Aristotle's categories. She opens chapter 4 of *Finite and Eternal Being* by pointing to

21. Stein explicitly attempts to find the image *(Abbild)* of God in all creation and not simply in human beings. See *Finite and Eternal Being* VII.
22. Stein says, "The essence of Socrates prescribes for him how he is to unfold, in a measured way, the pure form" (EeS 153/ESG 144/FEB 159).

two ways in which the Aristotelian categories can be understood: first, as categories of *assertion* and, secondly, as categories of *being*. These two understandings of the categories correspond insofar as what can be asserted of a thing should indicate what the thing is. Thus, when we say that we can distinguish qualities, relations, and other accidents of a thing, we can do so, presumably, because the thing is truly made up of such elements. That the thing is divided through the categories enables one to assert such categorical divisions in the thing.

There is, however, an important incongruity between the categories as forms of assertion and the categories as forms of being. The *tode ti* as a form of assertion describes the *what* of a thing, its fundamental nature, which for Aristotle is the species-form. This can be known separately from the thing and, therefore, predicated of a thing as a whole. I can say, for example, that Crito is human. Crito's human nature as his *tode ti* allows itself to be distinguished from Crito as existing; it could not be predicated of Crito if one could not so recognize and assert it of Crito. In contrast, when seen as a form of being, the *tode ti* does not allow itself to be known. It is the form *of* and *within* the thing, the final base on which all accidents depend and that which underlies all accidental changes. As such a foundation, it cannot be separated from the thing. The *tode ti* as a form of being can only be pointed to as the foundation to which all other being (as quality, quantity, etc.) belongs.

Stein exploits this ambiguity between the categories as logical predicates and the categories as groups of ontological forms in order to develop a tripartite understanding of things. She claims that things (as real, independent objects) consist of essence, matter, and substantial form.[23] The form, understood in terms of essence, is the

23. In the later chapters of *Finite and Eternal Being*, Stein talks of form, matter, and substrate *(Träger)*, which I interpret as an analogous distinction to that given here, and chapter 7 has numerous references to *person* as the substrate of the essence *(Wesensträger)*. See, for example, EeS 331–32 and 334/ESG 306–7 and 308–9/FEB 356–58 and 360. *(Träger* could also be translated as "carrier," which is a more appropriate rendering of *Träger* in other parts of *Finite and Eternal Being*. See the glossary for a fuller discussion of Stein's use of *Träger*.)

tode ti as that which can be finally or most fundamentally asserted of a thing (which Stein, in contrast to Aristotle, understands as the individual form rather than the species-form). Form in this sense is not understood in contrast to matter but is, rather, the essence. It is ultimately *what* the thing is, and if that thing is a material entity, the essence would include matter.[24] In contrast, form in the sense of substantial form is precisely form in contrast to matter, and substantial form is—for corporeal things—the structure which has the power to organize matter and appropriate nutrients in order to form the entity.[25] The substantial form plays the role traditionally ascribed to form as the principle of growth and development;[26] it is the principle for the unfolding of organic, living structures— human beings, squirrels, etc. (as opposed to, for example, the experience of joy)—and is characterized as interior-dwelling, goal-directed power.[27] The substantial form can be described as a seed which has the power to fashion matter according to the "code" or "type" written upon it, while the form in the sense of essence is a

24. For example, in *Finite and Eternal Being* IV, §4, 11, she notes that the universal essence of corporeal things includes matter. In this context, however, I take matter to refer not to actually existing matter, but to the empty "place holder" for the matter (that is, matter of indeterminate dimension) that must enter this thing if and when it has real being.

25. See, for example, *Finite and Eternal Being* VII, §2. Stein struggles with the notion of matter, distinguishing both a pre- and post-Fall state of the relation of matter and form (see *Finite and Eternal Being* IV, §4, 5) and presenting two conceptions of what matter might be, an atomic and dynamic hypothesis. She prefers the atomic, but entertains both hypotheses (see *Finite and Eternal Being* IV, §3, 12).

26. She says: "Thus, matter-forming substantial forms are not thinkable without material fullness formed through them. One such form is *living*: i.e., its being is movement out of itself, and *power*-endowed, i.e., capable of determinately forming efficacy. The coincidence of *form* and, in certain senses, creative *power* flashes here: *substantial forms are as such powerfully formational.* From this, one understands that the form is described as the proper entity [*Seiende*] to which the matter owes its being and that one can waver as to whether one should not call them alone, and not first the whole, οὐσία or substance" (EeS 220/ESG 205–6/FEB 235; the phrase "in gewissem Sinne, schöpferischer"—translated as "in certain senses, creative"—is not in the ESG edition).

27. See, for example, EeS 217/ESG 202/FEB 231 and EeS 230/ESG 215/FEB 246.

static notion, functioning as the principle of intelligible (and structural) content.

These three are related insofar as the substantial form strives to actualize the essence by working through matter. The substantial form functions as the efficient cause of change within organic things once they exist.[28] The nature of the thing, however, is not determined by this guiding form alone, but by its state as that which unfolds in the form of such and such. (The substantial form has this essential structure "written on it," but Stein makes clear that the essential what or essence is nonetheless distinct, in some sense, from the substantial form. It seems to me that this distinction becomes most clear in light of her claims regarding essential being: the essence of Socrates, for example, *is*—in its essential being—"being Socrates," regardless of the degree to which the substantial form succeeds in "unfolding" the essence in real being.)

Stein develops her distinction between essence and substantial form by considering the case of fictional characters. She has claimed both that "real" beings (for example, squirrels and cats) are also *wesenhaft-ig* (that is, they have essential being) and that other non-real things, for example, fictional characters, are not merely mental but also have essential being. There is a structure and logic to ideal objects and fictional imaginings.[29] How then do we distinguish the first and second kinds of entities, both with essential being? How do we say one is *real*, while the other is not?

Both squirrels and fictional unicorns are *unfolding*. A squirrel begins as a small being and goes through a certain type of cell di-

---

28. She makes the interesting claim at the beginning of *Finite and Eternal Being* IV, §4, 7, that "each structure as each matter is an embodiment of a quiddity, a *pure form*. The realization is guided through the substantial forms. It is possible that a pure form (for example, that of a landscape [but surely not limited to landscapes]) demands a multitude of materials and therefore also of substantial forms for its realization" (EeS 224/ESG 209/FEB 239).

29. Stein discusses the example of art and poetical characters in some detail, suggesting that the very fact that we can evaluate art and recognize better and worse art implies that it is not merely *mental* but also *essential*. See *Finite and Eternal Being* IV, §3, 2.

vision and a certain type of gestational experience, and grows and matures according to the pattern of squirrel development. So also, we might imagine the early life of a unicorn, the sprouting of its horn, its growth and development, etc. Stein claims that "the real as well as the poetical figures have their exemplar in *pure forms* and unfold in accordance with them."[30] A poet, for example, makes a true or genuine figure insofar as she chooses traits and actions from the possibilities of the essence, unfolding a character amid its possible ways of behavior. Stein describes the difference between geometrical objects or poetical figures and squirrels or cats as that between merely unfolding entities and *self*-unfolding beings. The heroine of a novel "unfolds her possibilities" only if the novelist sits down to write out her story, whereas a cat—given enough food and water—will grow and develop without work on my part. Fictional characters do not unfold in efficacious happenings nor do they truly *possess* an essence through a substantial form which actualizes it.[31] Stein argues that the difference between what is real (the squirrel, for example) and what is imaginary (the novel's heroine, for example) lies not in their respective essences per se, but in how that essence is present. The poetical figure is "bestowed" or loaned *(verliehen)* a nature, whereas real things possess their essence and unfold within the essence through their substantial form. The real, living entity has the power in itself (its substantial form) to claim the pure form.

Thus, Stein distinguishes between the principle responsible for growth (the substantial form, *Wesensform*) and that responsible for intelligibility (the essence), although also claiming that the two are intrinsically related. The substantial form develops according to the prescriptions of the essence, although the substantial form itself is never properly known.[32] It is the power to realize the form in

---

30. EeS 155/ESG 146/FEB 161. Stein makes clear on the previous page that poetical figures have essences which are copies of pure forms.

31. See *Finite and Eternal Being* IV, §3, 2.

32. This claim is dependent, first, upon the unknowability of the form *within* the thing and, secondly, on the equation of substantial form and substrate. In *Fi-*

real being, but is not itself that intelligible structure.[33] The essence, however, is *what* the thing is, and as a *what* is distinguishable and knowable.

Substantial Forms and Individuation

As seen in the second chapter, Stein argues that any adequate theory of individuation must be able to account for the indivisibility of an entity (that is, its inability to be divided into further things of its kind) in addition to its impredicability. While matter can give the second, it cannot provide the first. Matter is, by its nature, divisible; the genus of matter is precisely that which is extended through space and divisible.[34] Thus, she argues that the principle of individuation must be formal.

Stein, however, distinguishes at least two senses of form within the thing: the essence and the substantial form. The essence in its essential being provides the set of "rules" for the structure and development of the entity, and the substance, insofar as it develops,

---

nite and Eternal Being VII, §1, she claims that the substrate *(Träger)* is incommunicable. Insofar as the substantial form is to be identified or closely related to the substrate, it is never properly known.

33. We could ask: if the substantial form is that which empowers the unfolding of the entity according to the prescriptions of the essence, and the substantial form itself is not intelligible nor is the entity yet fully worked out, then how do we know the entity? Stein answers this by pointing to a *worked-out essence (ausgewirkte Wesen),* which differs from both the essence and substantial form. She says: "For living things, the determination of essence is much more that which prescribes to them what they should *become* and what they continually *acquire.* At the same time they *have* indeed, however, in each step of development already a characteristic essence and one grounding outer appearance and activity" (EeS 233/ESG 217/FEB 249). Likewise: "We hit here again upon the opposition of *pure form*—the idea of the plant or of the determinate species of plant which stands 'over' the line of development, the *substantial form* which is efficacious in the individual plant, and the changing *worked-out essence* which corresponds more or less to the pure form" (EeS 233/ESG 218/FEB 250). Thus, we both unfold according to a structure and unfold some structure, the worked-out essence. See also the discussion in chapter 3.

34. Despite some of the overtones, Stein's discussion of matter here draws from an understanding of matter more medieval than phenomenological.

must develop according to the laws and prescriptions of its essence. In contrast, the substantial form is the principle of development; it is primarily a seat of powers, including the power to develop according to an essence. As such, the substantial form is non-transferable and impredicable.[35] As the principle by which the entity achieves its essence, the substantial form cannot be both in the mind and in a thing (as, in contrast, an essence can). Furthermore, the substantial form is distinguished from matter, which, Stein declares, is by its nature divisible. (And thus it avoids Stein's critique of Thomas's position.)[36] If it cannot be divided (as matter can) and cannot be predicated, then the substantial form appears to satisfy Stein's paradigms for individuality. It has properties sufficient to give us both an indivisible (that is, closed as a species-whole and incapable of being further divided) and an impredicable entity.

When Stein ascribes the individuation of material things to the form of the thing, I take this to mean the substantial form, *not* the essence.[37] In *Finite and Eternal Being* VIII, §3, she says:

35. "The substantial form is not 'communicable' to a multitude of individual things but, rather, the pure form or essentiality in which the things 'participate' through their substantial form" (EeS 445/ESG 408/FEB 486). Stein often sets words concerning *participation* (for example, *mitteilbar* and *teilhaben*) in scare quotes. See also *Finite and Eternal Being* III, §2.

36. It can be argued that Stein has not understood Thomas correctly. Höfliger in his dissertation on the problem of universals in *Endliches und ewiges Sein* says: "Edith Stein understands the materia signata quantitate as a first formation. In my opinion, she does not understand Gredt correctly. Neither Gredt nor the Thomistic school mean the materia signata quantitate as informed, therefore actualized matter. Still for Stein it holds fast: 'The "separation," the being-extended spatially and the divisibility, is the form of matter as such' (441). That would point to the actualized material and not to that which Thomism meant." (*Das Universalienproblem in Edith Steins Werke "Endliches und ewiges Sein,"* [Fribourg: Universitätsverlag, 1968], 73). I have argued here that, while this may be true, neither Stein's own critique of Thomas nor Höfliger's evaluation of that critique address the points of deepest disagreement.

37. Further, the substantial form has in itself individuality. She says, "While the substantial form was described as incommunicable, it is already to be taken as something individual 'in itself'" (EeS 446/ESG 409/FEB 486). See also *Finite and Eternal Being* VIII, §2, 6. Her discussion here is relevant only to material things, and the question must be asked anew for non-corporeal things. See also EeS 244/ESG 228/FEB 262–63.

Individuality and independence are both anchored in the structure it-self, and certainly because of that, it is a *something* or an *object* (in the narrow sense):[38] substrate of a what and an essence. The independence belongs to the whole—to the substrate with what it carries—the individ-uality, however, already [belongs] to the substrate itself and to all that it carries or closes in itself: the essence as well as all its parts and all added attributes. Thus, independence and individuality have a common basis in the formal construction of the being.[39]

Here she claims that the substrate of the what has individuality. We cannot say that the substrate is itself fully independent because it needs something to carry (presumably, an essence as well as mat-ter and accidents). But the substrate is the principle and ground of individuality as well as independence.[40] I take the substrate here to refer to the substantial form. As noted above, Stein distinguish-es substantial form and essence, and the substantial form is that which realizes or unfolds the essence. In that sense, the substantial form "carries" the what or essence. If this equation between sub-strate and substantial form is correct, then it appears that the sub-stantial form is the principle of individuation.[41]

Stein does grant that matter has a role in individuation inso-far as a substantial form cannot exist without matter; the substan-tial form is the "matter-forming form," in contrast to the essence.[42]

38. See the penultimate section of chapter 3 for the narrower and broader meanings of "object."

39. EeS 450/ESG 412–13/FEB 491–92.

40. With substantial form as the principle of individuation, Stein also adds a third condition necessary for full individuality: independence. She spends time showing how independence is a necessary condition for full individuali-ty through a discussion of the incomplete individuality of specific geometrical shapes. See *Finite and Eternal Being* VIII, §2, 6.

41. Likewise, she says that "the difference (among things) rests on their sub-strate" (EeS 451/ESG 413/FEB 492).

42. See EeS 446/ESG 409/FEB 487. She gives us a footnote at this point, say-ing: "If I rightly understand him, Duns Scotus does this also: he sees a positive entity as *principium individuationis,* that divides the individual substantial form from the universal" (EeS 446/ESG 408–9/FEB 610). I should make note of this comment, but exactly what she means with this footnote is not clear to me. Stein herself does not posit individual forms for all entities, but only makes that claim for human beings and angels. Whether non-human animals have such an indi-

This enmattered form is unrepeatable, impredicable, and very much a this. Thus, Stein's claim that the principle of individuation is formal should be understood carefully. The principle of actual individuation (in real being) is formal insofar as *substantial form* is a kind of form, and with substantial form as the principle of individuation, she gets both impredicability *and* indivisibility.[43]

Substantial Forms and Unrepeatability

In chapter 2, I argue that Stein, like Scotus, understands individuality—that is, what it means to be an individual—to include indivisibility in addition to impredicability. That which individuates and thus makes a thing an individual must be the source both of the indivisibility and of the impredicability of the thing. Substantial form appears capable of achieving both.[44] Likewise, it appears that the substantial form acts as the principle of uniqueness, in the stronger sense of unrepeatable. The substantial form is precisely

---

vidual form is an open question for her. Thus, it is possible but unlikely that she is referring to Scotus's claims regarding *haecceitas*. Further, her footnote is connected to a comment regarding *matter*. She may merely be pointing to Scotus's insistence that the principle of individuation be something positive, not a mere division from other things.

43. Stein's critique that Thomism fails to give us full individuality is, it seems to me, slightly misguided. For Thomas, matter gives to a thing its impredicability, but indivisibility lies in the union of the matter and form (which provides the closed-ness in a species-form). Stein's own claim that matter may participate in making each of us individuals has itself a rather Thomistic ring, and it is not clear to me that in the end her claim regarding the principle of individuation is radically different from Thomas's (although her claims regarding the distinction of essence and substantial form as well as essential being put the claim in a different metaphysical context).

44. If we understand the principle of individuation as the principle by which we get an individual and Stein uses the paradigms of indivisibility and impredicability in order to understand what it means to be an individual, then substantial form appears to be a sufficient answer. But it is not clear to me that this truly solves the problem of *individuation*. I take the problem of individuation to ask not simply how we get an individual, but how we get many individuals *all of one type*. It is not yet clear to me that substantial form alone can do this. Since my primary concern is individual forms, I will not pursue this question here.

that which directs the unfolding of the essence; it is that through which an entity "claims" its essence. While any particular form (understood as structure) may theoretically be repeated, the history of actual development cannot. Stein gives the example of a melody played twice. It is the same melody, but as unfolded at different times, we have two. In a similar ways, "we see the course of life of a man as something one-time that cannot be repeated."[45] Each thing as the embodiment of its essence, accomplished via the substantial form, is unique.

Stein says:

We attempted such a demonstration and found the root of being individual in the formal construction of the objects as such: therein, the final substrate as the empty form of its essence is incommunicable. . . . The difference in content of individual things, however, is not grounded in their formal construction.[46]

I read this to mean that the root of being an individual thing is found in the formal construction, that is, in having a substantial form. The root of being unrepeatably unique, however, is not grounded in the formal construction but, rather, is something non-formal. It is the *actual activity* of the substantial form, and thus the strongest uniqueness of each individual is accomplished via the substantial form. One is unrepeatably unique because of one's actual choices and experiences. Experience, although perhaps unfolding along the lines of the essential structure, is not itself an essential structure. Thus, for example, the melody as played is not identical with the marks on the score sheet. (Another non-formal element is matter. Stein, however, rejects matter as the principle of uniqueness.[47] Mat-

45. EeS 453/ESG 415/FEB 494. Her claim here can be compared both with Husserl's position in the latter sections of *Ideas II* and with her own position in *On the Problem of Empathy*, where she claims that the I is "varied" (i.e., unique) "because each one has its peculiar experiential content" (*On the Problem of Empathy*, 39).

46. EeS 454/ESG 416/FEB 496.

47. "The species characteristic would indeed get here a different stamp according to the material of construction that the individual form [*Einzelne Form*] 'finds.' (It is not thereby said that the various shapes of the species characteristic

ter may help make the being unique insofar as it influences the development of the substantial form, but it is not itself the principle of uniqueness. Like its role in individuation, matter assists and affects the "work" done by the substantial form.) In both cases the substantial form is the root of our individuality: it gives to the individual both impredicability and indivisibility, and in the course of its unfolding of the essence, it makes the individual unique.[48] Insofar as it is a substantial form (rather than the pure form or essence), it is capable of being the principle of individuation, providing impredicability and indivisibility, and as lived (although not simply qua substantial form) it provides true unrepeatable uniqueness.

Individual Forms and Individual Uniqueness

If I have correctly interpreted Stein thus far, there appears to be little role for the individual form in either individuating us or in making each person unique. In both cases, the substantial form plays that role. Yet Stein posits individual forms. Although individual forms are not the principle of individuation or the principle of unrepeatable uniqueness, they are principles of the weaker kind of uniqueness. Individual forms are an a priori principle of individual uniqueness—or, perhaps better stated, they are that which provides the a priori structure for our personality, the core traits marking who each of us as an individual ought to be. Our individual form need not mark our actual personality (we can be deformed versions of ourselves), but it provides, rather, the structure marking how each of us ought to develop.[49]

---

is derived from the variety of materials for construction alone)" (EeS 456/ESG 417/FEB 498). See also EeS 457/ESG 418–19/FEB 499–500.

48. In the later part of *Finite and Eternal Being*, Stein describes human beings as a unity of body, soul, and spirit. This tripartite division can be seen to line up with the discussion thus far insofar as "body" corresponds (more or less) with "matter," "soul" with "essence," and "spirit" with "substantial form." Our fundamental uniqueness (as unrepeatability) lies in our spirit, in our free choices and decisions about how to form ourselves, etc.

49. Terry Wright helpfully describes the personal core as that which (or who) you fall in love with (correspondence, fall 2007).

In her dissertation (in a passage quoted in chapter 1), Stein asks us to imagine Caesar in a village rather than in Rome, or we might imaginatively place Caesar in Russia in the early twentieth century. Although surely certain things would be different if Caesar had lived in such different circumstances, nonetheless "just as surely he would remain Caesar." Stein posits a consistent personal structure characterizing Caesar as Caesar, regardless of where he finds himself. This personal structure "marks off the range of possibilities of variation," and this range is independent of the actual circumstances in which he happens to be born.[50] Regardless of where Caesar is found, even if time travel were possible, Caesar would in any place at any time remain essentially Caesar. Maybe the circumstances in which he makes his choices would differ, but the essential individual structure would remain the same.

In chapter 4 of *Finite and Eternal Being*, a work written nearly twenty years after her dissertation, Stein says (in a passage quoted in my chapter 4 above):

"Socrates," as the name of the final determination of the essence, means something different from the human being Socrates himself, and the being-Socrates of this human being must be something different from his spatio-temporal existence [Dasein].[51]

Here she points to *being-Socrates,* not *being-human,* as the essence. (Presumably, *being-Socrates* includes the possibilities of how he speaks to others, how he engages in philosophical debate, how the particular qualities of his rationality may unfold, etc.) Insofar as the essence has essential being, then *being-Socrates,* Socrates's essence, should have essential being and be therefore a priori or different from Socrates's real being. As such, *being-Socrates* is independent of his historical and material conditions. The historical and material conditions may affect the degree to which the essence is unfolded, but they do not shape the essential possibilities. The essence is that *in which* we unfold; it marks off our possibilities. Individual forms, therefore—insofar as they are part of the final de-

50. *On the Problem of Empathy*, 110.   51. EeS 148–49/ESG 140/FEB 154.

PRINCIPLES OF INDIVIDUALITY

termination of the essence—are not the result of our experience, but instead prescribe the possibilities available to experience. Thus, the individual form does *not* function as a principle of individuation or of uniqueness on the level of real being; rather, its role is on the level of essential being, where it acts as a principle of individuality and of uniqueness.

~

In his introduction to Stein's thought, Philibert Secretan makes a distinction between ontology and metaphysics. He says:

Within a theo-centric philosophy—that here is identified with the concept of "scholasticism"—difficulties arise, which are made visible by Edith Stein in the following: if scholasticism distinguished between essence [*Wesen*] and empirical fact, so they did not know to distinguish between ontology and metaphysics. If ontology investigates the nature of real things, so metaphysics looks to the possible (as Husserl showed after Leibniz). Only from this distinction can the real-existing be grasped as the individual realization of the universally valid possibility.[52]

I am inclined to use the terms differently, associating *metaphysics* with "the nature of real things" and *ontology* with the investigation into "the possible." Nonetheless, regardless of the name given, we can distinguish between an investigation into the *possibilities* of an essence[53] and a study of the *potentialities* of an entity. There can be no potentialities in a non-existent, or not-yet-really-existing, entity; potentiality is connected to reality, to the really existing, in a way that possibility is not.

The contrast between ontology and metaphysics, and correspondingly, between *possibility* and *potentiality*, ties into Stein's division of essential and real being. She speaks of two understandings of *Möglichkeit* (possibility):

52. *Erkenntnis und Aufsteig*, 128–29.
53. Stein consistently speaks of *Möglichkeiten* (possibilities) rather than *Potentialität* (potentialities or potencies). I take it that her choice of words here is deliberate and an indication of this distinction. See, for example, EeS 34 and 38/ESG 39–40 and 43/FEB 34–35 and 38, where she claims the language of *Möglichkeit* for her project. On EeS 304/ESG 282/FEB 328, Stein does use *Potentialität*, but note that it is in the context of a discussion of substantial form (*Wesensform*). See also EeS 326/ESG 302/FEB 353.

Possibility as the temporal-real is grounded in the essential being of the delimited unities of meaning (possibility of essence) and possibility as a preliminary step [*Vorstufe*] to higher reality (potentiality in contrast to actuality), as a deeper way of temporal being.[54]

She distinguishes possibility on the level of essential being, or possibilities of the essence, from possibility (i.e., potentiality) on the level of real being. Because Stein distinguishes these two kinds of being, she has two corresponding levels of possibility.

Stein has claimed that the essence is the structure of a thing but not in the same way in which a Thomistic form is. It is the static, intelligible structure which is distinct from its principle of real being. As such, the essence acts as a principle of *possibility* but not as a principle of *potentiality*. It delimits the possibilities available to the entity, but it does not provide the power to achieve anything (and therefore it is not a principle of potentiality).[55] In contrast, the substantial form, as the principle of being, dictates the metaphysical possibilities (that is, potentialities) of the essence.

If this is an accurate assessment, then it appears that the individual form individualizes the universal form on the level of essential being and acts as a principle for the *condition* of uniqueness, that is, it prescribes how a person *could* develop as unique, not how she *is* unique. We can interpret her claim in chapter 4 of *Finite and Eternal Being* regarding blessedness as suggesting this. She says:

The individual human being then, if he has reached *his* perfection (that is, in glory because there is no perfection for us beforehand), does not realize *everything* that is prescribed in the pure form "human being" but, rather, only that which is determined in *his* individual essence (therefore something of the pure form "Socrates").[56]

54. EeS 326/ESG 302/FEB 353.

55. In her 1922 essay on sentient causality, Stein distinguishes empirical possibilities from essential possibilities, that is, possibilities of an essence. See *Philosophy of Psychology and the Humanities,* esp. 94. I take that same distinction to be operative here.

56. EeS 213/ESG 199/FEB 226. Likewise, she says that in each person "the possible lines of development are marked out in the substantial form and differ for individuals" (EeS 366/ESG 337/FEB 397). I am interpreting her claim here to mean that the possible lines of development are marked in the essence, accord-

She claims that reaching perfection would involve the realization of all the possibilities of the individual form. The individual form, however, differs from the human form. Thus, the possibilities which one individual may unfold need not be identical with those available to another. Achieving perfection, she says, is not realizing all human possibilities but, rather, realizing all of *my* possibilities. The substantial form, as it unfolds the essence in matter and in real circumstances, determines how we truly are unique (that is, unrepeatably unique), but a *condition* for our unrepeatably unique development lies in the individual form with its distinct possibilities.

It appears that the individual form more fully determines the common human form, making the human form of Socrates, for example, a distinct instance of the universal form, on the level of essential being.[57] Our individual form—the being-Socrates—is, according to Stein, distinct from the species-form and more fundamental than the species-form. It is that *in which* the being-human is enclosed.[58] The essence of individual things can only become real in an object (through a substantial form). But the universal essence is even more dependent. Presumably, the individual form more fully determines the common form in the realm of essential being and characterizes it in unique ways such that the possibilities for one human form may differ (to a greater or lesser degree) from those of another human being. Thus, the universal form must first be individualized by an individual form in order to then become the essence of a truly existing object.

In the first chapter, we distinguished two senses of unique. The stronger notion of uniqueness requires unrepeatability. The weaker notion requires only difference. The individual form creates unique possibilities only in the weaker sense. Our possibilities are unique only insofar as there is not, in fact, another person with exactly the same form I have. This lack of repetition is due only to

---

ing to which the substantial form unfolds, and in that sense are marked in the substantial form.

57. See EeS 439/ESG 402/FEB 478 and EeS 79/ESG 79/FEB 81–82.

58. To be discussed in greater detail in the next chapter.

sheer luck or divine providence, but not to the nature of individual form per se. Likewise, the determination of the human form by the individual form should be understood in a weak sense. The individual form does not individuate the human being by making it *impredicable*. The common form is not through the individual form incapable of being predicated of something else nor is it an individual in any full sense. The individual form simply makes the human form more determinate in the realm of essential being. In both cases, real individuation and real uniqueness are due to the substantial form.[59] The individual form merely provides the conditions for the possibility of real individuality.

~

One might ask whether "individual form" is not simply another way of referring to the accidents characteristic of some subject. Aristotle distinguishes *substance,* what a thing is, from the *accidents,* which inhere in the substance. The tree is thus a substance, while the brown of the bark is an accident. Trees all of the same type may nonetheless have quite distinctive accidents. We might ask: insofar as Stein understands individual forms as specifications of the substance, may they not be simply *accidents?* As far as I can tell, this is not what Stein means by a determination or specification of the species-form. Accidents may come and go, while a thing remains the same substance. What it means, however, to be Caesar cannot come and go, while Caesar remains Caesar. Being-Caesar is, on Stein's account, the most basic formal intelligible structure; it provides the most fundamental "set of instructions" for the substantial form. Anything at the level of accident cannot provide such a basic formal component. Thus, when Stein argues that the individual form is more basic than the species-form, she is not denying the traditional distinction between substance and accident (although reinterpreting it slightly in light of her differing metaphysical account) but, rather, arguing that the structure of

59. She says: "With the characteristic of their being coincides, however, also a characteristic of their individual being" (EeS 450/ESG 412/FEB 491). I am reading "being" here to refer to their *real being.*

the substantial form (i.e., the essence) is individual and not merely species.

Conclusion

Stein's rejection of the Thomistic theory of individuation is deeply tied to her distinction between substantial form and essence. Stein can reject matter as the only principle of individuation in composite physical substances because she has a formal principle within such things which (like matter in Thomas) is not an accident but is, rather, on the level of substance, yet nonetheless is impredicable. Further, insofar as the substantial form offers indivisibility and independence, Stein has a way to distinguish, for example, the individuality of Socrates from that of a pile of gold or the triangle in the southwest corner of a pyramid—neither of which count as full individuals. Yet in none of these ways is the individual form the primary principle of individuality. In contrast to Scotus's *haecceitas,* individual form in Stein plays a role in making us individuals only on the level of essential being. The individual form makes Socrates's essence a unique instance of the human form, but in order to exist (in real being) it must be realized by Socrates's substantial form. Only as united to the substantial form or "written upon" the substantial form does the individual form work toward either the individuation or the uniqueness of a really existing being.

Thus, in the end Stein's theory of individuation is less Scotist than Thomistic (but not quite Thomistic either). She does not attribute either individuation or individual uniqueness to an individual form but, rather, both roles are played by the substantial form. Nonetheless, her understanding of the being most appropriate to the essence—essential being—gives her theory a Scotist cast. And it is primarily on the level of essential being that individual forms play their role as a kind of principle or condition for the individuality of the common form and the uniqueness of each human being.

Six ∼ INDIVIDUAL FORM AND MEREOLOGY

Many philosophers—Descartes, for example—argue that if something is genuinely distinct, it must also be separable, at least by God.[1] In contrast, Thomas argues that two things may be distinct but inseparable. For example, the substantial form and the matter of a bird are truly distinct, but nonetheless inseparable.[2] If there is no matter, there is no bird; if there is no form, there is no bird; but the form is nonetheless utterly distinct from the matter, even though dependent on the matter for its actualization. In claiming that form and matter for the bird are inseparable, Thomas is not claiming that the very *same* matter must be present at all times with the form. He is simply claiming that the form must be united to some matter (and likewise, the matter must be united to some form). Both the matter and the form could change over time, but there could be no point at which one has the form of a bird but no matter at all. We could contrast the relation of matter and form to that between a bird and its chick. The mother bird is distinct and separable from the chick, even if the chick is quite dependent on the mother for quite some time. There may be relations of dependence between the mother bird and chick, but there is not the same kind of inseparability as between form and matter. Thus, the claims regarding separability are somewhat different from claims regarding dependence. We can further distinguish different types of dependence and differing types of relations among and kinds of parts and wholes. The

1. See Descartes's sixth meditation in *Meditations on First Philosophy*.
2. This would be true of all corporeal animate beings except human beings. Thomas notes a qualified hylomorphism (or, one might say, a qualified dualism) regarding human beings.

positions that one takes on these mereological issues are critical for one's evaluation of different philosophical claims.

In the following I would like to discuss Husserl's mereology briefly and argue that Stein is probably employing the general Husserlian account of parts and wholes. I would then like to show how such an account of parts and wholes fits with Stein's claims regarding individual and universal form, and, finally, show how such an approach to individual form can answer certain common challenges to the Scotist account of *haecceitas*. Although Stein's individual forms differ both in content and in philosophic role from Scotus's forms of this-ness, they do share certain features, and Stein's employment of the Husserlian mereology does, I think, respond more fully to the challenges raised to the formal distinction in at the least the common readings of Scotus.

It is clear that Stein posits an individual form in addition to the common human form, but it is not evident precisely how she intends these two to relate. If the common form does not retain its integrity and distinct identity, we cannot have many individuals all of the same type (rather than many more or less similar things). Thus, the common form and the individual form must be, in some way, distinct from one another. But if the two are not also somehow united, then the individual form cannot individualize the common form nor can the entity be *one* being.

In Investigation III of *Logical Investigations,* Husserl presents a theory of parts and wholes that can be applied to Stein's theory in order to gain an understanding of the relation of individual and universal forms.[3] Further, Husserl's theory, mapped onto Stein's theory of individual forms, fits well with a large number of Stein's claims and creates a fairly consistent picture of the concepts she uses. In the following I would like to look at Husserl's theory of the

3. There is evidence both in his examples and explicit statements that Husserl may have intended this theory to have ontological ramifications. For example, he says: "Our distinctions have first of all related to the being of particular individuals thought of in 'ideal universality,' i.e., of such individuals treated purely as instances of ideas. But they obviously carry over to ideas themselves" (III, §7a; p. 448).

different kinds of parts and their relation to a whole as well as at evidence that Stein may have been employing this model. Finally, I would like to show why such a model is successful in answering a problem arising from Scotus's similar claim regarding *haecceities* and their relation to the common nature. If Stein has in mind a theory of parts and wholes similar to that developed by Husserl, then her theory of individual forms would have a distinct advantage over Scotus's. Throughout, however, I am merely suggesting that Stein *could* have used this model, not arguing that she explicitly did or that she *should* have employed this understanding of the relation of individual and common form.

Husserl's Mereology

In the Third Investigation, Husserl defines a part in general as that which can be distinguished as disjoined or discontinuous. A part is anything "that can be distinguished 'in' an object, or, objectively phrased, that is 'present' in it."[4] He then distinguishes two different kinds of parts: *pieces (Stücke)* and *moments (Momente)*. (The latter term is somewhat unfortunate in its temporal connotations. "Moments" in this sense ought not to be confused with "moments in time.") Because *pieces* are parts of a thing in a way different from *moments*, the relations between *pieces* (or *independent contents*) and wholes, on the one hand, and, on the other, *moments* (or *dependent contents*) and wholes also differ, and therefore various "parts" must be discussed in different ways.[5] The *pieces* or *independent contents* are "the elements of a presentational complex (complex of contents) [that] by their very nature *permit their separated presentation*," and we have *moments* or *dependent contents* "wherever this is not the case."[6]

4. III, §2; p. 437.
5. The language of *dependent* (or non-independent) and *independent contents* comes from C. Stumpf (see *Über den psychologischen Ursprung der Raumvorstellung*). Husserl notes his dependence on Stumpf's theory in the introduction to the Third Investigation as well as §4.
6. III, §2; p. 439.

Thus, Husserl makes a distinction between different kinds of parts: *pieces* or *independent contents* and *moments* or *dependent contents*. *Pieces* can, minimally, be imagined as separate from the whole, if not actually found as separate from the thing, whereas *moments* cannot—in principle—be so separated, although they are, nonetheless, distinct in content from the whole as well as from other moments of the whole. For example, the head of a horse is a *piece* of the whole and may be chopped off (although it would then be a "head of a horse" in name only),[7] whereas his animal-ness is a *moment* which cannot be removed from the horse. One can imagine a head without a body, but one cannot imagine a horse that is not an animal.[8] Although the head of the horse separate from the body could no longer function as a head, the sensible properties might be the same. Thus, a *piece* is an *independent content* or part of the horse, insofar as it can be what (in content—although not in function) it is independent of the whole. In contrast, the second, a *moment,* is a *dependent content* because it cannot be what it is nor can it be presented as independent of the whole.[9]

Husserl claims that animal-ness is—in its content—different from the horse; thus, it is truly a part and not identical with the whole of the horse itself. But, on the other hand, it is not a part in such a way that it can be separated from the whole or divided out from the horse (even in the imagination), as its head can be cut from its body. Thus, Husserl argues that there are parts of a whole that are truly parts but not separable.

7. See *Logical Investigations,* 439, for Husserl's qualification of this point, as well as Aristotle's *Metaphysics* 1035b24–25 and 1036b31ff. I thank John Drummond for pointing to these sections.

8. One could object that there could be a horse that is not an animal but rather a doll or a picture of a horse. But in such cases, we do not really have a horse but, rather, the image of a horse and likewise the image of a mammal and an animal.

9. Robert Sokolowski describes *moments* as "parts that permeate each other. They are inseparable from one another and from their wholes" ("The Logic of Parts and Wholes in Husserl's *Investigations,*" *Philosophy and Phenomenological Research* 28 [1968]: 538).

Not all things need to have parts. But for those things that have non-independent parts or *moments*, there are a priori laws regarding the relations of these parts, governed by laws of essences;[10] *"non-independent objects are objects belonging to such pure Species as are governed by a law of essence to the effect that they only exist (if at all) as parts of more inclusive wholes of a certain appropriate Species."*[11] For example, color is compatible with a triangle, square, rhombus, and pyramid. But color cannot exist without some figure. There must be a triangle, square, rhombus, or some other figure for there to be color. A *moment* can be what it is only within the context of a greater whole (that is, it must enter as a part of another thing if it is to exist), and there are specific kinds of wholes in which it must "fit." Independent objects or *pieces*, in contrast, do not lie in the same kind of lawful relations. They may, but need not, exist as parts of greater wholes. The head of the horse need not be attached to a body, but mammal-ness just as color must fit in with another *moment*.[12] Thus, Husserl distinguishes independent contents *(pieces)* and dependent contents *(moments)* by claiming that dependent contents, in contrast to the independent, cannot exist without other contents. Dependent contents are, essentially, partial contents—they cannot come into existence without resting upon another part (of an appropriate kind)—while an independent essence "requires no other essence to be interwoven with it."[13]

10. Our access to such a priori laws is through thought: what cannot be thought cannot be. He says, "Wherever therefore the word 'can' occurs in conjunction with the pregnant use of 'think,' there is a reference, not to a subjective necessity, i.e., to the subjective incapacity-to-represent-things-otherwise, but to the objectively-ideal necessity of an inability-to-be-otherwise" (III, §7; p. 446).

11. III, §7; p. 447.

12. The horse's head may be a *piece* in this respect yet also a *moment* insofar as it is a figure against some background. See III, §7.

13. III, §5; p. 443. Husserl does not mean that the independent *pieces* do not need their dependent *moments* in order to be what they are. Rather, that which is independent needs no other content *but itself and its parts* (i.e., its *moments*). One cannot cut off the horse's head without also cutting off all the *moments* of that head, its brown-ness, its heavy-ness, etc. But you can cut the head off the *body* (that is, another *piece*). The animal-ness, however, can never be cut off from

But once Husserl has declared that *moments* are so dependent that they cannot exist without something else, it is not clear that we should call them *parts*. If Husserl claims that the content of figure and the content of color differ, then there must be something that makes them different or "isolatable." Husserl acknowledges that often a figure or color does not gain notice without also the whole object which has these qualities being noticed. In order to "set into relief" one content, the whole must itself be "set into relief." But, he argues, the contents may still be distinctly and differently noticed. He says of the "isolatability" of each content:

Isolatability means only that we can keep some content constant in idea despite boundless variation—variation that is free, though not excluded by a law in the content's essence—of the contents associated with it, and, in general, given with it. . . . *In the "nature" of the content itself, in its ideal essence, no dependence on other contents is rooted;* the essence that makes it what it is, also leaves it unconcerned with all other contents.[14]

Figure is different in essence from color. Although we always meet contents in some context—we do not, for example, meet the essence *color* running about without a figure whose color it is—it does not thereby follow that color is identical with figure. Because the one *moment* comes with a background, within a context, does not imply that the content of one is identical with that of another. Thus, in calling *moments* "dependent contents," Husserl does not mean that they are dependent *in content.* They are dependent only insofar as they need other contents *in order to exist.*[15] You will not meet a pyramid that is not some color, nor "color" that is not a specific color, but the sandy-brown color of the pyramid is, nonetheless, a distinct content in itself and maintains its own identity even as a part of the pyramid. Thus, *independent contents (pieces)* and *dependent contents (moments)* are only independent or dependent in existence, not in identity.

---

the horse, nor could there be animal-ness without horse-ness (or dog-ness or cat-ness).

14. III, §5; p. 443.
15. See III, §7.

Husserl draws a distinction between, on the one hand, "*intuitively 'separated' contents, contents relieved from or cut apart from* associated contents" and, on the other, contents which "*blend* with their associates, or which *flow undividedly over* into them."[16] The intuitively separable content does not simply flow into the other contents without a point of difference.[17] Thus, no section of the white color of a sheet of paper is intuitively separable, whereas the whiteness of the paper is separable from its smoothness. (Contents, however, can be both independent and not separable in the above sense. For example, each piece of the white surface is an independent piece, but not separate in the sense given here.) Although we cannot see a horse without animal-ness and we never notice an animal that is not also a certain animal, the content of horse and that of animal, nonetheless, do not flow together without distinction. Thus, he argues that there is a difference in *content* (and therefore a difference in essence), even if they are not separable in real or imagined existence.

In the second chapter of the Third Investigation, Husserl introduces different kinds of relations among the parts. Some moments, he claims, may found others. For example, in the above case, color and figure are reciprocal moments; there cannot be a color without a figure just as there cannot be a figure that is not colored.[18] In contrast, the relation between "mammal" and "horse" is a founded one. A horse must be a mammal, but a mammal need not be a

16. III, §8; p. 449. He further says, "*An individual item already lacks separation from all other items if there is a single item from which it does not stand forth in relief*" (p. 450).

17. Barry Smith and Kevin Mulligen in their article on Husserl's theory of parts and wholes summarize Husserl's notion of the "isolatability" of contents nicely: to be isolatable means something like to be "capable of being held constant in presentation under conditions of absolutely free variation, within the limits set by the nature of the content in question, of all contents associated with it, so that it should indeed in the end, but only in principle, remain unaffected by the very elimination of such contents" ("Pieces of a Theory," in *Parts and Moments: Studies in Logic and Formal Ontology,* ed. Barry Smith [Munich: Philosophia Verlag, 1982], 38).

18. See III, §16.

horse. The *moment* mammal is consistent with and may be present in whales, human beings, and cats. Thus, there is a founded relation between the *moment* mammal and horse, and horse-ness is founded upon mammal-ness.[19]

Husserl uses foundational relations in order to explain how an object with many co-existing parts (that is, many different *pieces* and *moments*) need not thereby end up simply as a conglomerate of parts, losing the unity of the thing. Rather, Husserl argues that if there is some foundational relation, there can be a whole. He says:

By a Whole we understand a range of contents which are all covered *by a single foundation* without the help of further contents. The contents of such a range we call its parts. Talk of the *singleness of the foundation* implies that *every content is foundationally connected, whether directly or indirectly, with every content.*[20]

The unitariness of the whole arises from the kinds of relations among the parts and, thus, can be built "up" rather than out. If the parts in question are *moments* rather than *pieces* and the relations between them are either reciprocal or foundational (in the case of one-sided relations), then we may have many parts but still *one,* unified thing. Contents such as *moments* can be distinct without being independent. (*Pieces,* in contrast, cannot be distinct and dependent, although *pieces* "may still have a common identical 'moment,'" "their common boundary.")[21] Thus, *moments* can truly be

19. The example I have given of *horse* and *mammal* is a founded relation and, in some sense, non-reciprocal. The relation between *horse* and *mammal* differs from that between *mammal* and *horse.* The example Husserl gives for non-reciprocal, founded relations is slightly different; he says, "The character of being a judgement is, on the other hand, one-sidedly founded on underlying presentations, since these latter need not function as foundations of judgements" (p. 466). As in this case, the relation between the foundational and founded contents can be (but need not be) one between an independent and dependent content.

20. III, §21; p. 475. Likewise, he says, "It may at first seem extraordinary in this respect that mere necessities of coexistence, demands for supplementation, consisting in no more than the fact that the existence of certain sorts of contents conditions the mere coexistence of contents of certain coordinated sorts, that requirements of this kind, I say, should serve to produce unity" (§22; p. 477).

21. III, §17; p. 468. A whole in this case would mean something slightly different for Husserl. Insofar as the wholeness is not based in founded and foun-

"founded" on each other, and therefore "they require no chains and bonds to chain or knit them together, or to bring them to one another. In their case all these expressions have in fact no sense at all."[22] Thus, Husserl can say that nothing exists beyond the parts of the whole without also saying the whole is merely a conglomerate or aggregate of parts. (The problem with such an aggregate of parts is precisely that it is not a true unity. An aggregate "is an expression for a categorial unity corresponding to the mere form of thought, it stands for the correlate of a certain *unity of reference* relating to all relevant objects."[23] Wholes, in contrast, are governed by laws of essence.) Thus, Husserl claims that there can be one unified thing that is truly one and also "merely" a unity of parts. There need not be a whole in addition to the parts so long as the parts in question are *moments,* non-independent contents.[24]

Stein's Appropriation of Husserl's Mereology

Although Stein refers to Husserl's *Logical Investigations* in *Finite and Eternal Being,* she never directly refers to the Third Investiga-

---

dational or reciprocal relations, the thing is not a genuine whole, in the strict sense.

22. III, §22; p. 477. He adds, *"The only true unifying factors, we may roundly say, are relations of 'foundation'"* (p. 478).

23. III, §23; p. 480.

24. There is, nonetheless, a priority of the whole over the *moments.* One may be able to consider *moments* in relief or as distinct, but they are also fused within the whole, "which reveals itself in a mutual dependence as regard change and destruction" (III, §9; p. 452). The animal-ness, color, and quickness may all be distinct *moments* in the horse, but they are also dependent on the horse; when the horse is destroyed so also are all the *moments.* (According to Husserl, even the whole, however, should be understood somewhat flexibly. Dependence and independence are relative concepts for Husserl. What is dependent cannot be independent; however, an independent may also be dependent. For example, a person is an independent that may also be a part of another whole, the community. The community is thus composed of various parts that are themselves relatively independent.) *Moments* or dependent parts can also have parts and further dependent parts. Thus, the abstract part of the horse, mammal, has the part warmbloodedness, and the further dependent *moment* animal-ness. Thus, generally, there are numerous and varied relations among parts of a whole, although all independent contents possess abstract, dependent parts (i.e., *moments*).

tion.[25] But Stein does make numerous claims that seem to presuppose Husserl's mereology. For example, she says that the final determination of a rose is not the species-rose but, rather, the form of *this* rose which distinguishes it from all others. The species-form, however, *belongs* to the final determination, as do the forms of the qualities, characteristics, etc.[26] Likewise, she says that in the individual form Socrates, the human form is contained.[27] In chapters 3 and 4 of *Finite and Eternal Being,* she claims that there are many traits in the essence [*Wesenszüge*] (each, presumably, distinguished in terms of content and structure), and she describes any given object as a layered construction which can be compared with the scaffolding of a house or the skeleton of an animal (although not visual or spatial).[28] Thus, a person may include the general form of object-ness, the form of mammal-ness, human-ness, and an individual form. These are not randomly put together but must relate in lawful ways.

These claims lend themselves to a Husserlian understanding of parts and wholes. We can see the individual form of *this* rose as founded upon the species-form of the rose in the way that a *moment* is contained within a more foundational part. I hesitate here. There is a slight dissimilarity between the two claims. In the previous section I described "mammal" as the *moment* founding "horse" (the more universal founds the specific), whereas Stein says that the *being-Socrates* encloses the *being-human*. I do not know if her claim is similar to Husserl's or whether she has claimed that the more specific founds the universal. I will assume that she follows Husserl here, but the ambiguity should be noted.

25. For references to the *Logical Investigations,* see EeS 16, 99, 106, 261, and 273–74/ESG 23, 97, 104, 242, and 254/FEB 549, 565, 566, 588, and 591. At the beginning of II, §6 of "Bemerkungen über das Wesen, die Wesenheit und die Idee," an article oft-quoted in *Finite and Eternal Being,* Hering asks us to compare his comments with Husserl's doctrine of parts and wholes as found in the Third Investigation.

26. See *Finite and Eternal Being* IV, §3, 1.

27. See, for example, EeS 159/ESG 149/FEB 166 and EeS 439/ESG 402/FEB 478.

28. See EeS 196/ESG 184/FEB 207.

And, like Husserl, Stein distinguishes these essences through content.[29] She says, "Where the species is in content supplemented by the individual determination, the *real essence* contains within itself both, united in an individual whole."[30] (That is, the real essence or the essence in its real being contains the species-form and individual form in, presumably, some kind of foundational relation.)

Finally, the claim regarding the a priori lawfulness of essences is echoed in *Finite and Eternal Being* IV; as Stein discusses Jean Hering's use of *morphe* (μορφή), she says:

> The μορφή of color is not immediately the μορφή of the rose, but *mediately* it contributes to its construction; Hering describes it as *immediate* μορφή of the color and *mediate* μορφή of the rose, correspondingly the rose and its color as *mediate* and *immediate carriers* of the μορφή. The rose as a whole has its own μορφή.[31]

Each trait has its own form which both makes it what it is and "participates" or gains its structure from its corresponding essentiality. Thus, she says, "the color of the rose has a μορφή in itself which makes it red and has therefore a share in the essentiality 'Redness.'"[32] The forms are parts within a greater form which "carries" them. Thus, the red of the rose is a trait and has an essence that makes it what it is and corresponds to the essentiality Red. The red color is within another form, the rose, and it contributes to the constitution of the rose, but is not the immediate (or essential) form of the rose. Rather, there is a form particular to this rose which may carry the form of the color of this rose.[33] There is, thus, a lawfulness among the traits of the essence, or here μορφή, which

---

29. By "content" here Stein appears to mean *what* the thing is and "what [it] can be and cannot be" (EeS 57/ESG 60/FEB 59).

30. EeS 365/ESG 336/FEB 396.   31. EeS 85/ESG 84/FEB 87.

32. EeS 85/ESG 84/FEB 87.

33. This theory of μορφή certainly needs expansion with an epistemological theory. Stein makes a few comments at the end of *Finite and Eternal Being* III, §7, regarding how we know this *Gesamtmorphe*, but says little about how this knowledge is gained.

dictates their relations within the structure. Similarly, she says that various genera *(Gattungen)* of being cannot be derived from one another and that the "species" below the general genera are related according to relative dependence and independence.[34]

In *Potenz und Akt,* Stein lays out an understanding of the relation between individual things and abstract parts that has similarities to Husserl's theory of parts and wholes. *Potenz und Akt* was written largely in 1931, approximately five years before *Finite and Eternal Being,* and although Stein was never satisfied with the work, I think that the chart in chapter 2 is instructive. In a section (II, §3) entitled "Division of the Ontological Forms according to Levels of Generality. Independence—Dependence,[35] Whole—Part, Complexity—Simplicity," Stein provides a schema, charting the structure of entities as shown in figure 3.

The left-hand column represents, I take it, real existing things, and, because the formal "components" of either a general or a more limited kind cannot exist (in real being) except in concrete individuals, a line goes straight down from independence to "this concrete individual."[36] But on the right-hand side, we have a formal analysis of entities, discussing dependent parts. Things that exist (in real being) can have various elements constituting them as what they are: the form of objectness in general, a nature or what, being, and a how.[37] Stein claims that, in a way analogous with Thomas's doctrine of the transcendentals, the most general essenc-

34. See *Finite and Eternal Being* IV, §2, 7.

35. While Stein focuses on *independence* and *dependence* in this section—echoing Husserl's language regarding *pieces* (independent contents) and *moments* (dependent contents)—she does not refer to independent and dependent *contents.* Rather, she drops the language of "contents" all together in this section. I suspect that this is due to her inclusion of *being* [*Sein*] as a formal category. Whether my suspicion is accurate, however, would require further examination.

36. She says, "Only concrete objects, in which all forms [*Formale*] are filled and all fullness is formed, can be independent. But their forms construct [*vorbilden*] the independence as we saw with the individual and, in a certain sense, also with the ideal object" (*Potenz und Akt,* 35).

37. She says, for example, that "the what is the form of fullness toward which the form of the object longs." And: "Being is a general form that allows various

Figure 3. Structure of Entities

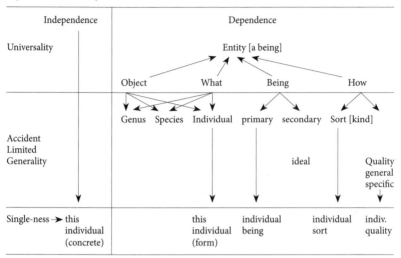

Source: *Potenz und Akt,* Edith Steins Werke 18 (Freiburg: Herder, 1998), 37, and Edith Steins Gesamtausgabe 10 (Freiburg: Herder, 2005), 35.

es are comparable to the transcendental *aliquid,* something. In order to be anything, an object must share in the essence of objectness.[38] Likewise, in order to be a being, it must have some kind of being,[39] a nature or what, and, she claims here, a how. These most

material completion through different *modes of being;* at the same time, however, corresponding to these modes [is] a formal differentiation. All the empty forms have their characteristic mode of being—which we have characterized as 'needy being'—that is a material completion of the *general* form of being, at the same time, however, [it is] a special *form* of being which corresponds to this mode" (*Potenz und Akt,* 35).

38. See *Finite and Eternal Being* V. See also Andres E. Bejas's *Vom Seienden als solchen zum Sinn des Seins. Die Transzendentalienlehre bei Edith Stein und Thomas von Aquin* (New York: Peter Lang, 1994).

39. Stein is quite clear that the content must be held distinct from the way of being of the thing (presumably referring to mental versus real being—not in terms of essential being). It is the difference between content and way of being that makes empathy, for example, possible. In her dissertation, Stein argued that one can empathize because the content is the same; what is different is whether we experience that same content primarily or secondarily. Stein repeats the same

general "empty forms" *(Leerformen)* can be filled with various content, what I am calling here "other essences," such as living being, animal, mammal, human being (the species), Socrates, or, equally, colored, whitish-yellow, and pug-shaped.

The most fully determinate essences are able to become individual, concrete things. And the concrete things are the most determined in the sense that they have a large collection of interconnected essences (or essential traits)[40] that make up the object. The *empty forms* are more and more determined until they reach the individual, where there is full determination.[41] The less determined traits have a relationship to other traits, which Rudolf Allers, in his review of *Finite and Eternal Being,* sees as analogous to matter and form.[42] As matter receives determination by form, so various kinds of forms or contents need determination by other contents. Thus, for example, within a particular red rose, we can distinguish the essence "object-ness" (among the most general essences), its genus- and species-form, the structure appropriate to *this* rose, the colored-ness, red as a specification of *color,* and the hue of this red. One part (or *moment*) of the rose is "being-colored," but "being-colored" as a content or essence requires (in order to be presented and in order to exist) further content, for example, red and this hue of red.

In chapter 8 of *Finite and Eternal Being,* Stein makes some of

---

idea here in this chart and again in *Finite and Eternal Being;* see EeS 72/ESG 73/FEB 73.

40. Her language in describing the constitution of an essence varies. A frequent expression is that the essence is made up of essential traits *(Wesenszüge).* See, for example, *Finite and Eternal Being* III, §5 and §7. Here I understand the *Wesenszüge* to include the universal form. I am also assuming that each essential trait has its own essential being in contrast to (although related to) the essential being of the other parts.

41. She says, "'Form' (= *Leerform*) we name, finally, the 'framework' of the whole thing (and the parts of the framework) in relation to that which gives it content and determines it to *this* individual" (EeS 202/ESG 189/FEB 213).

42. He says, "As prime matter is wholly undetermined and receives determination by the form, so the *Leerform* requires a form to which it stands in the relation of matter" (Allers in *New Scholasticism,* 483).

her strongest statements indicating that she is utilizing the Husserlian mereological model. She claims that each individual human being "must embody the 'universal human nature' in order to be able to be a member of this whole," but the "universal human nature" "is only a frame that must be filled through the manifold of the essence of individual members."[43] The universal human form by itself does not come into being; it is too "empty" to do so, that is, it is—without further forms—incomplete. Rather, individuals who have the human form as well as further specifying forms come into being. She draws an analogy with color: each visible object has a color, but no visible object merely has color. It must be black or brown or sea-green. It belongs to the nature of color to be *a* color and to the nature of a color to be *color*.[44] In a way analogous to color, each human being must be a human being (have an instance of the common human form) and be *a* human being (that is, have an individual form specifying their universal form).

Thus, in light of this analogy and Husserl's mereology, we can say that, from the perspective of any individual essence, the *moments* or *dependent contents* are necessary for the identity of the individual essence (for an individual human essence, this would include the human form). Any individual essence requires the more general essences as *moments*. From the perspective of the more universal essence, however, there might be several individual essences in which it may be a *moment*. (This is analogous to the claim above that a horse must be an animal, but an animal need not be a horse.) In order to be actual, some individual essence is necessary, but the more universal essence can accept a range of possible individual essences. While the universal essence "human being" appears to be capable of accepting many differing individu-

---

43. EeS 464/ESG 425/FEB 507. This comes in the context of a discussion of the mystical body of Christ. But given the analogy following immediately, it seems she intends both the notion of humanity as a frame which is filled with many individual human beings and human nature as a frame (of one human being) capable of accepting the individual nature.

44. See EeS 464/ESG 425/FEB 507–8.

al (human) forms, it cannot come into actual existence without an individual form.[45] (I am not hereby implying that individual form acts in any way as a cause for the actual existence of the universal form. Rather, if there exists in real being a human form, then there also exists in real being an individual form. The cause of the existence of either, however, must be attributed to something else.)

Given this model, the individual form *specifies* the more universal one, and the common human form acts as a *moment* of the individual form. This reading of individual and universal form provides a clear way to understand her claim that

if already the essence of individual things is *dependent* because it can become *real* only in *another* (namely, in *its* object), so the *universal* essence is doubly dependent because it needs the individual essence and its object in order to be real.[46]

The concrete object has at least two moments: the individual essence and the common form. We could likewise say that the individual form is immediately related to the object and the universal form is mediately related. The more universal may only relate to the object through the mediation of the less universal form, but nonetheless both are *moments* of the object and distinct in content.

Likewise, we can also read her language regarding "substrate" or "carrier" and the "carrying" of different forms through a model of forms as *moments* in various relations of foundation.[47] Entities are multilayered "constructions" involving reciprocal, non-reciprocal, founding, and founded relations among the contents involved. All of the forms or parts, however, including the individual form, are *moments* of the concrete individual. In the case of human beings,

45. She says, "The universal is only indeterminateness that is capable of and needs a determination" (EeS 137/ESG 130/FEB 141). And she describes the universal essence as that which occurs "here and there and can become or is real in all individual essences belonging to it" (EeS 79/ESG 79/FEB 82). In contrast, she says of the individual essence that there can be another "equal" to it, but there cannot be another the same as it. See *Finite and Eternal Being* III, §5.

46. EeS 79/ESG 79/FEB 81–82. For an interpretation of "object" here, see chapters 3 and 5 above.

47. See, for example, *Finite and Eternal Being* VII, §1, and VIII, §2, 6.

each of us has a unique (in the weaker sense) individual form which carries and thereby characterizes our species-form in its own distinctive way.[48]

Stein's language implies a Husserlian understanding of parts and wholes, and her descriptions clearly draw from the phenomenological tradition.[49] She describes objects as having a formal "construction," in which the more general genus- and species-forms (as well as qualities, etc.) are carried by the more specific forms; only objects which are fully specified may have real being. Thus, we can talk about levels of generality and a kind of hierarchy among the essences and essential contents. Like Plato, Stein accounts for the varieties and varied kinds of lawfulness in things through an appeal to a myriad of forms. Such forms account for the intelligibility of this changing world. (Although unlike Plato, Stein does not posit these forms as independent of mental or actual being, nor essential being as existing independent of the other types of being.) In the individual form, Stein has a way to account for the lawfulness of an individual's actions (thus, we can say "so-and-so would not do *that*") and, in the universal form, she has an explanation for consistent human types of action.[50] They fit together insofar as one is a *moment* and therefore dependent in real being upon the other.

Comparison with Thomas Aquinas

I take it that Stein, in claiming that entities are many-layered "constructions," does not mean the same thing Thomas does in pointing to differing degrees of precision in our concepts. Thomas con-

48. She claims that individuals contain the "measure of their species-shape internally" and in their own characteristic way (EeS 244/ESG 227/FEB 262).

49. See also Stein's discussion of genus and species in her Münster lectures on anthropology.

50. This interpretation also helps give a framework within which to understand her distinctions between the essence *(Wesen)*, essential what *(Wesenswas)*, and full what *(volle Was)*. See *Finite and Eternal Being* III, §4. In complex beings, composed of many various interlaid traits, we can distinguish the fundamental structure, the *essential what (Wesenswas)*, from the *full what (volle Was)*, the essences or forms present at any particular moment.

cludes that human beings are rational animals, but they are not composed of animality and rationality but of body and soul. We can legitimately categorize a human being as an animal but not because there is some part within the essence—the animality—such that we correctly recognize a human being as an animal. Rather, the essence (the body and soul) is such that, when considered in a general way, it has similarities with chimpanzees, chipmunks, and lizards.[51] In considering each of these essences, we can develop a notion of animal that includes—in an indeterminate and unspecified way—human beings, chimpanzees, chipmunks, and lizards.[52]

In claiming that all beings of a certain general similarity belong to one *genus,* Thomas is not taking this classification to be merely arbitrary. There are real similarities on the basis of which we can place differing entities in one genus, but this does not imply that each member of that genus shares an essence or even some real part of an essence. The similarities among members of one *species,* in contrast, are of a stronger sort. Each cat, for example, is composed of its own designated matter and an animate, cat soul. Each member does not share numerically one soul, but each cat has a soul that is *identical* to (that is, the same in type and quality but numerically different from) that of other cats.[53] Each cat need not

51. He notes that the designation of the individual (in comparison to the species) is through "matter determined by dimensions" ("On Being and Essence," 39). In contrast, the designation of the species (in comparison to the genus) is through a difference taken from the form.

52. Whatever "is in the species is in the genus in an undetermined fashion," and the genus in an indeterminate manner signifies all that is in the species ("On Being and Essence," 39). Because the unity of genus is due to the indetermination of the predicate, there is no need to claim that members of the same genus share a common essence (mammal-ness, for example).

53. The character of *species* is a part of human nature only as it exists in the intellect; he says, "Human nature itself exists in the intellect in abstraction from all individuating conditions. Thus, it has a uniform relation to all individuals outside the soul, inasmuch as it is equally the similitude of all and leads to the cognition of all inasmuch as they are men. And since the nature has such a relationship to all individuals, the intellect forms the notion of species and attributes it to the nature" ("On Being and Essence," 48–49). We can call the species a universal only because it is a "common representation of many" (ibid., 49), and the charac-

look identical because the matter, as well as the various accidents, may differ. But when we recognize similarity among cats and categorize them under the *species* cat, we recognize a similarity that is of a different (and stronger) kind than that among all members of a genus. Each cat has a part of its essence (its form) that is identical in kind, but not in number, with that of other cats. In contrast, the similarity among animals need not imply that there is any part "animality" in any member of that class. We can legitimately recognize similarities and group many individuals into the category of "animal," but not on the basis of any distinct essence of "animal" but, rather, because—when understood in a more general way—there are significant similarities among differing essences.

For Thomas, form plays the role of ensuring a real similarity among members of a *species,* and our form is fundamentally our species-form. This form can ensure that similarity quite smoothly by acting as the principle determining *what kind* of being the entity is and *how* it enjoys its being. The form makes the individual a member of a species and indicates the kind of unity and development proper to that entity. For example, the form of a stone ensures that this bit of matter is a stone and remains so as long as the form is present. Likewise, the form of the lizard gives that bit of matter order as a lizard. How a stone and a lizard enjoy their unity and being, however, differs. The lizard begins as a small group of cells within an egg that knit themselves together, take in nutrition, and grow according to the dictates of the form. Unlike the stone, the lizard moves from a quite small entity within the egg to a lively four-footed reptile. The form of the stone and that of the lizard dictate that each *is* in different ways. Because the form is the principle dictating how each entity receives its act of existence, it can also be the principle of becoming for plants, lizards, and other living things.

---

ter species follows from the essence only as an accident which follows from it as it exists in the intellect. For Thomas, species is a mental category with a basis in the forms of real things. We see the similitude among individuals and posit a species. It is real similarity, but it is not something real beyond the collection of individual similarities among individual instances of the same human form.

In contrast, Stein does not make the species-form most fundamental. The species-form is not responsible for our basic unity as an entity, and thus Stein must preserve the unity of the common species-form in another way, which she does through her notion of essential being.[54] Because each form or essence (individual, species, genus, etc.) retains its own being despite its instantiation or intellectualization, she can, therefore, say that "animal-ness" is truly a part of all animals and our classification is not simply based upon a similarity among different types of essences, but a true and real identity in content. Thus, each form (including the common human form) maintains its identity despite its unification to or foundation in an individual form.[55] The universal form becomes a *moment* in the individual, but it retains its characteristic identity as the common form. The *content* of the universal form is, thus, in all cases identical even if it is in a dependent relation to other *moments* of the object.[56] Thus, for Stein, in seeing (real) similarities, we are "abstracting" a content which has its own unity and being as that content is preserved in essential being. There are, thus, truly distinct essences or contents (each with their own essential being) for "flower" and "plant," both of which are contained in this rose.

Comparison with Scotus

In her claim regarding the being of the common nature, Stein echoes Scotus's claim regarding the unity of the common nature. Similarly, in positing an individual form, her claim has a Scotist ring. Stein posits *individual forms,* and not merely forms of thisness; her individual forms function primarily as principles of uniqueness as difference, rather than as principles of individua-

---

54. She clearly connects different structures within a thing and essential being. See, for example, EeS 98–99/ESG 96–97/FEB 101–2.

55. Presumably, the evidence for this identity lies in the essence's "isolatability" or difference in content, as Husserl articulates it in the Third Investigation.

56. Once again, the identity I am pointing to here is not numerical identity nor identity over time but identity in content.

tion. Nonetheless, like Scotus, Stein has the challenge of articulating the distinction yet relation between common and individual forms.

With the Husserlian model (insofar as she employs it), however, she avoids one of the weaknesses in Scotus's version. One criticism frequently raised of Scotus's individuating principle is that it is unclear how the individuating principle and the common form relate. Scotus clearly wants to maintain that there is a common form in all individuals of the same type. But he also claims that individuality, individual unity, is a perfection, and therefore it cannot stem from a mere privation or negation (for example, simply being divided off from other things).[57] Positive features are prior to negative ones.[58] Therefore, the individuating principle must be positive and real.

That which makes us individual, however, must be united with the nature. If the two aspects are not inseparably united, then the nature is not truly made individual, but simply given an additional accident.[59] Nothing accidental can be the principle of individuation because, given the priority of substance over accidents, commonality would be prior, and we would not truly be individuals af-

57. As Scotus argues, "It is necessary through something positive intrinsic to this stone [and all individual things], as through a proper reason, that it be incompatible with the stone for it to be divided into subjective parts. That positive feature will be what will be said to be by itself the cause of individuation. For by 'individuation' I understand that indivisibility—that is, incompatibility with divisibility" (*Ordinatio* II, d. 3, p. 1, q. 2, n. 57, brackets mine). Likewise he says, "Since in each unity less than numerical unity there is found a positive entity that is by itself the reason for that unity and for that incompatibility with the opposite multitude, this will be found most of all—or at least equally—in the case of the most perfect unity, which is numerical unity" (ibid., n. 58).

58. See *Ordinatio* II, d. 3, p. 1, q. 6, n. 57.

59. In his debate with Godinus, Scotus insists: "The singularity about which we are asking in this discussion is being a something per se one among many beings [*aliquid per se unum in entibus*] to which it is repugnant to be divided into subjective parts; of this repugnance there can only be a single cause" (Godinus/Scotus, "Utrum materia," E, f. 73v [ed. Stroick, p. 596]. Quoted and translated in Timothy Noone's "Individuation in Scotus," *American Catholic Philosophical Quarterly* 69, no. 4 [1995]: 531).

ter all.[60] Thus, the principle of individuation must be on the level of substance rather than accident, yet it cannot be the species-form or common nature because that is what makes things alike, not what makes things individual.

Scotus's requirements for the individuating principle include: (a) that it not interfere with the integrity of the nature, (b) that it form a whole with the nature, (c) that it be real and not accidental, and (d) that the principle itself be distinct in order to function as that which distinguishes and individualizes. The individuating principle is not part of the nature, and so it does not preclude there being many individuals of the same sort; although formally distinct from the nature, the principle of individuality forms a per se unity with the nature. Thus, the unity formed by the nature and individuating principle is incompatible with "division into several subjective parts,"[61] and able to be designated as a this.

Crucial to Scotus's solution is the formal distinction. He has to be able to show how the individuating principle and the nature are both inseparably united and truly distinct. If either is compromised, then the nature would not truly be common (the individuating principle would be infringing on the integrity of the nature) or the nature would not truly be individuated (the principle would fail truly to unite and make the nature itself individual). The problem is how to understand this distinctness which also has unity. In order to justify Scotus's realist epistemology,[62] he needs an ontological

60. See *Ordinatio* II, d. 3, p. 1, q. 4, n. 82.

61. Ibid., q. 6, n. 169.

62. If our knowledge is to be true, the distinction between the universal and individual form must be prior to our thought about things. If the nature were not common, then our knowledge of it would be untrue. See *Ordinatio* II, d. 3, p. 1, q. 1, n. 29, quoted in chapter 4, n. 23 above. Thus, there must be both an extensional and intensional distinction between the common nature and what makes us individual. The distinction must be extensional prior to intellection if the intensional distinction is to have objectivity—to be true. Allan Wolter makes this point nicely: if our concepts and reality are isomorphic, "then the mere possibility of conceiving one property without the other requires some actual nonidentity or distinction of properties *a parte rei* which is logically prior to, and a condition for, our thinking of one apart from the other" ("The Formal Distinction," in *Studies in Philosophy and the History of Philosophy*, vol. 3, ed. John K. Ryan and

ground for this distinction between the nature and the individuating principle, yet he is also required (by his principles) to hold that there is not an absolute distinction or separation between them. Scotus calls this distinction in true unity the formal distinction.

Regarding the distinction between the individuating principle and the nature, or the formal distinction, Scotus says:

I. Thus whatever is common and yet determinable can still be distinguished (no matter how much it is one thing) into several formally distinct realities of which this one is not formally that one. This one is formally the entity of singularity and that one is formally the entity of nature. These two realities cannot be distinguished as "thing" and "thing.". . . . Rather when in the same thing, whether in a part or in the whole, they are always formally distinct realities of the same thing.[63]

∽

II. But in the present case neither does the specific entity include the individual entity through an identity, nor conversely. Instead only some third item, of which both of these are as it were per se parts, includes both of them through an identity.[64]

∽

III. In things there is a double manifest distinction, namely, of supposites and natures; in the intellect, the double manifest distinction is of the modes of conceiving and of formal objects. From this we conclude to a difference which is not manifest because it is the smallest of its kind, i.e., among all those that precede intellection. It is concluded from the real difference in this manner: the distinction of divine supposites is real. But since the supposites cannot formally agree and differ really from each other, we must conclude to some difference in the essence wherein the supposites agree from those reasons *(rationes)* by which the supposites are distinguished. Similarly, from the difference of formal objects, of which neither is contained in the other eminently even in the intellect which considers them intuitively, one can conclude to a difference of things known intuitively antecedent to all operation of the intellect.[65]

Bernardine M. Bonansea [Washington, D.C.: The Catholic University of America Press 1965], 49–50).

63. *Ordinatio* II, d. 3, p. 1, q. 6, n. 188.

64. Ibid., q. 6, n. 191 [*sic*].

65. Scotus, *Opus oxoniense,* I, d. 2, q. 7, n. 43, VIII, 602–3, translated by Maurice J. Grajewski in *The Formal Distinction of Duns Scotus,* 87–88.

Scotus is fairly clear in his claim that the nature and principle of individuation are distinct, although in the same thing. It is more difficult, however, to get a sense of what that distinction amounts to. The second quotation seems to suggest that there is some sort of third thing which underlies the *formalities*.[66] Thus, there is not identity between nature and individuating principle although they are both part of something else. In the third quotation, he argues that the distinction precedes intellection and is real, but is "the smallest of its kind." We can conclude that there is a difference prior to intellection because the two formalities—for example, the individual form and the common nature—do not agree formally, or in definition, and one cannot be contained "eminently" in the other. Thus, he seems to be claiming that it is not possible for the definition of the essence of each formality to include the other. Yet they are clearly one, while also differing in some way. This he calls the formal distinction.

The formal distinction can be compared with the real and conceptual distinctions taken simply. They can be contrasted: in a *conceptual distinction,* one thing can be conceived in two different ways (for example, the victor at Jena and the vanquished at Waterloo); in a *real distinction,* two definitions refer to two things; and in the *formal distinction,* two "formalities" which are truly distinct, and the definition of one does not include the definition of other, are nonetheless inseparable and in one and the same thing. Thus, for example (to use one of Scotus's examples), the divine attributes of justice and mercy are definitionally different but necessarily united.

It is generally accepted that the criterion of a formal distinction is definitional difference but essential unity or inseparability; but what this means and how to classify the distinction is controversial. Some have associated the formal distinction with the mental

66. Likewise, he says, "The specific reality does not of itself have the wherewithal to include through an identity the individual reality. Instead, only some third factor includes both of these through an identity" (*Ordinatio* II, d. 3, p. 1, q. 6, n. 189).

distinction—claiming that it is a particular sort of mental distinction, one that has a basis in reality but is nonetheless conceptual.[67] Others have understood the formal distinction as a subdivision of the real distinction. It is a sort of minor real distinction, not to be confused with a real distinction in which the two distinguished things are separable.[68] The third camp of interpreters has concluded that it is actually a third sort of distinction posited between the mental and the real distinction.[69]

One advantage of interpreting Stein's project in light of Husserl's mereology is that there is a way of understanding the relation of individual and universal form without attempting to articulate what the "formal distinction" would mean.[70] With a theory of parts and wholes, and in particular with the distinction between *pieces* and *moments,* Stein has an explanation available for how individual and universal form relate which—insofar as it is successful— neither compromises the identity of each form (especially in light of her claims regarding the essential being of each) nor problematizes the unity of the being. The distinction between them is not a real distinction insofar as they are not separable (as *pieces* are), nor a conceptual distinction because the two forms are not identical.

Conclusion

Stein claims that each essence has *essential being,* which differs from both real and mental being, and provides the essence with a

67. For example, Gabriel Casanova interprets Scotus's distinction as, in essence, the Thomistic virtual distinction and thus a subdivision of the mental. See *Cursus Philosophicus ad mentem D. Bonaventurae et Scoti,* vol. 1 (Matriti, 1894), 401. This likewise seems to be Allan Wolter's position, although his description of the claim is more nuanced, in "The Formal Distinction."

68. For example, Maurice Grajewski in *The Formal Distinction of Duns Scotus.*

69. Suárez interprets Scotus in this way, although Suárez sees it as an indefensible distinction. He suggests that Scotus should have made a conceptual distinction instead. See *On the Various Kinds of Distinctions,* trans. Cyril Vollert (Milwaukee, Wis.: Marquette University Press, 1947).

70. Or, perhaps, Husserl's mereology articulates what Scotus may have intended with the formal distinction.

being "prior" to intellectualization or instantiation in real things.[71] Thus, there appears to be an identity and being to the common nature prior to its existence in individual things. The being and identity of the content, for example, of the universal form, can be preserved in its essential being even when it is united to an individual form. What preserves the distinctness of the universal form in its various instantiations in so many unique persons is its essential nature that is repeated *in identical content* in every individual. Thus, all human beings share an identical content which is not compromised in the unique individual forms.

The identity of the common form and that of the individual form are preserved as distinct in their essential being. Their relation, however, is one of foundation. As this specific burgundy is the foundation for the red-ness of the chair (as well as its colored-ness), so the universal form has a founded relation with the individual form. The universal is contained within the individual form and receives its specification and, therefore, uniqueness (in the weaker sense). Thus, Stein's version has advantages over Scotus's insofar as she avoids discussion of the formal distinction, positing instead a notion of interlocking forms (retaining their identity in their eidetic structure in essential being). Insofar as the notion of essential being and the Husserlian mereology are coherent and compatible, it appears that Stein has a way of accounting for the real similarity (and sameness) of all human beings as well as an account of the a priori individuality of each person.

---

71. It seems to me that utilizing her notion of essential being here is both useful and warranted. But she does not explicitly claim that all components or parts of an essence have their own essential being. Given her argument in *Finite and Eternal Being* III, §10, the universal form, however, should have its own essential being and likewise, the individual form, as stated in *Finite and Eternal Being* IV, §3, 2, can be lifted from the thing and grasped as an *essential what*.

Seven ～ CHALLENGES FOR INDIVIDUAL FORMS

Insofar as she has presupposed Husserl's mereology, Stein has a clear way of understanding the relation between individual and universal form which preserves not only the genuine commonality of our human nature but also the essential uniqueness (in the weaker sense) of each person. Furthermore, with this model Stein can also account for the genuine unity of each person. We are not merely a collection of parts but a true whole, one being. There is a single carrier (the substantial form) of our nature, which can be distinguished according to a number of distinct but interconnected moments, including both our nature qua human and our nature qua individual. Finally, this model offers a more satisfying explanation of the formal distinction than at least certain readings of Scotus provide. Thus, it appears that Stein's account avoids challenges in Scotus's comparable claims regarding *haecceitas* and presents an account that values our uniqueness, and not merely our individuation.

Nonetheless, there are further questions that should arise about Stein's claims regarding individual forms. Although I find Stein's focus on individuality beautiful and the particular way in which she employs individual forms to be both theoretically sophisticated and powerful, there are dangers in accepting Stein's account of individual forms.[1] Stein has not lost the genuine commonality of

1. See my "What Makes You You? Individuality in Edith Stein," in *Contemplating Edith Stein,* ed. Joyce Avrech Berkman (Notre Dame, Ind.: University of Notre Dame Press, 2006), 283–300, for a much less developed version of some of these critiques.

all human beings: each of us is truly and equally human. But our fundamental formal structure is not our structure as human but our structure as individual. In this sense, Stein's position regarding human beings is analogous to Thomas Aquinas's regarding angels. Thomas understands angels to be both structurally different—each angel is, he affirms, its own species—and on different levels in the Great Chain of Being. Some angels are, ontologically, more valuable than others. Because all human beings share the same basic formal structure, in contrast, there is an equality among all human beings that is not present among the angels. Stein, however, disagrees with Thomas about the most basic formal component in each human being. According to Stein, our fundamental structure is not, in fact, identical, but rather individual. But Stein also claims that there is true equality among all human beings. We are not on different steps of the Great Chain, nor is any one human being ontologically more valuable than any other. The question then arises of how Stein can affirm an account of human beings similar to Thomas on angels in this respect without also accepting Thomas's correlative claim regarding hierarchy. My thesis in the following is that this problem, although perhaps not decisive, nonetheless presents a significant challenge. I would like to look, first, at Stein's comments responding to the potential threat of hierarchical relations among human beings. Stein was well aware of this challenge, and she presents several arguments to show that it is not a threat to human beings in the way it might be for angels. Secondly, I would like to consider the threat more fully, looking at a few of the implications of Stein's claim regarding our fundamental structural differences, with a particular eye to the challenges Stein's position presents for our understanding of certain ethical, political, religious, and social claims. Finally, however, I would like to ask how significant these challenges are for Stein's position.[2]

2. Much in the following owes a tremendous debt to Terrence Wright. Terry Wright very kindly read and commented on an earlier draft of this chapter, offering a number of provocative arguments in defense of Stein's position. I am grateful for his feedback, and apologize in advance for the times when my summaries have not done justice to his arguments.

The Danger: A Comparison with the Angels

In *Person in the World,* Mary Catharine Baseheart summarizes Stein's position on individual form by claiming:

According to Stein's theory of individual form, each human being has not only universal essence but also individual essence. These are not two essences but are a unity in which the essential traits join together in a determinate structure.[3]

A person does not have two substantial forms[4] but, rather, one form with a determinate structure, part of which comprises the

3. *Person in the World,* 55.
4. Stein refers several times to Gallus Manser's article "Das Wesen des Thomismus," *Divus Thomas: Jahrbuch für Philosophie und spekulative Theologie* 2 (1925). (This was expanded and revised as *Das Wesen des Thomismus* [Fribourg: F. Rütsche, 1935].) Among the topics Manser discusses is the debate regarding many substantial forms. Stein makes note of this question in *Finite and Eternal Being* IV, §4, 11, citing Thomas's objections. In several places, among them *De anima, Summa contra gentiles, De unitate intellectus, De spiritualibus creaturis,* and *Summa theologica,* Thomas criticizes the claim that there are many substantial forms in one being. In the *Summa theologica* I, 76, 3c, for example, Thomas argues that many substantial forms are impossible because, first, nothing is one except by one substantial form; "because a thing has from the same source both existence and unity; and therefore things which are denominated by various forms are not absolutely one." If we were to understand the soul as a motor, then many substantial forms would be possible; it is not then unreasonable to claim that one thing is moved by several motors. If, however, we understand the soul as the *substantial form* of the body, we cannot have many substantial forms and one person. Second, Thomas argues that there must be one substantial form because of the manner of predication. Things are predicated either essentially or accidentally. If there were one form for animal-ness and another for human-ness, then one must be predicated of the other accidentally. We are not, however, essentially an animal and only accidentally human (or essentially human and only accidentally animal). Thus, it makes no sense to say that some substantial forms are predicated accidentally of a thing. Thus, there cannot be more than one substantial form. Finally, Thomas argues from the operations of the soul. One operation of the soul can impede another; therefore, the principle must be such that the operations are not fully distinct and can affect each other. There is, thus, one substantial form, the soul, with many operations.

Stein has certainly posited many forms in the thing, but she has not posited many *substantial* forms. Rather, first, she has not defined form in the same way as Thomas, and, secondly, she has claimed that the many forms are *interlocking*

individual form and part of which is the universal form. Or, given the model laid out in the previous chapter, we can describe individual and universal form each as a *moment* of the individual. Each is truly present in the object and retains its essential being, but they are united into one interwoven essence.

But so described, each human being need not be identical in her structure. Each human being has a *moment* or certain content which is identical, but the particular structure of each individual's basic form need not be identical.[5] This can be seen in the analogy Stein suggests for the relation of individual and universal form: universal and individual form are related as *color* in general is to a *specific color*.[6] Among the things that are red, there are cardinals, sunsets, the hair of Red Skelton, and the dusty-red sands of the Painted Desert. Most specific (or foundational) in each of these is its own particular color—deep red or pinkish red, orange-red or a muted sandy red—which "carries" the *moment* redness. Each is truly red, but none is the same color of red. All four are red, however, because, in the particular color, there is a more universal *mo-*

---

forms. They are *moments* of the object which fit together in a lawful manner. See also the discussion in chapter 6.

5. Jay Wood raised the objection that surely this is what happens in our DNA. We have human characteristics specified in individual ways by the particular DNA we have. Thus, it appears that scientific evidence supports that it cannot but be the case that we are different in our fundamental structure (and thereby have an "individual form") (conversation, January 30, 2001). This does not, however, solve the dilemma. Aristotle, and Stein following him, distinguishes substances from accidents. DNA "information" need not be solely or primarily information regarding our substance. One can still distinguish accidental traits from substantial ones, even if many of these are specified in our genetic structure. Furthermore, the traits in Stein's notion of individual form must be essential to the person and not merely accidental. If substance is prior to accident and individual form provides some positive principle of uniqueness, then placing the characteristics provided for in the individual form on the level of accident relegates the principle of uniqueness to a secondary status. If the individual form involves accidental traits, then we lose individual form as a positive and fundamental basis for uniqueness. If, however, the individual form is essential, then each human being is not *alike* in basic structure.

6. See *Finite and Eternal Being* VIII, §3, 2. See also chapter 6 above.

ment that is common to them all.[7] Likewise, in each individual human being, the individual form would be most foundational, but it is an instance of and specification of the common human form, which makes all of us human beings.

Stein compares her position on individual forms in human beings with Thomas's claim regarding the angels.[8] Thomas claims both that matter is the principle of individuation in composite physical substances and that angels do not have matter.[9] He accounts for their individuality by claiming that each angel is the sole member of its species. Thus, there cannot be many members of the same angelic species; rather, for pure spirits, the individual *is* the species. The multitude of angels is due to the multitude of species of angels, and all are considered angels, of the genus "angel," insofar as they are incorporeal, finite intelligences. Thus, he answers the problem of individuation for angels, essentially, by avoiding the problem: there are not multiple instances of the same species but, rather, multiple species.

Stein's claim regarding human beings is similar. Each individual human being is, analogously, her own "species" and the only member of this "species."[10] No one else shares any one person's individual form.[11] Thus, Stein can say of human beings what Thomas does of angels: the multitude of human beings is due not to matter individuating the form but, rather, to the multitude of different individual forms which can all be classified as "human." (This analogy should be qualified by emphasizing that Stein has a stronger

7. The use of *moment* here is mine and not Stein's.

8. See *Finite and Eternal Being* VIII, §3, 2. We should note, however, that Stein posits non-corporeal matter (see *Finite and Eternal Being* VIII, §2, 7), and thus her theory of angels differs significantly from Thomas's.

9. See *De ente et essentia* IV.

10. She puts the comparison forward as a question: "Are human beings, through the acceptance of an unrepeatable character in each human soul, like angels?" (EeS 462/ESG 424/FEB 506).

11. The non-repeatability of the individual form here should be taken in the weaker sense of unique. She acknowledges that it is theoretically possible that there would be more than one person with the same individual form. See *Finite and Eternal Being* VIII, §2, 6, and §3, 2.

sense of the commonality of genus than Thomas does. For Stein, there is a *moment* of "animal-ness" in each animal and a being to each of these *moments* in their essential being.)

Despite our differences, human beings are alike in a real sense; we all share a common nature. There are, thus, traits characterizing all human life. She claims, for example, that each human spirit is united to a body and must develop out of a matter-bound soul.[12] Thus, all human life is alike in a fundamental sense—it is bound to corporeal matter—and differs in that respect from angels. But despite this difference, angels and humans are alike, according to Stein, insofar as each is its own "species," that is, the most fundamental form in each human being is not repeated in any other. Thus, for all the similarities among human beings, we are—at base—different from one another. Since all angels can truly be classified as "angels" because they have certain characteristics in common (as non-corporeal, finite intelligences), so all human beings can be classified as "human" (as corporeal, matter-bound, finite, intelligent beings). But for neither angels nor human beings is this commonality due to a commonality of the most basic form (although the commonality is, nonetheless, formal for Stein).

Stein herself makes this analogy, and I think that it is a fair analogy. It is limited, however, insofar as Stein claims that all human beings share a common form. Our individual forms are intended not to place us in differing groupings, but to provide specification within the common category of "human." Thus, her analogy with colors is quite useful. Nonetheless, the similarity between Stein's claim regarding human beings and Thomas's regarding angels raises significant questions. The claim that we are not, for all our similarities, identical in our fundamental form carries certain challenges or dangers. Among those, I would like to consider some of the ethical,

12. To be matter-bound is, for Stein, to be a soul. If there is no matter (as in the case of pure spirits), then there is no soul. Stein's discussion of matter is very interesting and well worth further study. She distinguishes, for example, several different models for understanding matter and posits some kind of spiritual matter relevant to angels. Such discussion, however, goes beyond the scope of this study.

social, political, and religious problems to which such a claim leads.

But before turning to these objections, I would like to make clear where the problem lies. The problem, it seems to me, is not primarily that Stein posits an individual form but that she posits individual forms for human beings that differ *in content* from each other.[13] If, however, individual forms are not understood as different in content, it is difficult to know how to interpret several of her claims, among them:

> The individual human being is not capable of unfolding within his life all possibilities which are grounded in his essence (understood as individual essence). His power is so limited that he must purchase his accomplishments in one area with gaps in another.[14]

Stein makes a point here of saying that the possibilities in question are not the human ones per se, but the possibilities of our individual essence. It is not worth making such a distinction unless there is a difference in content, that is, a difference in the possibilities (and, therefore, potentialities), in each essence. Likewise, she says:

> The being-human as such is the essence of all individual human beings, common, always and everywhere remaining the same; beside that, however, each has something which differentiates him *through content* from others.[15]

Presumably, this difference in content is a priori, that is, prior to any of our experiences or choices, and is a character of our soul which must be, as such, *discovered.*

Stein's Response to the Possibility of a Hierarchy

Stein claims that each human being is an embodiment of the universal human nature and a member of the whole, humanity, as

13. If the formal structure did not differ, the individual form would not be problematic in the ways I have objected here. See chapter 8 below for a fuller discussion of an alternative understanding of individual form.

14. EeS 463/ESG 424/FEB 507.

15. EeS 458/ESG 419/FEB 500. The italics are mine.

each angel is an embodiment of the universal angelic nature. Stein, however, goes on to qualify this comparison by saying that the relation between the individual and the community differs for human beings and for angels. In the angelic world, each individual angel presents a particular step in a *hierarchy*, and together they all build a harmony and Great Chain.[16] In contrast, for human beings, Stein claims that there is no such hierarchy.[17] The reason for this difference is that angels are independent of each other in a way that human beings are not. She says:

No angel, however, owes its nature to another; none needs the others for the unfolding of its nature—they build a unity as the "heavenly court" that surrounds the throne of the Almighty.[18]

Angels have a hierarchy while humans do not because humans need each other in order to *become* themselves in a way that angels do not. Human beings experience enrichment and completion through each other; we "owe" our possession of our own nature to the other.[19]

There are a number of ways to read Stein's claim here, and I would like to consider two different readings. We might, first, read "owing our nature" in light of Stein's account, in her dissertation,

16. See *Finite and Eternal Being* VII, §5, 2, and Stein's 1941 article, "Ways to Know God: The 'Symbolic Theology' of Dionysius the Areopagite and Its Factual Presuppositions," trans. Rudolf Allers, *The Thomist* 9 (July 1946): 379–420, for a discussion of the Areopagite's theory of the angels and their hierarchical relations.

17. Thus, even while insisting that the individual forms of human beings are of the same kind—that is, within the general human category—Stein still recognizes the potential danger of the ranking of the forms. I take it that as soon as a formal difference in content (and particularly an a priori one) is posited, this possibility is opened.

18. EeS 466/ESG 426/FEB 509.

19. She concludes *Finite and Eternal Being* VIII, §3, 2, with the claim: "The experience of commonality, on the other hand, is significant for grasping humanity as a whole which encloses and carries us, that binds us with people of all times and heavenly realms, despite all differences, and [offers] the enrichment and completion we can experience through contact with humanity formed in other ways" (EeS 466/ESG 427/FEB 510).

of empathy and development; the second reading of "owing our nature" interprets the phrase in a more metaphysical light.[20]

First Reading of Stein's Response to the Challenge of Hierarchy

In *On the Problem of Empathy*, Stein claims that "the constitution of the foreign individual" is "a condition for the full constitution of our own individual."[21] In order to know ourselves fully as individuals, another person is necessary. This is the case in at least two different ways. First, in another person's perception of me as something that can be seen, responded to, at least partially understood, and critiqued, praised, and blamed, I come to understand myself.[22] Through such responses, we come to recognize tendencies in ourselves, persistent traits, talents, and capacities; we begin to discover a character (which we ourselves are) that reveals itself in our actions. The discovery of our character, personality, and tendencies offers us the opportunity to engage in self-critique. We can, in some sense, "stand back" from our immediate impulses, instincts, and reactions, and decide how we want to act. As such, the way in which another "teaches" us about ourselves is a condition of our freedom, responsible action, and self-formation.[23]

20. I owe the idea for this second reading to Terrence Wright, conversation, October 2006.

21. *On the Problem of Empathy*, 88. Antonio Calcagno points to the centrality of this claim in, among other places, Stein's critique of Heidegger. He summarizes her position: "Stein maintains that the individual person cannot be thought of apart from his/her community. One implies the other, and both are constitutive of one another" (*"Die Fülle oder das Nichts?* Edith Stein and Martin Heidegger on the Question of Being," *American Catholic Philosophical Quarterly* 74, no. 2 [2000]: 274).

22. She says, "To consider ourselves in inner perception, i.e., to consider our psychic 'I' and its attributes, means to see ourselves as we see another and as he sees us" (88).

23. See *On the Problem of Empathy* III, §5p. It is worth noting that in her later work, Stein qualifies this claim a bit. In the appendix to *Finite and Eternal Being* on Teresa of Avila, *Die Seelenburg*, Stein repeats her claim that others may help "give" us to ourselves, but then notes that "many sources of error are bound with this knowledge" so long as God does not provide assistance (in *Welt und Person*, 63).

Stein articulates a second way in which the other informs me of myself. Our potential is something that is not yet but which I may become. As such, it does not yet exist. We know of our potential, Stein claims, because we see what others do. If I see someone, for example, act courageously before a group of peers or colleagues, I may recognize the yet-unrealized potential for courage in myself. If I see someone practice the piano daily and come to play elegantly, that possibility is opened up for me as well.

The other, thus, both enables me to develop an objectivity toward myself that is necessary for truly free actions (that is, acts both rationally motivated and chosen) and the other "informs" me of the possibilities or potentialities among which I may choose.[24] Thus, when Stein says that the human being *owes* her nature to another in a way angels do not, we can interpret this claim to mean that because we do not begin as wholly ourselves but must unfold our nature, others are critical for that often difficult process. We owe the development of our nature to another. The process is not instantaneous and our knowledge of ourselves is incomplete, and thus other people are necessary even to be ourselves.

Second Reading of Stein's Response to the Challenge of Hierarchy

As noted in the first chapter, although Stein speaks often of our individuality, she also emphasizes very heavily the communal aspects of our being. She takes seriously the notion of the mystical Body of Christ and sees each as a member in the whole of humanity. It is not simply that each of us happens to be a human being, but each of us is also a part of humanity itself, and there is a unity to the human race as a whole.[25] I do not yet understand all that Stein wants to say in making this claim, but at least part of the commitment is tied to the distinctiveness of human material life. Angels

24. See Rachel Feldhay Brenner's *Writing as Resistance: Four Women Confronting the Holocaust* (University Park: Pennsylvania State University Press, 1997), esp. chapter 3, for a helpful discussion of this concept in Stein's thought.

25. See *Finite and Eternal Being* VIII, §3, 3.

are not born of angelic parents, gaining their nature through materially conditioned propagation. Humans are. We gain our nature through other human beings, and thus there is a fundamental dependence on others. Not only do we owe the development of our nature to another, but the possession of that nature is itself dependent on other human beings. As such, there is a level and kind of dependence among human beings that is not present among angelic beings.

Questions about the Appeal to Dependence

Stein's claim in *Finite and Eternal Being* that we are dependent for our nature on other human beings is the basis for her argument that, although the fundamental uniqueness of angels may lead to hierarchical relations among the angels, it does not do so in human beings. While angels have different fundamental forms (although, presumably, sharing enough commonality to be properly classified as "angels") and stand in hierarchical arrangements, human beings—despite their differences in individual forms—do not. The equality of human beings, in contrast to that of angels, lies in our interdependence. I am not wholly sure whether it is better to read her claim in light of her theory of empathy or in a more metaphysical way, but both readings together provide a substantive account of how we as human beings are interdependent.[26]

I am still, however, a little worried that the appeal to interdependence is not yet strong enough to avoid fully the possibility of hierarchy or the dangers inherent in the claim regarding fundamental differences. Stein herself argues in her dissertation that enrichment only occurs in the context of commonality.[27] In *On the*

26. We might also consider Stein's comments from *Der Aufbau* (quoted in chapter 2, "Evolution," above), interpreting the "breathe of God" not as something bequeathed on individuals, but given to a species and providing a solidarity among all members of that species.

27. I do not believe that Stein cites her dissertation in *Finite and Eternal Being;* she does, however, refer to her texts on causality and motivation, written just a few years after her dissertation and developing ideas put forth there. See EeS 403, footnote 96/ESG 370, footnote 99/FEB 606, footnote 101.

Problem of Empathy, she says: "Inasmuch as I now interpret it [another living body] as 'like mine,' I come to consider myself as an object like it."[28] It is seeing the other as *like* me and similar to me that allows me to so objectify myself and thus be enriched in the meeting of the other. I see the other as an object to be considered, understood, and evaluated, and *recognizing that I am like the other,* I can also consider, understand, and evaluate myself. Thus, it is the basic commonality between us which allows the other to enrich and complete me. If, however, I did not consider the other as like me—if I considered her, for example, to be a superhero or a saint far beyond my meager powers[29]—I would also not feel the pull to become like the other and thereby enriched. It is precisely in recognizing the similarities, and thus an unrealized but real potentiality, that I gain understanding of myself and enrichment from my experiences with another.

Saying that we need others like ourselves in order to develop fully need not imply that I need others who act and think as I now act and think, but, rather, others with the same potentialities. Stein understands our potentialities to be part of our essence, existing in their essential being, and brought to actual being only in our choices and various efficacious events. In a very real sense, it is the others who do *not* act as I do or think as I do who are most helpful in revealing to each of us our not-yet-realized potentialities and encouraging us to further development.[30] Such others can re-

28. *On the Problem of Empathy,* 88. Likewise, she says, "The individual is only possible for a subject of the same type. For example, a pure 'I,' for which no living body of its own and no psycho-physical relationships are constituted primordially, could perhaps have all kinds of objects given, but it could not perceive animated, living bodies—living individuals. It is, of course, very difficult to decide what is here a matter of fact and what is necessary essentially" (87).

29. This is, it seems to me, one of the dangers of overly hagiographical styles of writing about saints. If saints are souls of a different nature than the "rest of us," they can be neither examples nor encouragements for us (although they might provide some kind of inspiration).

30. We could likewise develop Stein's claim here in light of Hegel's "master/slave" dialectic. Insofar as there is inequality, the self-development will be incomplete.

veal our potentialities and thus what we can and ought to become in act. But others do this only insofar as we share potentialities. Where we differ in essence, so too we differ in potentiality. Thus, it seems that if the individual form adds traits to the common form, then we can experience enrichment only in terms of what we share in common.[31]

Stein contrasts our dependence as human beings with the independence of angels. An angel does not "owe its nature to another," whereas each human being owes its nature and the development of its nature to other human beings. Our debt to other human beings creates the equality among all human beings. But it seems to me that we owe our nature to another *only insofar as* we are similar.[32] Where we are different, the other may offer help for self-understanding and development only in the weak sense of telling us what we are not. Thus, we are dependent on another to the degree that we are similar, but the claim regarding individual forms is that we are not structurally similar in all respects. Thus, it is not clear to me that the equality of human beings has truly been defended. I may learn quite a bit about myself through an empathetic relation with a dog. For example, I recognize in my dog the ability to make someone feel loved, a talent for careful watchfulness, and abounding joy. I can then recognize such traits in myself—to greater and lesser degrees—and desire more fully to unfold them. Thus, my dog has been helpful in my own self-knowledge and self-development. But we need not thereby conclude that my dog deserves the same treatment I deserve or that ethical injunctions apply equally to me and my dog.

The second reading of Stein's response, however, emphasizes that we owe the whole of our nature to another human being. It

---

31. It might be objected that the individual form does not add traits per se, but the specification of traits. I am not convinced, however, that this gets her out of the difficulty. The specifications would still be formal and thus formally different.

32. Her claim in *The Hidden Life* that the development of full individuality requires divine help, quoted in the first chapter, takes a disturbing turn here. If help is always necessary for us to claim our own nature and our nature qua individuality is not shared, then it is not surprising that only God can help us.

is not merely the case that we can develop our nature through interaction with others like us, but that our possession of that nature owes itself to other human beings. The second reading points to where the previous analogy between me and my dog is faulty. I may owe my dog much for the development of my nature, but I am not dependent on my dog for the origin of my nature.

I am not sure, however, that this quite solves the problem. If Stein's individual forms are different in content, each presenting a different and unique (in the weaker sense) specification of the human form, then a child ought to have a different individual form than her parents. The child might owe her nature *qua human* to her parents, but I am not sure that the child need owe her nature *qua individual* to her parents. As such, we would be dependent on others for the conditions of our existence and our common human nature. But we would not be dependent in terms of our specifically individual form. Thus, it is at least theoretically possible that the content making each of us unique (in the weaker sense) could indicate sufficient independence to undermine our confidence that there are not hierarchical relations or problematic differences among human beings.

Thus, if the individual form adds traits to the common human form in such a way that there are some traits present in the individual that are not in the human form (even if allowed by the common human form), then the notion of an individual form compromises the commonality and equality among all human beings achieved through the notion of a common form and, thus, is not desirable. It is clear that Stein does not want either to compromise the commonality or the equality of all human beings. Nonetheless, I am worried about the degree to which she can succeed in fully affirming that commonality and equality.

Further Challenges for Individual Forms

In the following section I will articulate further variations on the previous challenge, spelling out the potential problems in four areas: the ethical, the political, the religious, and the social. In none of these cases do I think that the objection is fully unanswerable, and I end each section with possible responses Stein might make. But I do think that all four areas raise significant questions in need of further investigation.

Ethical

In Dostoevsky's *Crime and Punishment,* Raskolnikov justifies his murderous act by distinguishing himself and his talents from those of the old pawnbroker. He sees certain privileges and treatment as appropriate to some people of sufficient intelligence. That is, he claims that all people are not equal, and because of their intellectual talents some should be exempted from certain aspects of the law.[33] In the course of the novel, it becomes clear that Dostoevsky thinks his main character is mistaken in this. There is no such privilege, and by implication, there is no such inequality.

The claim that we are—at base—different, that our individuality and individual form is more fundamental than our common form, lends itself to Raskolnikov's error. If some traits are individual, rather than universal, it is possible that some people cannot be held responsible—or perhaps not held responsible to the same degree—for certain things. For example, ethical injunctions need not apply to all because the higher status of some may exempt them from the law. Likewise, we could say that a person may be exempt from certain responsibilities if she lacks the corresponding trait and, therefore, the real potentiality for those types of actions. For example, if Mao lacked the ability to be compassionate—or if it was formally less capable of being developed—he would not, thus, be morally responsible for his actions in the way another person with a fuller potentiality to be compassionate would. If one *cannot* do something, that person is not guilty of failing to do so.

---

33. In a way similar to Stein, Raskolnikov has not claimed that some human beings have an intellect and others do not but, rather, that the intellect of some may be sharper than others. Thus, there is a human capacity—the intellect—which is realized differently in different individuals.

Thus, in positing individual forms, Stein has complicated universal ethical injunctions. To return to her analogy with colors, it is possible to think of many different reds—burgundy, fire-engine red, and orange-red—without ranking them or claiming that they are "unequal." But you do not, thereby, use just any of those reds in combination with a dusty-rose sofa. One knows, prior to seeing the paint samples, that not all reds are equal or, in this case, not all reds look good with pastel furniture.[34] Likewise, without a fundamental commonality, we cannot assume that ethical injunctions apply a priori to all persons. If we are, at base, different, one must consider not only extenuating circumstances in applying a law or ethical principle but also real structural differences.

This critique does not require that any universal ethic actually praise and blame all people with an identical standard, but that such equality acts as an ideal to be negotiated and qualified as particular circumstances dictate. Suppose, for example, there is a child whose mother used and continued to use dangerous drugs throughout her pregnancy. After the child is born, he lives with his mother, who struggles for most of his childhood with drug addiction, and he himself develops a serious drug habit. It seems that the situation of this child differs in several significant respects from another child who is not born already addicted and who grows up in a home where the use of addictive drugs is not standard and access to them is not easy. If both choose to take drugs, surely we must assess the blame for that choice somewhat differently. Thus, I do not want to say that we, in fact, do or should assess praise and

34. When I claim that we know this prior to seeing the paint samples, I am not claiming that we know this prior to seeing *any* paint samples or red objects. Rather, prior to seeing the *particular* red in question, we know something about whether bright or tame reds are appropriate. Likewise, in making claims about a priori assumptions regarding all human beings, I am not saying that we do or can know anything about human capacities prior to meeting *any* human being whatsoever (it may, in fact, require the meeting of a great number of human beings to have any good ideas regarding human potentialities). But we can know quite a few things about some particular person prior to meeting her insofar as we know about human nature.

blame in a purely univocal way.[35] But the significant differences in these two cases are a posteriori; the "blame," or way of assessing the conditions of freedom and responsibility, in making the choice to use drugs is in each case different because one child had different *experiences* than the other. But we do not assume a difference independent of any knowledge of the persons or their experiences. There is an a priori assumption in universal ethical injunctions that we are—at base—(structurally) identical, and this assumption is only modified once there is evidence of extenuating circumstances (or the imagined possibility of such circumstances). Thus, it is fundamental to any universal ethical claim that all human beings share a basic common nature.

Likewise, it seems that moral and ethical injunctions common within the Christian tradition are based on this assumption. In the Sermon on the Mount, Jesus says "blessed are the merciful," "the pure in heart," "the peacemakers."[36] If we are not assumed to be identical in structure (that is, in potentialities), then this cannot be assumed to apply to all human beings and, therefore, neither spiritual development nor religious training should expect (or even encourage) such traits in all persons. If there is something that can be "unfolded" differently in the individual, is it perhaps not simply lamentable, but unavoidable and even right, that some people

35. My concern here is very limited. I am not asking how a court of law should deal with each case, but, more simply, how much responsibility for the actions and addition should be assessed, in an ideal sense, to each child. I am also not claiming that—in any particular case—any one of us would know or understand enough to make an accurate judgment regarding each child's responsibility. We may, in fact, never be able to make such judgments due to the difficulty of appreciating all the factors involved in concrete cases. But, in theory, we could at least recognize that such differences in responsibility are possible.

36. Matthew 5. There is debate among Catholic moral theologians about how to interpret, among other things, Jesus's statements in the Sermon on the Mount. To claim that they are moral injunctions applicable to all people is only one of the available positions. It was, however, a mainstream position among Catholic thinkers during Stein's lifetime. Given her consistent attempts to remain orthodox and the lack of evidence to the contrary, it is unlikely that she would have taken a minority position in this debate.

never develop mercy, for example, or courage? The question arises: how do moral and ethical injunctions retain their force if they cannot be assumed to apply to all human beings?

(Stein does say that someone would be required, for example, to be compassionate even if he lacked the "natural power" to do so insofar as the grace of God was offered or made available for overcoming this natural weakness.[37] It is not clear to me, however, that this comment quite addresses the objection. The individual form must give the *possibility* of being compassionate even if one lacks the *ability* to do so at that moment, given, perhaps, her experiences and habits. The eidetic structure must allow for this, even if—in fact—we are not now capable of such an act.)

Insofar as Stein's account of individual forms with their individual potentialities posits something more fundamental than the common human form, she has opened the door for the undermining of certain types of moral injunctions and the a priori assumption of commonality present in a universal ethical theory.

Stein might respond to this by arguing that all human individual forms are *specifications* of the common human structure. We do not have different *general* potentialities, simply different variants on those general potentialities. We all do, in fact, make judgments—even about very small children—that certain things are fit for that individual which are not for another, while also insisting that certain types of behavior (e.g., running with scissors) is inappropriate behavior for all children. We regularly judge that one child—Roma, for example—should read certain stories, while Lucas ought to read quite different stories. Both children ought to develop their imaginations, but, because of their individuality, certain stories and

---

37. Thus, she says: "God desires nothing from human beings without giving to them at the same time the power for that. The faith teaches it and the experience of a life of faith confirms it. The interior of the soul is a vessel in which the spirit of God (the life of grace) streams, if it opens itself to him by the power of its freedom" (EeS 409/ESG 375/FEB 445). God gives new life to a soul, enabling it to do things it could not do on its own natural power.

characters are more fit for developing Roma's imagination and others for Lucas's. But these differences do not in any way compromise the more general point that children all have an imaginative faculty and that it ought to be developed. We could take ethical and moral injunctions to be similar: insofar as they are aimed at the general and not the specific, universal moral and ethical claims still apply. Thus, all human beings ought to develop the capacity to be merciful, for example, but Mariah ought to develop that capacity with a particular kind of depth whereas John ought to do so with a particular quickness and expansiveness.

I am not yet sure that this response would get Stein fully out of the problem. It will require greater investigation into both a right picture of the ethical life and the implications of individual forms in that account in order to evaluate fully the effect of affirming individual forms on our account of the ethical life. Affirming such individual forms would certainly have an impact on a traditional virtue theory, affecting both our descriptions of the virtues and our account of the development of those virtues. It does seem clear, however, that maintaining the a priori universality of certain moral and ethical claims would be made more difficult, although not impossible, on a Steinian account. (One might argue, however, that perhaps this is a complexity that is needed in our moral reflection.)

Political

The potential for hierarchical relations leads to political questions as well, particularly for democratic societies. It is not obvious that democracy is the best form of government, and problematizing the theoretical support for any particular political arrangement need not be a devastating objection to any account of human beings. Political theory should follow our account of the person and the structure of reality, and not vice versa. Further, many people have argued that democracy is not, in fact, the best form of government, and many who hold to a common human form have, nonetheless, not been strong supporters of a liberal democracy. I point to the challenge individual forms would present for certain political orders, not because I want to defend democracy per se, but because accepting Stein's individual forms would require those who do want to make such a defense to look carefully at the implications of her claim.

The challenge arises: if not all individual forms contain the same traits and talents and, therefore, the same basic possibilities, is there a sufficient basis for a democracy? It is the assumption of a political democracy that "everyone is created equal" and that, in principle, there is one vote per person. Each person—because she is human—is presumed to have some relatively equal role in the political process, but dolphins, even when affected by the decisions, nonetheless do not have a significant political right to shape the decisions. Political democracies thus make a sharp distinction between humans and non-humans, and all humans—simply because they are human and not based on any special ability or origin—have a crucial role in the political process. If it has been shown that some person's capacities have been hindered, through significant mental handicap, for example, or if they are not yet fully developed, as in the case of minors, they may not be allowed a say in the political process. But no human being is, on principle, disallowed. There is no a priori reason for preventing someone from voting, only a posteriori reasons. After meeting someone or knowing of that person's experiences or life situation, we might judge that she ought not to have a vote, but democracies nonetheless begin with the assumption of commonality. There is, thus, an assumption of basic sameness or similarity among all human beings, whereas dolphins, on principle and in contrast, are not allowed a vote because they have different capacities and potentialities.

If, however, the individual form adds *traits,* or significant specifications of those, to the universal form, then there may be reason to revisit this assumption. Democracies assume (a) that the basic distinction between humans and non-humans is the most important distinction for having an active role in the political process, and (b) that there are no significant distinctions among human capacities such that a priori some humans would be more fit to be involved than others. But if Stein is correct that we each have an individual form that offers greater specification to human potentialities, then it is not clear to me that these assumptions are fully justified. If we each have an individual form that offers structural specification to the common human form, then these structural differences may have implications for our political systems. Perhaps we might think that only people testing sufficiently intuitive on the Meyers Briggs personality test and, therefore, most oriented toward large-picture theory and ideas, should be allowed to decide public policy. Or perhaps those with less capacity for compassion ought to be relegated to a lesser significance in the process (maybe given only a half-vote, for example). It seems plausible, if we have individual forms, that only certain kinds of specifications of the human potentialities are truly fit for making such momentous decisions. Just as we judge that parrots, simply because they are parrots, do not have an equal say in the process, so too perhaps we might judge that certain kinds of individual forms, simply because they are of that kind, ought to have a lesser role.

There would, of course, be significant questions about how we recognize the differences among individual forms and thus how we would determine whether someone had the more appropriate kind of individual form for having a say in the political process. These difficulties might raise sufficient challenges such that the best practical course was simply to continue with the common assumptions of the democratic system. But the practical difficulties would not eliminate the theoretical ones. Even if it is, in practice, exceedingly difficult to distinguish and determine the types of individual forms and thus individual capacities most valuable to the political process, the introduction of individual forms raises a theoretical challenge to the theoretical bases for a political democracy.

I am not sure how Stein would respond to this challenge. Stein certainly affirms the fundamental equality of all human beings. Stein notes, for example, that failing to recognize the fundamental unity of human beings and our true commonality leads to problematic political notions, among them one-sided nationalism. In her essay on the state (which she footnotes both in *Finite and Eternal Being*[38] and in the appendix to the text *Martin Heideggers Existentialphilosophie*),[39] Stein maintains that a state must organize itself around the good of the individual members.[40] Presumably, the interest and well-being of *all* members of the state are significant— not simply those of a few, or the most privileged, or those "most able to contribute to society." The human capacities and potentialities are taken as more fundamental than individual specifications of these; thus, regardless of whether intuitive thinking is difficult or easy, whether one's judgments are clear or cloudy, the fact that one has human potentialities is sufficient for the state's interest in that person's well-being. In contrast, the state does not organize itself around the interests or good of my cat. His rights within the state derive from mine. Thus, there is an assumption—in Stein's own theory of the state—that all human beings have some basic equality or identity such that the rights of each human being must be considered in a way that no other beings' are.

Stein certainly does affirm a common human form, but insofar as the notion of individual form introduces differences in basic potentialities, it raises a challenge that may—although I am not confident that it must—be detrimental to Stein's own theory of the state. As in the previous case, Stein may be able to appeal to our commonalities as human beings in order to defend her account of the legitimacy of democratic ideals, but her introduction of individual forms has made this appeal more complicated than it would be on a Thomistic scheme. On the Thomistic scheme, our most basic formal structure is identical. Each of us is fundamentally human, and the differences among us are all a posteriori (due, for exam-

38. EeS 380, footnote 75/ESG 349, footnote 77/FEB 602, footnote 78. Marianne Sawicki suggests that this footnote may have been added by the editor. See the editor's introduction in *An Investigation Concerning the State*, xi.

39. See n. 58 of *Martin Heideggers Existentialphilosophie* in *Welt und Person*, p. 98/ESG 469, n. 62.

40. *An Investigation Concerning the State*, esp. II, §1, and Calcagno's essay on Stein and Heidegger, "*Die Fülle oder das Nichts?* Edith Stein and Martin Heidegger on the Question of Being," 274.

ple, to the relation between our matter and form, the working out of the potentialities of our form, our various experiences, choices, etc.). These a posteriori differences may lead us to talk of differing capacities, but these differences are not based in our fundamental potentialities or our capacities in the most basic sense. All human beings are, for Thomas, structurally identical at the most basic levels, and there is thus a clear justification for the assumptions of a political democracy. Stein cannot, however, make the same claim. Thus, although she clearly affirms the full equality of all human beings and articulates a theory of the state proceeding on this assumption, the theoretical basis for that affirmation is less clear than in Thomas's account.

Christianity and the Incarnation

The ethical and political concerns raise theoretical challenges for Stein's position on individual forms. Although not obviously impossible to overcome, they do present questions. I take both the religious and social implications of individual forms to present more significant challenges. Stein acknowledges that real commonality among human beings is necessary in order to understand the Christian doctrines of creation and salvation,[41] and she clearly wants to preserve real commonality and therefore an orthodox understanding of creation and salvation. She points to the claim that in one man (Adam), all have sinned. Such an understanding of the *community* of human beings makes little sense apart from a notion of our fundamental commonality. Our experience of divine grace is likewise connected to our fundamental similarities. She says:

The life of grace streams to the members because they stand in connection and are able already *from nature* [understood as human nature]—as spiritual beings and empowered to free self-revelation—to accept within themselves its divine life. The connection between head and member is grounded in a three-fold way: in *nature, freedom* and *grace*.[42]

41. See, for example, *Finite and Eternal Being* VIII, §3, 3.
42. EeS 478/ESG 438/FEB 523.

Stein recognizes that the unity between the Head (Christ) and the members of His body lies in a unity of nature, that is, all human beings share a nature that is capable of taking in divine life and therefore becoming members of Christ's body.

But it seems to me that the commonality necessary among all human beings in order to account for Christian claims lies even deeper. Among the powerful claims in the Christian story is that God became one of us, that is, he took on human nature and in so doing became like all human beings. The Christological debates centered around this very question, and the Church's rejection of Arianism and Apollinarianism were, in large part, based on the failure of both to preserve the fundamental and uncompromising nature of Jesus' humanity. He is not, as the Arians suggested, merely a human body, while remaining fundamentally divine in nature (and thus, not possessing a truly human soul).[43] Nor is he some hybrid of divinity and humanity, mixing together the two natures (and, thus, not human *like* we are human), as Apollinaris suggested.[44]

Rather, Christian orthodoxy claims that Christ must be spoken of as

made known in two natures without confusion, without change, without division, without separation, the difference of the natures being by no means removed because of the union, but the property of each nature being preserved.[45]

Jesus is fully human and fully divine and neither in such a way that either his divinity or his humanity is compromised. In mak-

43. See, for example, Athanasius's "Orations against the Arians," in *The Christological Controversy*, ed. and trans. Richard A. Norris Jr. (Philadelphia: Fortress Press, 1980), 83–101.

44. See "On the Union in Christ of the Body with the Godhead," in *The Christological Controversy*, 103–11. See also J. N. D. Kelly's discussion in *Early Christian Doctrines*, rev. ed. (San Francisco: HarperSanFrancisco, 1978), esp. chapter 12.

45. From the Council of Chalcedon, quoted in Kelly, *Early Christian Doctrines*, 340. The Christological solution was stated in terms of how we can speak of Christ, not in terms of how he *is*, thus affirming the real mysteriousness of the Incarnation.

ing this claim, Christianity insists that Christ in his human nature is not more like a first-century Jewish fisherman than a twentieth-century autistic girl, nor more like a charismatic religious leader than someone lacking personal charisma. Rather, all human beings share—at their most fundamental level—a basic commonality which Christ took on in becoming human.

In order to make such a claim, it appears that a fully Christian theory must affirm that the similarity of our human nature is more fundamental than any differences—be they contextual or in terms of personal traits and characteristics. Christ truly and equally became like all human beings. Presumably there must be something in terms of which he became *like us.* If, as Stein posits, each of us has an individual form which adds traits or content to the common form, then it is not clear how Christ is equally like all human beings.[46]

~

Stein might claim that Christ himself lacked an individual form. Perhaps all other human beings have an individual form in addition to our human form, but Christ was *pure human,* without any individual form. This possibility could get Stein out of the difficulty, but there is no textual evidence for such a claim, and it is not clear how this could work. If the human form is partial or incomplete as *moments* are, then it cannot exist without further content, that is, an individual form. There is no pure color that is not also some particular color—red, or blue, or green; so too, it seems that there could not be any pure human form without a further individual form. Thus, it is not clear that this avenue of response is open to Stein.

An alternative response might be to claim that Christ's individual form is so distinctive and unique, it can truly be claimed to be equally similar to all others. Thus, Christ does have an individual form in addition to his human form, but the content of his

46. I do not think that Stein's claims regarding individual forms are helpful in understanding the Incarnation. Husserlian mereology and Stein's appropriation of it, however, may nonetheless prove useful in other ways for a philosophical theology of the Incarnation.

individual form is sufficiently and equally different from all other individual forms such that no one person could be said to be more or less, at the level of structure, like Christ than another. Christ would thus be truly like all human beings at the level of human nature and, it appears, equally unlike all of us at the level of individual form. Although this route may avoid the theological difficulty, it may also raise some interesting and provocative queries of its own. What kind of reason (or specification of human reason), for example, is so distinctive that it could be *equally unlike* anyone else's reason? What kind of specification of compassion does Christ have such that His capacity for compassion is not more like one person's than another's? And what does this mean for our attempts to imitate Christ? If we can only hope to, and ought only to, imitate Christ in Christ's common humanity but not His individuality, then how do we distinguish each? What are the marks of Christ's *human* reasoning versus his *individual* reasoning?

Once again, these questions may be answerable, but the introduction of individual forms does raise a new set of questions for our understanding of the Incarnation, the Atonement, and the call to imitate Christ.

Social and interpersonal

Finally, any thesis compromising a fundamental commonality among all human beings may present certain social and interpersonal challenges. This threat is present in the notion of individual form in *Finite and Eternal Being* and is evident in Stein's earlier work. In her dissertation, Stein uses a notion of *type*.[47] Stein's notion of types probably differs in many important respects from

---

47. See chapter 4 of *On the Problem of Empathy*. Individual forms are unique to each individual, whereas types offer broader groupings. It is unclear in the dissertation, however, whether different types are a natural and good state of the person or a "fallen" state. She says, interestingly enough, that "the ideal person with all his values in a suitable hierarchy and having adequate feelings would correspond to the entire realm of value levels" (108). Likewise, it is unclear whether the type is permanent. Certainly in her essays on woman, Stein distinguishes "types," which are not permanent, from "species," which are.

her account of individual form; nonetheless, consideration of her account of type may help point to a weakness. Stein distinguishes persons of differing types based upon the levels at which values are felt. Thus, for example, someone for whom knowledge is a deeply felt value would be a "scientific type."[48] When we meet someone of our own type, we can empathize more deeply and fully (even when these traits have not yet been unfolded in our own life).[49] Where the other is of an alien type, I can only understand her experiences "in the manner of empty presentation," and I cannot fully empathize with her experiences.[50]

Marianne Sawicki in her book on Stein's phenomenology strongly criticizes the concept of type; she says:

Frau Doktorin, this is an offensive and dangerous idea. Besides which, it is wrong. There are no aliens so *alien* that we cannot feel inside their live experiences *at all*. We are all of one type. What disables the ability to understand another human being is not differentness, but only . . . one's own refusal of depth experiences of valuation, and one's consequent failure to become an authentic person.[51]

What makes type so problematic is that it "variously enables or disables interpersonal understanding,"[52] and thus real communi-

48. See *On the Problem of Empathy*, 107. I owe this example to Marianne Sawicki's *Body, Text and Science*, 138.

49. "Empathy" *(Einfühlung)* is, for Stein, a technical term used to designate the way in which foreign experiences are given to us. She distinguishes three phases in any (fully) empathized experience: "(1) the emergence of the experience, (2) the fulfilling explication, and (3) the comprehensive objectification of the explained experience" (*On the Problem of Empathy*, 10).

50. *On the Problem of Empathy*, 115. Sawicki summarizes this claim: "With *truly alien aliens*—people not of *my own type*—all I can do is to represent their experiences to myself and watch them from the outside" (*Body, Text and Science*, 184).

51. Sawicki, *Body, Text and Science*, 140. I have cut "the condition stipulated as item (b) above." Sawicki distinguishes different uses of "personal structure" in Stein; (b) is "the live experience of the eruption of particular valuations, characteristic of all human beings *except* those inauthentic wretches who have come by their values through contagion rather than their own deep feeling" (139).

52. Ibid., 140.

cation and understanding are not available with those beyond our type. If the possibility of real communication is de facto impossible between different types except as an empty presentation (as Stein appears to claim), then society and genuine social interactions are thereby limited to those like oneself. In pointing to the dangers of such a theory, Sawicki says, "'Type' is a pernicious notion when it usurps the category of humanity and demotes people of 'other types' to subhuman status. What was needed in 1930's Germany, and what is still needed today, is a phenomenology of the humanity *of strangers*."[53]

The downplaying of "other types" to a subhuman status need not follow from the recognition of difference or the limitations in our understanding of others; such a dehumanizing response can certainly be seen as inappropriate and unjustified, even if all too common. But Sawicki's objection that the notion of *type* "disables interpersonal understanding" would seem to apply likewise in the case of individual form. If the individual form is more fundamental than the universal form, and if the individual form contains traits different from those in the universal form, then real community and communication among members in a community is limited.[54] I can understand and empathize with others insofar as we share a common human structure. But insofar as each of us has an individual structure, I cannot empathize with another. I may be able to appreciate that someone experiences emotional pain at certain comments, for example, but there may be an a priori limit to my understanding of how intensely or how much the person experiences that pain. Any discussion or understanding of the per-

53. Ibid., 184. Stein recognizes the difficulty of both realizing and acknowledging the commonality of all persons, just as she indicates its importance. She says, "Being a member of humanity is something which we experience as a fact. Nonetheless, the individual must be quite progressed in his development in order to grasp humanity as a whole and to know his obligation to it" (EeS 466/ESG 426/FEB 510). What I am less certain of is that her theory gives us any help in explaining how we come to know our commonality.

54. My critique here is applicable only insofar as Stein retains an understanding of empathy similar to that presented in the earlier work.

son's history, previous experiences, life goals, values, etc., could not overcome this gap. Insofar as the limit lies not in our differing histories, material circumstances, etc., but in our individual structure itself, the gap in understanding is permanent. There would thus be a significant limitation in our ability to understand and feel with others. If our individual forms are "close enough," we may have less of a barrier with certain people in contrast to others, but with no human person would the limitation be utterly overcome.

It is surely right that some such limits in understanding exist. Stein argues in *Philosophy of Psychology and the Humanities* that no one else can experience my physical-bodily life in precisely the way I do. To use one of Sawicki's examples, another person can know what it is like to cut her finger, and she may jump with me in the moment of such a cut. But I feel the physical pain, whereas she does not. Similarly, it strikes me as quite likely that no one can comprehensively understand another person's act of will. There is in freedom a fiat, a moment of free choice, which is that person's act. Someone else might be able to understand the reasons for that act, but the act itself is not exhaustively comprehensible.[55] Thus, it is surely right that there are *in principle* limits—at the level of both body and will—to our understanding of others. (And there are other significant *practical* limitations as well.)

Stein's positing of individual forms and, presumably, their role in our ability to empathize and understand others would seem to create further limitations on our *in principle* understanding of others. Presumably, I cannot empathize with the feelings or kind of intellect characteristic of someone else's individual form, although I can empathize with human feelings in general and human intellect in general. Any further a priori specification of these general capacities, particularly where my individual form differs from another's, would create a limit to our mutual understanding and thus a limit on the type of relation and community possible between us.

55. See particularly the line of argument developed in the first essay in *Philosophy of Psychology and the Humanities*, "Sentient Causality."

Stein certainly affirms a common community among all human beings. She says:

The "we" is the form in which we experience the unity [*Einssein*] of a multitude of persons. The unity does not abolish the variety and difference of persons. The difference is once a difference of *being,* as we have recognized it belonging to the nature of the I: the being-integrated in a higher unity does not abolish the *monadic* closedness of the egoic life. It is, however, also a difference of *essence:* the commonality of kind, as the foundation of the being-a-we, allows room for a *personal characteristic* that the I shares with no other.[56]

The community is based on commonality of species, but Stein proceeds to claim as well a "difference of *essence,*" a *personal characteristic* which is shared with no other. If it is shared with no other and if it differs *in content* from all others, then do not individual forms present a significant limit on our ability to be a "we"?

~

Stein might simply accept that there is such a limitation on our ability to understand others and on the degree and kind of interpersonal relations which are possible. She might, however, also consider another approach. In her dissertation, Stein writes:

Now, in Dilthey and others we find the view that the intelligibility of foreign individuality is bound to our own individuality, that our experiential structure limits the range of what is for us intelligible. On a higher level, this is the repetition of possible empathic deception that we have shown in the constitution of the psycho-physical individual. However, we have not demonstrated that this belongs to the essence of empathy or said that the individual character is made the basis for experiencing other individuals. Of course, in the case of the psycho-physical individual, we could assert that the typical character was the basis for "analogizing" rather than the individual one. What can we do about this here where every single person is already himself a type?[57]

Here Stein claims that empathy may not, in fact, be limited by our individual character. It may be on the basis of our *general* charac-

56. EeS 323/ESG 299/FEB 349–50.
57. *On the Problem of Empathy,* 114.

ter, rather than our *individual* character that empathy occurs. We can empathize with others' emotional pain, not because we experience such pain in the same way (or have the capacity to do so), but because we have a general capacity to experience pain. Thus, individual forms would present no limit for our interpersonal relations insofar as empathy occurs on the basis of our general, rather than specific commonalities, and because we do truly share a common human structure.

This strikes me as perhaps the best avenue for responding to the challenge. There are, however, still further questions. It seems to me that we do in fact empathize with others not simply on the level of the human, but also on the level of the individual. This individual empathy strikes me as going beyond an "empty presentation." Stein writes on the next page of her dissertation:

> In principle, all foreign experience permitting itself to be derived from my own personal structure can be fulfilled, even if this structure has not yet actually unfolded. I can experience values empathically and discover correlative levels of my person, even though my primordial experience has not yet presented an opportunity for their exposure. He who has never looked a danger in the face himself can still experience himself as brave or cowardly in the empathic representation of another's situation.
>
> By contrast, I cannot fulfill what conflicts with my own experiential structure. But I can still have it given in the manner of empty presentation.[58]

In this section Stein is discussing the limitations of *type* rather than those of *individual form,* and thus it is not clear that all she says in her dissertation is equally relevant to the question of individual forms. But her comments do raise questions. Presumably we do not want another to understand our pain simply *as human pain* or in an empty presentation, but as my individual and individually experienced pain. If aspects of my individual form are significant for how I as an individual experience pain, I am not yet clear on how those would be accessible to another. Thus, it seems that it is

58. Ibid., 115.

at least a question how the deep empathy that we do in fact experience with others and which provides the basis for so many of our communal relations can be fully affirmed while also maintaining individual forms.

Conclusion

The challenge of hierarchical relations among individual forms, as well as differences that create tensions for at least certain accounts of our ethical, political, religious, and interpersonal lives, raise significant questions for Stein's account of individual forms. Stein may be able to respond to each of these, but her account of individual forms will require a rethinking of our understanding of issues quite pertinent to our daily lives. Thus, the introduction of individual forms presents us with significant theoretical work. Stein was aware of many of these difficulties, but it is not yet clear that she had worked out a full response to each of the challenges.

Rather than doing that work, however, I would like to suggest that we go in a different direction. Instead of responding to the challenges a priori content-based individual forms create, we might adapt Stein's theory of individual forms. There are sections in Stein's own work—although not the dominant ones—suggesting a different understanding of individual forms. These may provide a way both to maintain much (although not all) of what Stein wanted with individual forms, while also avoiding at least some of the challenges raised here. I would like to sketch briefly such an alternative account in the next chapter.

Eight ~ ALTERNATIVE ACCOUNTS OF INDIVIDUAL FORM

Stein shares with the Christian tradition, in a way that Aristotle did not, a concern for the individual and for the value of each and every individual. Each individual is not merely a means for the continuation of the species but is, rather, immeasurably valuable in the eyes of God. Stein has a beautiful passage about watching long lines of soldiers marching by; they form a mass where each conforms to all the others, all steps perfectly paced off. And yet the eyes of love— the eyes of the mother or bride—pick out a particular individual. They anxiously wait for just that one and recognize that individual's distinctiveness, even amid the great sea of soldiers.[1] Further, Stein rightly points out that the *person* is not reducible to her human nature; she is not simply one like all others with the human form. A person has a level of unrepeatability and dignity that the classic Aristotelian position did not adequately emphasize. If, in objecting to Stein's position, I end up undermining Stein's insights into the value of our individuality or our personhood, then I have failed. My contention in this chapter is not that Stein is wrong about the philosophic and moral significance of our individuality; it is, more simply, that our individuality can be adequately accounted for without positing a priori content-rich individual forms. Stein is, I believe, correct about the intelligibility and value of our individual distinctiveness, but I think that individual forms can be understood in a slightly different way than Stein (predominately) argues.

Stein distinguishes the substantial form, with its actual being, from our essence, with its essential being, which is then un-

1. See EeS 464–65/ESG 425–26/FEB 508–9.

folded in actual being. Individual forms, on Stein's dominant account, lie first and foremost at the level of essential being, as the final determination of the essence for finite personal entities. It is in this sense that Stein's individual forms can be described as a priori. They are not a priori in the sense of existing somewhere temporally prior to all actual being.[2] Essential being, although *other than* actual being, need not be prior to all actual being. Further, as properly atemporal, essential being is not relevant to time (even if the intelligibilities having essential being can be unfolded in time). Thus, in describing Stein's individual forms as "a priori," I simply mean that the being most fit to them is *other than* actual being: it is essential being.

Stein further claims that in virtue of our substantial form and our spirit, we can "stand over against" the possibilities of our essence; we can decide who and how we want to become ourselves. Thus, our true identity and deepest individuality lie in our spirit, not our individual form. It is our actually conscious, living, choosing self that is utterly unrepeatable and thus unique in the stronger sense. In addition to our spirit, however, Stein also affirms an individual form, which lays out possibilities distinctive for each of us as an individual and not merely as a human being. These individual forms do not make any of us unique in the stronger sense, but they do do so in a weaker sense.

While this understanding of individual forms is, I believe, the most consistent way of reading Stein's texts, there are very subtle hints of other possible interpretations. Stein makes a few comments throughout her writings which suggest—ever so subtly—slightly different understandings of individual form. These versions either do not make individual forms a priori or they play down the degree to which individual forms specify the *content* of the human form. None of the alternative understandings is consistent with the

2. And thus a priori here is being used in a sense closer to that of Kant, Reinach, and Husserl than to that of Plato insofar as he affirms a world of a priori Forms.

majority of what Stein says, and the comments leaning in these directions are comparatively few. But they offer hints of another understanding of individual form.

Further, and perhaps more significantly, I think that these comments hint at a better version of individual form than Stein's dominant position. I argue in the previous chapter that Stein's account of individual form is open to critical—although perhaps not insurmountable—challenges. The alternative versions, however, would not present the same kinds of challenges, and, moreover, the plausibility of the alternatives would show the non-necessity of Stein's a priori individual forms. If we can account for all that Stein wants without positing a priori content-rich individual forms, then such forms would be superfluous.

I would like to divide this argument into two chapters. In this chapter, I would like, first, briefly to sketch an outline of two alternate understandings of individual form which can be gleaned from a few of Stein's comments, although neither is fully consistent with all that she says. Second, I would like to argue that a priori content-rich individual forms are unnecessary. It seems to me that there are theoretical resources for articulating a substantive account of individuality which does not require Stein's (dominant account of) individual forms. The alternative I propose would require adapting or loosening certain aspects of the traditional Aristotelian-Thomistic account of the human being, but it may not require rejecting it as fully as Stein does with her positing of a priori content-rich individual forms.

In the next chapter, I would like to continue my argument that individual forms are unnecessary by showing, albeit briefly, how an alternative a posteriori understanding of individual forms can preserve (most of) the things that Stein wants to account for in positing a priori individual forms. In so doing, I hope to show that Stein can have (nearly) all that she wants in the individual form yet without the difficulties of an a priori content-rich individual form. The project of these chapters is ambitious, and I can at best offer suggestions and lines of investigation. But I hope to provoke the question of where and how much we ought to appropriate Stein's dominant account of individuality.

Hints in Other Directions

Thomas distinguishes essence and existence in all created beings. In *Summa contra gentiles,* for example, he writes:

> Although intellectual substances are not corporeal, nor composed of matter and form, nor existing in matter as material forms, it is not to be supposed that they therefore equal the divine simplicity. For a certain composition is found in them by the fact that in them *being* is not the same as *what* is.[3]

All created beings—even beings such as angels which have no matter—are a composition of essence and existence. Thus, all created beings are contingent and must receive being; they are in the process of becoming insofar as the potencies of their essences have not yet been realized.

Stein follows Thomas in this by distinguishing essence and real existence in all created things, but she does not separate the essence from its essential being (although she distinguishes them). As such, what is structural in an entity, what is part of its essence, is independent of its real existence; in its essential being the essence is timeless and stable. Insofar as individual forms are structures with essential being, they are distinct from (and in some sense prior to) the thing's real being. Therefore, the individual form cannot be the result of any choice or condition in real being. Stein can thus talk about an individual form containing *possibilities* for the individual which are distinct from and independent of the contingencies of the real existence of the thing (and thus, she talks of *being-Socrates,* which can be contrasted with the man Socrates).

While Stein's metaphysical claims allow her to posit a priori individual forms, I am not convinced that she should. If I am correct that individual forms function as principles of uniqueness

3. II, 52, 1.

and individuality on the level of essential being, then each individual form appears to provide a structure which determines "the goal and the way to the goal" of the individual.[4] It is that according to which the life of an individual can and ought to unfold, and the possibilities for one individual may differ from those available to another. As such, the individual form "fills out" or more fully determines the possibilities and prescriptions stipulated in the universal form, the human form. The individual form is not the principle of unrepeatable uniqueness: the substantial form or spirit with its actual being is that which is unrepeatable. But the individual form does add content to the human form in the sense that it adds traits or characteristics, providing a priori possibilities for one individual that differ from those available to another.[5] This seems to me to be the understanding of individual form most consistent with her claims throughout her writings—that is, the individual form is an essential structure specifying, prior (in some sense) to any experience or conditions of instantiation, the possibilities available to an individual human being.

Several texts in both her early work and her great opus, however, give me pause. But before turning to those texts, I would like to sketch very briefly the two alternatives I have in mind: first, individual forms as adverbs, rather than content-rich specifications of the human form, and, second, individual forms as a posteriori. Both of these versions of individual form would, I believe, avoid the challenges raised in the previous chapter, but I have a strong preference for the second, and that account of individual form will be filled out in a bit more detail in subsequent sections.

---

4. EeS 213/ESG 199/FEB 226. See also chapter 5 above.

5. As cited in the first chapter, she says, "The being-human as such is the essence of all individual human beings, common, always and everywhere remaining the same; beside that, however, each has something which differentiates him through content from others" (EeS 458/ESG 419/FEB 500). Similarly, she says of the essence of Socrates: "We observe it as not merely numerically different but, rather, different from the essence of every other human being through a special particularity" (EeS 439/ESG 402/FEB 478).

Adverbial individuality

There are passages in Stein's texts which discuss our individuality in terms of a personal core, providing a *how* we live out the human form.[6] If we emphasize this element, we might be able to understand Stein's principle of individuality not as a set of traits per se but, rather, as an adverb shaping individually how each of us performs and lives out the human capacities. If, for example, the use of language or abstract thought is a distinctively human capacity, then the individual form would shape Mary's use of language in a distinctively "Mary-like" way. She might engage in the very human activity, but there would be a coloring to her speech which is distinctive. On this account, one could not properly say that the individual form provides additional *traits* or even specification of traits; individual forms would not work in any way analogous to the specification of the category "animal" which occurs in considering a squirrel. But we could nonetheless acknowledge an individual form in the sense of some consistent and distinctively individual coloring of the common traits. Thus, we could say that Lucas runs, eats, laughs, listens, and plays Lucasly—with that distinctive Lucas energy. In contrast, Michael runs, eats, laughs, listens, and plays Michaelly—with a distinctive Michael sense of wonder. The "with energy" or "with wonder" would not quite count as a trait. Michael can do all these things with energy, just as Lucas can with wonder, but there would be a kind of coloring common to Lucas's way of engaging in human activities which is different from how Michael does so. Thus, on this account, the individual form would not make us different in content in any strong sense, but it would certainly make us different in a weaker sense. Perhaps the best description is to call it an individual adverb.

Stein certainly does describe the individual form as providing some kind of personal core, expressing the common human traits

---

6. See especially EeS 150–51/ESG 141–42/FEB 156–57, quoted in chapter 1 above.

in a distinctively individual way. Her comments do not, however, *limit* individual form to a merely adverbial role. This proposed account of individual form, however, would involve a limitation of individual form to the role of individual adverb. Individual form is, on this account, nothing more than an individual adverb, and the individual form would not add any traits or any significant content to the common human form. If we were to use an analogy with colors, the individual form here, rather than specifying a general category (e.g., "red" with "fire-engine" or "dusty rose"), would provide something closer to a finish for a common color (e.g., "glossy," "semi-glossy," or "flat"). On this account, the individual form may be a priori, but it would not be content-rich. There is no distinct content or trait to the individual form, but it may act as a core coloring all of our human content (yet without, properly speaking, adding traits).

I do not yet know if one could make full sense of this suggestion. How, more precisely, for example, do we distinguish *adverbs* from *traits,* especially for beings whose traits are often activities? I can imagine, in my analogy with colors, that a specification of the general category "red" with some particular shade of red would differ from changing the finish on that shade. I am not yet sure if this analogy, however, could be intelligently transferred to living beings or the traits of human beings. It might be possible, and if so, it could avoid the difficulties raised in the previous chapter. Because, however, I think the next route is a more promising way to interpret individual forms, I will not explore this possibility in more detail.

A Posteriori Individual Forms

The second alternative account of individual forms agrees with much of what Stein has claimed about individual forms: that they reveal differences in content among human beings, that they provide specifications of the common human traits, etc. On this account, however, individual forms are a posteriori and not a priori. The structure of the individual form, on this account, does not set the limits and goals for the development of any particular individual but is, rather, an intelligible pattern marking that person's individual structure which arises in and through the person's experiences and choices. Because of the material, social, cultural, and historical conditions of a person—as well as the history and effect of her choices—certain patterns of affect, behavior, etc., become characteristic of that person. Each person has so frequently made certain types of choices amid particular material, cultural, and social conditions that habits have formed and mark her character.

To use Stein's example, on this account, we could certainly recognize certain responses as characteristic of Caesar—perhaps that he is quick in his judgments about how to avoid danger, sees creatively how to take advantage of opportunities, etc. But these are not the case because there is a form of Caesar-ness existing in eidetic purity in its essential being; rather, they are the case because in and through the actual life of Caesar, certain traits and habits became dominant. The most basic a priori formal structure in Caesar would be his human form. The human form sets the limits for what is possible for human beings; it articulates the particular human potentialities (in contrast to, for example, llama potentialities). The individual form, in contrast, arises from the various dominant ways in which we develop our human form, and there is, thus, quite a bit of freedom involved in how we come to our individual form. Through, in part, our choices, we decide which of the human traits to develop and thus *how* to be a human being.

This account agrees with Thomas Aquinas's claim that there is no fundamental formal or structural component to our substantial form more basic than our human form. But it would also acknowledge that there is quite a bit of variety and flexibility in how the human traits may be developed and that we can recognize certain distinctive patterns characterizing each individual person. These arise in an a posteriori way, but they are nonetheless certain specifications of the human traits and distinctive to the individual. Thus, for example, although the capacity for humor is a general human trait and any individual's ability to enjoy a joke originates in that common human trait, the particular types of jokes that catch one person's fancy may be quite different from those that entertain another. These differences arise from differing cultures, familial situations, material conditions, etc., as well as different choices in how one responds to those varying conditions. Over time, one can recognize individual patterns and even describe these patterns in terms of traits marking something which might be described as an "individual form," but this individual form is not metaphysically equal to the human form. The origin of this form would not lie in its distinct essential being but would be the intelligibility resulting from the patterns of development of this individual human person in her actual being.

Texts Leaning toward these Alternatives

There are texts offering some minimal support to both of these accounts. For example, in her dissertation on empathy Stein discusses various failures to develop. Central to her examples of such failures are emotional failures.[7] Stein's emphasis is on the person as a particular type of emotional response to differing values; different personalities come from different types of value perception. She says:

Thus we have sketched the constitution of personality in outline. We have found it to be a unity entirely based in experience and further distinguished by its subordination to rational laws. Person and world (more exactly, value world) were found to be completely correlated. . . . *The ideal person with all his values in a suitable hierarchy and having adequate feelings would correspond to the entire realm of value levels. Other personal types would result from the abolition of certain value ranges or from the modification of the value hierarchy* and, further, from differences in the intensity of value experiences or from preferring one of the several forms of expression, such as bodily expression, willing, action, etc.[8]

7. In both her dissertation and subsequent phenomenological writings, Stein emphasizes our emotional capacities and the centrality of our emotional life for our person. There is, she reports, a psychological tradition that understands the I as constituted in our emotions, and from her examples, she seems to be identifying herself as within that camp (see *On the Problem of Empathy*, 98).

8. *On the Problem of Empathy*, 108. Emphasis mine.

Stein's discussion here is of personal types rather than individual forms, but it is nonetheless striking that Stein claims that the ideal person would be open to *all* values. This suggests that the possibilities for value perception would not—at least in an ideal case—be limited in any respect, and if there were more than one ideal person, both would have identical (in content) capacities for value perception. Different types in this case—e.g., the "scientific type" in contrast to the "aesthetic type"—are construed as deviations from the ideal. What is striking about this example is that Stein seems to have some account of the ideal person, and then understands what occurs in individual types as, in some sense, falling short of that ideal. Here what marks individual persons as different in content is not obviously celebrated.

It should be noted, first, that what Stein claims about *types* may be quite different from what she would claim for individual forms. Stein may certainly hold both that individual forms mark a perfection of the individual and that certain types mark an imperfection in individuals. Second, Stein does not here say that the ideal person could be a finite person, and thus it is not clear that Stein is claiming that all ideal human persons would have equivalent powers of value perception. Nonetheless, her comments provocatively raise the question of how we ought to distinguish that which is less than ideal from that which presents differing individual ideals.

Another passage in *On the Problem of Empathy* raises similar questions. Stein says:

This substantial unity is "my" soul when the experiences in which it is apparent are "my" experiences or acts in which my pure "I" lives. The peculiar structure of psychic unity depends on the peculiar content of the stream of experience; and, conversely, (as we must say after the soul has been constituted for us) the content of the stream of experience depends on the structure of the soul. Were there streams of consciousness alike in content, there would also be souls of the same kind or instances of ideally-the-same soul. However, we do not have the complete psychic phenomenon (nor the psychic individual) when we examine it in isolation.[9]

9. Ibid., 40.

In this passage, Stein hints that the ultimate structure of the soul (i.e., the individual form) is not a priori but, rather, formed by the "content of the stream of experience." That is, perhaps the distinctiveness of each of us *qua individual* does not lie in something eidetically necessary or in a priori essential being but, rather, our distinctiveness comes in and through the content of our material, cultural, social, historical, linguistic, self-conscious, and free lives. Stein does not explicitly make this claim, and the line coming closest to doing so here is discussing our "psychic unity," not our individual form. But one can see here some very subtle hints of a notion of individual form shaped in an a posteriori way.

When we turn to *Finite and Eternal Being,* we can find other tantalizing comments. For example, she says that for God, there is no diversity of nature, no contrast of universal and individual nature, *and thus no opposition of essential and real being.*[10] If this comment is meant to employ a parallel structure, then Stein is suggesting that the difference between universal and individual nature is due to the opposition of essential and real being, with the individual nature being tied more closely to real being than to essential being.

Similarly, in IV, §4, 11, Stein suggests "another way" to think of individual essence:

With *individual form* [*individuellen Wesen*] one can now think further of something different. What *finally* makes the thing to be the determinate thing which it is, is its substantial form. Because, however, the substantial forms of the so-called *composite substances* work themselves out necessarily in material fullness, so their material fullness belongs to that which they are and their material determination is to be seen as part of their individual essence.[11]

Stein does not go so far as to say here that individual forms are a posteriori, but she does suggest that we can think of the individu-

10. EeS 323/ESG 299/FEB 350.
11. EeS 235/ESG 219–20/FEB 252. In the 1950 edition, the second sentence quoted here begins: "Was *letztlich* das Ding"; in the 2006 edition, "*letztlich*" is omitted.

al form in connection with material determination or the matter upon which the substantial form "works." The substantial form is the power to work with matter; thus, matter can be seen as part of the individual essence. But presumably the substantial form and essence differ in significant ways, and the closer one places individual form to such a posteriori concerns, the better Stein is able to avoid the problems raised in chapter 7. As connected to real being rather than essential being, the individual form may characterize the person without changing the human possibilities.

None of these passages suggest a posteriori individual forms in a very clear or firm way. And in each case, the individuality Stein is discussing might be the strong sense of unrepeatable uniqueness, which is clearly tied in Stein's work to our actual existence. Nonetheless, one might be able to pull out very subtle hints of sympathy for an a posteriori individual form from these passages.

The strongest arguments in support of the first suggested alternative above, the adverbial interpretation of individual forms, lie in Stein's account of how we come to grasp the uniqueness of others. She says:

The interior of the soul, its most proper and most spiritual, is not color- or formless but, rather, is characteristically formed: it feels itself, if it is "by itself," "gathered in itself." It does not allow itself to be so grasped that one could name it with a universal name nor is it comparable with another. It does not allow itself to be taken apart in qualities, character traits, and the like because it lies deeper than these: it is the *how* (ποῖον) of the essence itself that imprints its stamp on each character trait and on each action of the human being and forms the key to the construction of his character. Through these "externalizations" the interior of the soul is graspable from the outside. We "feel" the ineffability of the essence also in another. It is that which "draws" or "repels" us at the deepest level. We can feel touched thereby as by something kindred. But my *kind* and that of the others does not allow itself to be laid out in something common and something different. In this sense, we must see that the distinction of essence of the individual is not graspable.[12]

12. EeS 458–59/ESG 420/FEB 501–2.

Here Stein emphasizes the degree to which the individual form is *not* knowable, neither in qualities nor traits. Much of what we can know of the interior is felt; it is what repels and draws us to others, yet in inexpressible ways.[13] We can see actions, but only *feel* the character of the person. (Stein has a rather long discussion of the significance of feelings and their nature as a kind of knowledge. The insights gained through our emotions or feelings can be distinguished from intellectual knowledge, but Stein will not relegate such insight to an incidental or insignificant place.)[14]

Stein strongly insists that we "know" of the uniqueness of others through our emotional faculties and not simply our intellect. Such an account of our access to individual distinctiveness would seem to fit better with something non-formal.[15] It should be noted

13. She says: "Because the soul is a personal-spiritual structure, therefore, its interior and most characteristic, its essence, springs out of its powers and the changing play of its life; [it] is not only an unknown X that we take up to clarify the experiencible psychological [*seelische*] facts, but also, something that can be felt and enlightens us even if it also always remains mysterious" (EeS 465, footnote 59/ESG 524 [within the appendix on *Die Seelenburg*]/FEB 611–12). When *Finite and Eternal Being* was published in 1950, the two appendices were dropped and various sections of them included, without notation, in footnotes throughout the text. Most of this quoted passage also appears on page 67 of *Die Seelenburg* in *Welt und Person*.)

14. At times, she speaks as though feeling were more primary than intellectual knowing. See the latter sections of *Finite and Eternal Being* VII and VIII, §3, 2. Stein also places a tremendous emphasis on the knowledge of values obtained through feeling. See especially "Individual and Community" in *Philosophy of Psychology and the Humanities*.

15. Stein does not claim that the individual form is an utterly unique and unrepeatable element and, therefore, not subsumable under a universal concept, as Scotus does. See, for example, *Ordinatio* I, d. 3., q. 2, n. 21, and Bettoni's discussion, esp. pp. 121–23. It would be clear then why individuality is not intellectually accessible; human beings know by subsuming the particular under a universal. If there is no universal under which it could be subsumed, then the particular cannot be so known. Instead, however, Stein has claimed that the individual form is merely unique in the weak sense; it is different from that of others. Furthermore, the individual form is a *form*, and thus by nature should be structural and intelligible. (She suggests this at EeS 149/ESG 140/FEB 155, quoted in chapter 1 above.) Thus, she needs to provide an account of why it is not intellectually graspable. Baseheart explains this difficulty, claiming: "The process of bringing *individual*

here that in the quoted passage, Stein is not speaking of individual form per se but of the interior of the soul. If, however, the uniqueness of the soul is conditioned by the individual form and the individual form is analogous to the human form, then intellectual knowledge should, at least to some significant degree, be possible. Stein could certainly respond that she has not claimed that our individuality is unknowable for all; it is only unknowable to human beings. God does see the uniqueness of each human. Nonetheless, if the individual form is analogous to the human form, then it ought to be knowable in ways analogous to the human form. If, in contrast, it is more like an adverb, such descriptions of our access to our individual core are more intelligible. Adverbial colorings would seem to be harder to articulate than individual, formal patterns of development. If Stein were emphasizing the adverbial element of individual forms in contrast to individual traits or content, then it is much easier to understand why Stein so strongly emphasizes that we feel another's uniqueness.

None of these texts, however, quite say what I would like Stein to say. The closest she gets to attributing individual form to a posteriori elements is in her discussion in *Finite and Eternal Being* VII, §5, where she focuses on individuality as a question of power. After claiming that understanding and will belong to the essence of each human being, she says of the individual: "It belongs to the essence of this man that his understanding is clear and his will decisive. Each intellectual and voluntary action is a 'direction of power,' in which the living spiritual power is formed in a certain way."[16] What makes this person's understanding different from understanding as a generic human trait is the way in which power is "directed through that trait": the *power* of his will is decisive as the *activity* of his understanding is clear. Likewise, she claims:

---

essence to givenness involves the discovery of the conglomerate of essential predicates that qualify the individual; the difficulty of grasping the proper mode of its being—its core—leads Stein to affirm the ultimate incomprehensibility of the person" (*Person in the World*, 104).

16. EeS 365/ESG 336/FEB 396.

A determinate measure of power belongs to the essence of this human being that is characteristic of his character and, indeed, the preferred direction of activity that is proper to him from nature.[17]

Here she suggests that the mark of a person's character is the "preferred direction of activity." Individuality could, thus, be seen—not as a change in human possibilities—but in terms of where, to what degree, and how those possibilities are unfolded.

Yet right after the section quoted above, she adds the comment "but the possible lines of development are laid out in the substantial form and differ for the individuals."[18] If what she means by this is that there are possible (i.e., eidetically possible or essential) lines of development circumscribed by an individual essential form, then this does not lean in an a posteriori direction. That is, if "the possible lines of development" are different in (individual) essence and not merely in fact, then her descriptions retain the notion of an a priori individual form. Insofar, however, as this comment can be interpreted to mean that there is simply a measure of power characteristic of each individual, then it is not obvious that the traits per se would differ, except insofar as a posteriori concerns become relevant. If seen as a "tendency of the flow of power" and not implying any difference on the level of essential being, then individual form does not compromise the universal form.[19] Stein could then claim that the possibilities of each human essence are identical—our fundamental structure is the same—but our diverse personalities, talents, and skills are due to the ease with which "power" flows toward certain possibilities. For example, perhaps one person, due to material conditions (and therefore a posteriori conditions), has

17. EeS 366/ESG 337/FEB 397.

18. EeS 366/ESG 337/FEB 397. Similarly, she says: "The power that stands available for each human being respectively as an already present possession and the highest measure thought according to the determination of his essence itself is a *measure*, i.e., 'measured,' a finite amount" (EeS 408/ESG 374/FEB 444).

19. This notion of a flow of power could be compared with her discussion of "lifepower" in her 1922 contributions to Husserl's *Jahrbuch*. See "Individual and Community" in *Philosophy of Psychology and the Humanities*.

a weak connection between her ear and her brain. While she can hear voices, music, etc., it is, nonetheless, difficult for her to catch subtle nuances in tones or other sounds. Thus, she claims that she is "unmusical" and turns her attention instead to visual stimuli. The possibilities within her essence are identical with those for any other human being, but due to material circumstances, she is inclined toward some avenues of communication and expression rather than others.[20]

If we could read individual form as a matter of power and the habitual "paths" through which it is directed, we could claim that all human possibilities (on the level of essential being and essence) are identical and thus justify the assumption of sameness, while attributing difference to the way in which the substantial form unfolds in real situations—including physical, psychological, and spiritual factors.[21]

20. We could also argue that due to material circumstances (among others) certain possibilities contained in the human essence never become real potentialities for a person. If the girl were deaf, for example, she would not have significant potential for certain kinds of self-expression and communication, even if they were possibilities written into her human form.

21. In a rather long footnote, she says: "Husserl speaks in the 'Ideas' (p. 8ff) of the possibility of bringing out the *what* in an individual object of experience through *eidetic intuition* or *ideation*. This distinctive intuition distinguished from all experience draws the content [*Gehalt*] from the facts of experience without achieving the *position* of experience (the apprehension of the thing as something *real*), and sets it as something that could also be realized elsewhere, outside of the context in which it was experienced. For Husserl, therefore, *universality* belongs to *the essence as such*, regardless of the level of generality within the region of essence to which he refers. The possibility of such an apprehension rests evidently on the double 'nature' [*Wesen*] of essence [*Wesen*] that emerges for us. It removes only the one side, the *essential being*, for consideration and cuts the connection to reality which belongs not externally but, rather, internally to the essence. From this cut achieved in the first account of the separation of fact and essence it is indeed understandable that Husserl came to an idealistic meaning of reality, while his co-workers and students (Max Scheler, Alexander Pfänder, Adolf Reinach, Hedwig Conrad-Martius, Jean Hering and others) proceeded from the full sense of *essence* grounded ever more in their realistic interpretation" (EeS 82, footnote 43/ESG 82, footnote 45/FEB 562). Stein suggests here that *reality* may be an essential component of essences, or at least certain

The Non-Necessity of Individual Forms

The most consistent interpretation of Stein's texts attributes to her the claim that each human being has an a priori content-rich individual form—that is, a form which provides a structure for our individual development and therefore limits our individual possibilities. This is not the only way to read Stein's claims, but it is the most consistent. It is not clear to me, however, that an a priori content-rich individual form is necessary in order to account either for the logic and intelligibility of our distinct personalities or the value of each individual person. If we are, as Stein claims, free, although conditioned by our matter and our social, cultural, and historical influences,[22] are individual forms also necessary?

Thomas Aquinas understands *individuation* to be due to designated matter. That is, what is responsible for there being many individuals all of one type is not form, but designated matter. (Angels, because—according to Thomas—they lack matter, are each the single instance of its kind.) Our *individuality* as a person, however, is not accounted for in the same way as our individuation. In his discussion of the divine Persons, Thomas says:

Further still, in a more special and perfect way, the particular and the individual are found in the rational substances which have dominion over their own actions; and which are not only made to act, like others; but which can act of themselves; for actions belong to singulars. Therefore also the individuals of the rational nature have a special name even among other substances; and this name is *person*.[23]

Aristotle and Thomas both distinguish between substance and accident. Substance is more fundamental, whereas accidents are *of* the substance and have their being in the substance. Previously (in the last section of chapter 1), I claimed that for Thomas our unique-

---

essences. If we could interpret this to refer to individual forms, this would be a promising passage.

22. Stein grants this and claims that uniqueness is the "product" of many factors. See, for example, *Finite and Eternal Being* VII, §9, 4, and VIII, §2, 10.

23. *Summa theologica* I, q. 29, a. 1c.

ness in the sense of difference is due to our accidents. This is true in a sense. What makes one squirrel different from another squirrel in more than numerical ways is accidental rather than substantial. But this is not the end of Thomas's claims regarding our individuality (in the sense of difference), particularly when we are talking of the individuality of *persons*. Thomas claims here that the distinctiveness of persons—our unique individuality—is due to our existence as free, self-forming, conscious beings. Thus, individuality in the sense of uniqueness for Thomas is not due either to designated matter (in any direct way) or to any a priori or formal element, but instead to our lived experience as persons. Thomas thus distinguishes, in contrast to Aristotle, between the essence, including both matter and form, and the act of existence. It is the latter that is central to our personal individuality, and, as far as I can tell, our act of existence as personal beings is both that which makes us unrepeatably unique and that which contributes to making us different from others of our kind.

Stein agrees with Thomas regarding the first part, that is, she agrees that something in actual being (for Stein, our substantial form) is that which is responsible for our unrepeatable uniqueness. But she posits individual forms as contributing in some significant way to our uniqueness in the sense of difference (in a more than numerical sense) from others of our kind. Individual forms—understood as content-rich and a priori—may, however, be a case of positing more than is necessary to account for the phenomena. It seems to me that what Stein attempts to account for with individual forms can, for the most part, be accounted for through other means.

In his struggle with God in the garden outside Milan, Augustine describes his weakness as one of habit, a weakness of will, but not of nature.[24] He says: "I was held back not by fetters put on me

24. By "nature" here, I am referring to human nature per se, not our fallen nature. Human nature in its essential structure or original state cannot be fallen; otherwise, Jesus could not have become genuinely human yet without sin. See Augustine's argument in *De spiritu et littera*.

by someone else, but by the iron bondage of my own will."[25] He had acquiesced in his desire which "became a habit, and the habit, being constantly yielded to, became a necessity."[26] Without importing the negative tone, personality could be seen in much the same way. Our personalities are in part characterized by our choices (from among the human possibilities) and, being consistently chosen, become abiding traits of our nature. (Personalities would similarly be alterable, to a greater and lesser degree, in a way analogous to habits.)[27] It would thus be our factual conditions—our matter, experiences, and real choices—that determine who we as individuals are, not an essential a priori individual nature.

This account could certainly continue to affirm with Stein that our ultimate uniqueness lies in our spirit, that is, in our actual free choices, the various ways in which we "stand over against" our actions, habits, etc. Our uniqueness, however, in the weaker sense of our personalities and distinct individual (and not simply human) intelligibility would be due to the various habits and consistent patterns each of us develops over time. Insofar as our dignity lies in our strong uniqueness—our personhood and free consciousness—this account in no way compromises the irreplaceability of each person. But our uniqueness in the weaker sense of difference would arise through more historical and contingent means. It is in and through the various influences, conditions, and choices we make over time that we develop such distinct patterns marking our uniqueness and differences as individuals.

This account strikes me as fitting with certain everyday experiences. We regularly meet people whose behavior, mannerisms, and choices all seem quite distinctive. As we hear about that person's life story and observe her in her childhood context, however, we can come to understand the distinctiveness in a new light. Per-

25. *The Confessions of St. Augustine*, trans. Rex Warner (New York: Penguin, 1963), 168 [VIII, 5].

26. Ibid.

27. Clearly the degree to which any particular trait or characteristic can be altered is dependent upon numerous factors.

haps one person is quick with a joke and can always get a crowd laughing; he is the "class clown" or the "office wit." We often discover, however, that these traits have a history, and the person can frequently point to events significant in their acquisition. Perhaps critical choices were made quite early on and, through them, habits of mind and heart developed into what now seems like a permanent trait. Perhaps the person had ears that stuck out a bit as a child and learned quickly that it is better to get others to laugh with you than at you. Or perhaps he just enjoyed the sound of his mother's laugh, and loved to find ways to provoke it. We can think of cases of people of strong will who enter a room and shape the events and atmosphere to their own vision. One can often find in such a person's past a need to fight hard against a challenging situation and critical moments when there were various types of encouragement to cultivate a strong will. At least part of why we like to read biographies is that we are looking for clues that help make a particular individual's personality and characteristics more intelligible. It is through understanding a person's past that we can come to appreciate who and how that person is. This is certainly not to claim that our history *determines* our personality, but it may make our personalities intelligible.[28] Given these kinds of examples, it is not clear to me that our individuality need be accounted for through an a priori individual form but may, rather, be partially chosen and partially an "accident" of our histories.

We might, however, ask *why* one person chose to cultivate a strong will in the face of some challenging situation, whereas another chose to cultivate profound patience. Might not these striking differences in choices in similar situations be accounted for best, as Stein does, with a priori content-rich individual forms? There is something mysterious about why people—for example, siblings and twins—facing the same conditions nonetheless choose quite differently. Stein's individual forms seem to offer some kind

28. Stein presents what I find to be a convincing account of the differences between causation and motivation in "Sentient Causality," the first essay in *Philosophy of Psychology and the Humanities*.

of insight for understanding these cases. We might also think of newborn babies. A child, not even a day old, can have a distinctive personality, and one can recognize very early on traits that are consistent throughout that person's life. Such examples would seem to count against my suggestion of a posteriori individual forms. If distinct personalities reveal themselves so early in our lives and help account for such differing choices in common situations, then there does seem to be some evidence in favor of a priori rather than a posteriori forms.

Although these cases present some evidence for a priori individual forms, they are not conclusive. There are no cases—even with identical twins—where the conditions under which each person chooses are identical. Each of us face unique situations, where the various factors motivating us to choose to cultivate a strong will or a profound patience will differ, even if subtly. But, further, even if there were such identical conditions, it is not yet clear that our choices are better explained by an individual form rather than simply by our freedom. Stein herself claims that our individual form marks who each of us as an individual *ought* to be, not simply who we are. Individual forms mark out the lines of and limits of development for each individual, but we can choose not to develop our own individual form just as we can choose not to develop our human nature. We need not become a fully developed version of our own individuality. Becoming ourselves—even on Stein's account—is something we have something to do with, and we must choose how and to what degree we become even our own individual form. If that is so, then Stein's a priori content-rich individual forms would add another factor motivating our choices, but they could not in themselves account for or explain our free choices. In our choices, we decide *who* we in our actual being want to be, how we want to live out our possibilities, what we will value, etc. The individual form does not provide any kind of final explanation for our free decisions.

Thus, although a priori individual forms might seem to offer some help in understanding our choices and our differences, it is not clear to me that they offer a much fuller account than we get through looking at our material conditions, histories, family experiences and relationships, etc. And if we can account for our individual distinctness through these various *a posteriori* factors, then Stein's individual forms would not be necessary.

∼

It does seem to me that we regularly account for ourselves—our personalities and tendencies—by pointing to various choices and situations we have faced, that is, by pointing to various a posteriori conditions. We explain who we are by talking about our histories, our families, and our relationships. We talk about what rules and traditions our parents had, what our siblings were like, who was around when we were children, what happened in school, etc. Further, such formation surely began long before we were self-consciously aware and making choices in any mature manner. Even before a child is born, there are many months of formation and development. An infant is already familiar with certain voices before she is born, and she is presumably also familiar with certain struggles and material circumstances (both in the sense of her matter in contrast to her form and in the sense of the child's biological surroundings), and she has developed limited habits for responding to her conditions. We might not call these habits "chosen" in a strong sense, but they are surely nonetheless strongly motivating habits characteristic of that person. In claiming that our individual characteristics are a posteriori based in the development of habits of behavior and affect, I am not denying that these characteristics appear quite early. The traits marking us as individuals are formed even as we ourselves are formed.

Thus described, "individual form" would be a posteriori; it could be understood as differing expressions of the human form, with each individual presenting a "face" of the human form. Stein herself notes that

already [that is, in our earthly life] the individual human being is not able to unfold within his life all the possibilities that are grounded in his essence (understood as individual essence [*Einzelwesen*]). His power is so limited that he must purchase the great achievements in one area with the losses in another.[29]

If we remove the parenthetical clause "understood as individual essence," then Stein's claim here would be consistent with what I think would be a better conception of individuality. Our powers are limited, and we cannot simultaneously unfold all the possibilities grounded in the human essence but must make choices to concentrate in one area rather than another. We must "purchase the great achievements in one area with the losses in another." Our individuality lies in how this "purchase" and exchange takes place. We can thus genuinely speak of an individual distinctiveness or even individual form, but not something with essential being prior to our real existence and which would be "written onto" our substantial form. Given certain combinations of factual conditions, it is true that certain traits and habits are more likely to be developed and will be easier for one person to develop than another (and in some cases certain traits will be exceedingly difficult, if not practically impossible, to develop due to material circumstances), but nonetheless—at the level of substantial form—each human being is characterized by the same set of possibilities.

In so altering individual forms, Stein could more easily respond to the challenges raised in the previous chapter. For example, substantive empathy and community among human beings is more intelligible if we understand the individual form as a posteriori. Even if, because of factual conditions, there are some traits or skills I will probably never develop, insofar as they are *human*

29. Stein continues this passage: "Because of that we are allowed to accept that for each the fullness of being in glory will bring not only release from the slags of a ruined nature but also the unfolding of his unfulfilled possibilities. But he does not bring the 'essence of humanity' perfectly to expression. It belongs to the essence of human beings that the individual is a *member* and that he, as a whole with all the possibilities grounded therein, realizes himself in *humanity*, in which the individuals are 'member to member.' Each must embody the 'universal human nature' in order to be able to be a member of this whole. But it is only a frame that must be filled through the manifold of the essences of the individual members" (EeS 463–64/ESG 424–25/FEB 507).

and thus part of my basic structure, they cannot be truly and utterly foreign to me. Stein certainly grants that we are in community in the sense that we share a common nature. An even stronger notion of community arises by claiming that, in our differences, we can see differing ways in which that structure which is fundamentally our own may be unfolded. All manner of human development points to differing ways I could have been. (If I had been born under different conditions, if I had different matter, or had made different choices, I could have developed the traits someone else did, in fact, develop. And thus none of the human traits are fundamentally alien to me.) Similarly, the assumptions of commonality written into our political system and the orthodox Christian account of the Incarnation could be quite easily affirmed. It would truly be the case that we are—on our most fundamental formal and structural level—identical in content, and a priori assumptions of such commonality are justified. (In making this claim, I am certainly not denying the significance of the material, social, etc., conditions under which the human form is developed. We may be formally identical, but, because of the great significance of our matter and material conditions, etc., we can recognize genuine and significant differences among individuals.) Thus, it seems to me that a posteriori individual forms allow us both to affirm some intelligible account of individual forms and to defend important ethical, political, religious, and social ideas.[30]

Conclusion

Stein defends an account of a priori content-rich individual forms specifying the human form at the level of essential being and thus adding traits or characteristics marking each of us as individuals.

30. I am less interested in the pragmatic reasons for making the latter point—if the accounts are not *true,* then there is no point in defending them, no matter how useful. Rather, I am interested in this point for theoretical reasons. The traditional justifications of certain ethical, political, religious, and social ideas strike me as highly plausible and right in important respects.

These individual forms do not undermine our fundamental unrepeatable uniqueness nor do they compromise the true commonality of our human form, but they do add an additional principle of uniqueness (in the weaker sense) for each person, articulating who each of us can and ought to be not simply qua human but qua individual. There are a small number of passages throughout Stein's work suggesting a slightly different account of individual forms, allowing us to interpret them either as a priori adverbs of the human form or as a posteriori. I do not find, however, either of these interpretations of Stein's work to be overly convincing, both because the number of passages is few and because the alternative account of individual form is so vaguely stated. What I do find in the passages is not insight for understanding Stein's claims but, rather, ideas for an alternative reading of individual forms. I tried to argue that individual forms ought to be accepted not as a priori but as a posteriori. It seems to me that our intelligibility *as distinct individuals* can better be accounted for by turning to various a posteriori conditions, including our material, social, cultural, historical, and linguistics conditions as well as especially the use of our freedom in making choices and thus forming our habits amid these conditions. If this alternative explanation for our distinctiveness as individuals is adequate, then positing a priori individual forms would be philosophically unnecessary.

Nine ∾ AN ALTERNATIVE ACCOUNT REVISITED

The idea that there is something each of us as an individual ought to be strikes a deep chord. Most of us have met people who are deeply, deeply distinctive and yet profoundly authentic and truly themselves. And we can contrast these with others who seem to have taken on habits and mannerisms simply for the sake of standing out, being "unique"; something about their way of doing so rings false. Those closest to such people can often recognize what is part of "the act" and what is essential to "the real person." Stein's a priori individual forms offer one way to account for these differing experiences. Stein thinks that we can be true to ourselves *qua human* and *qua individual.* That is, there is a structure and positive form of individuality characteristic of each of us and marking out what it means to be truly and fully ourselves.

The notion that there is something each of us ought to be not simply as a human being but also as *this* human being, and the idea that our individuality is a positive feature of each of us and not some kind of lack of development, are both insights that I would like to preserve from Stein's account. I am not convinced, however, that the only or best way to do so requires a priori individual forms. In the last chapter, I tried to argue that an a posteriori account of individual forms is plausible and thus a priori individual forms are unnecessary. We do, in fact, develop habits in how we behave, how we use our reason, our will, etc., and we can talk of such patterns as a kind of individual form, albeit one arising through our lived experiences and not a priori or setting limits on what is possible for each of us as individuals. (Thus, "form" here would be a principle of intelligibility, but not a principle relevant to growth and development.) Stein, however, raises a number of concerns leading her to posit her a priori individual forms. It is not yet clear that my alternative account can truly preserve all that Stein wants to account for with her notion of a priori individual forms.

In the second chapter above, I laid out five considerations leading Stein to posit individual forms, including (a) the intelligibility of each of us as individuals, (b) the flexibility of the species-form suggested by evolutionary theory, (c) theological concerns about the value of individuality, (d) the role of our individuality in our spiritual development, and (e) the inadequacies of Thomas's account of individuation. In the following, I would like to reconsider each of these in light of an a posteriori model of individual form, arguing that most of what Stein is concerned about can be accounted for without a priori individual forms. Stein's questions strike me as right concerns. I am not yet convinced, however, that serious attention to these concerns requires us to posit a priori individual forms, and in the following I would like to offer a bit more defense of a posteriori—rather than a priori—individual forms.

The Intelligibility of Individual Distinctiveness

Individual forms are appealing to Stein, in part, for their usefulness in articulating a metaphysical understanding of the person compatible with her psychological studies. She understands the soul as a structure which is to be discovered and which has particular traits whether or not they are ever realized. Similarly, people can be categorized into personality groupings or types based upon certain (more or less) consistent features. My suggestion that individuality be due to a posteriori rather than a priori considerations appears to compromise this compatibility. If we are in our most fundamental structure identical, with only accidental divergences due to our conditions and choices, then it appears that psychological "types" are contingent products of chance, and the intelligibility of either types or individual persons would be somewhat difficult to account for. There would be no individual core holding certain traits together, nor a distinctive *individual* telos. Further, it would be less obvious how one distinguishes genuine from false fictional characters. It does seem that we do so, and yet without a priori individual forms it is more difficult to say *why* we can do so. Thus, the individuality of both factual and fictional human beings seems to be less well accounted for without Stein's individual forms.

There may nonetheless be a way to account well for our individual intelligibility without introducing a priori individual forms. Rather than positing individual forms which are more fundamental than the human form, the intelligibility of a person's behavior and patterns of behavior may instead be due to relations among the various traits within the human form. The human form is characterized by a large number of traits and potencies. Each of these must be developed, and the development of one is not unrelated to the development of others. Perhaps certain traits are closely related or eidetically correspond in such a way that when one of these is well developed (motivated perhaps by our historical or material conditions), other traits customarily are developed as well. Thus, our individual form need not be an additional formal structure but could, rather, be an individual pattern made possible (and intelligible) by relations among the many possibilities laid out in the common human form. For example, we might consider someone who is a great basketball player, who has a real attentiveness to spatial relations and anticipates well the best arrangements for achieving a goal. Such a person might also possess great confidence in a crowd and carry himself with grace. He feels at home in his body, and his confidence puts others around him at ease. His great development of certain human possibilities lends itself to the development of other related traits. We might even say that there is a core to his personality, perhaps a "generous, confident ease," which marks his way of speaking, engaging in business deals, making friends, etc. We could contrast this with someone who has the ability to function simultaneously at a number of different emotional levels. Such a person may be deeply aware not simply of the content of what another person says, but also the various motivating values—the insecurities, desires, hopes, visions of what one ought to live for, etc. He might be able to communicate both compassion and hope with just a few words and attend to numerous people at the same time. He might also, however, develop genuine friendships quite slowly and be fiercely protective of those to whom he is committed. The human possibility at which such a person excels may be connected to other corresponding traits, motivating someone who develops the one also to develop the others. If such correlations are plausible, then personality types could be explained in terms of the eidetic relations *within* the human form, rather than requiring a new form in addition to the human form.[1] Discerning well spatial relations and emotional states are *human* traits, not specifically individual ones. Those who have found the "unfolding" of one of these human possibilities easier than others may also find other, related possibilities and tendencies easier. Thus, skills or personality traits may be grouped in more or less predictable kinds of ways.[2]

This account could apply equally well to fictional characters. We find certain characters false because they do not present a particularly coherent way of relating human traits; they fail to follow along the eidetic relations *within* our common human form. Or perhaps they fail to offer adequate motivations or explanations for the various choices of the character. In contrast, great works of art can teach us something about what it means to be human; they can reveal connections among human traits that might be surprising or unexpected but nonetheless insightfully reveal a "face" of our

1. As such the individual form could be understood (as a form) in terms of the worked-out essence. It is how, at this moment, I have worked out the human form. This is compatible with and would help explain her claim that there can be a change in personality. See *Finite and Eternal Being* III, §4.

2. Stein says, "It is evident as a fact of experience that there are similarities between predecessors and descendants which indicate an inherited condition. And it is likewise evident that the similarity is not only bodily but also stretches to psychological [*seelische*] characteristics" (EeS 468/ESG 428/FEB 512). It would require some work to determine whether these "types" or groupings of traits could also apply to inherited dispositions and personality characteristics.

common humanity. Thus, there can be an individual intelligibility, though it is not a distinct form independent of the human form, but patterns of development allowed by the human form itself.

I would like to return to this in the section on spiritual development below, but it may be worth noting here that what it would mean to discover oneself, on this account, would have to change. Self-discovery could no longer mean discovering my type or individual form existing in some essential being, but rather a discovery of my human possibilities and the ways in which I have thus far tended to unfold those possibilities. This would tell me nothing of an essentially existing individual form but would, rather, provide a history of my actual life. Thus, contra Stein, "Caesar in a village instead of in Rome" would not be Caesar. There would be no "personal structure" which would "mark off a range of possibilities of variation within which the person's real distinctiveness can be developed 'ever according to the circumstances.'"[3] The circumstances (including our freedom in those circumstances) would be everything, and Caesar living in a village rather than Rome could well be quite different. There would be no "personal structure" outside of the human form as the real person Caesar chooses to unfold it, in whatever setting he finds himself. Thus, by *discovery of self* we could not mean a discovery of "pre-existing" personal possibilities, but we could talk of discovery of self in the sense of discovering *how* I can best live out the human form given my particular circumstances, history, etc.

Thus, it seems to me that we can affirm both that our common human form is our most basic formal structure and that our individuality is at least partially intelligible.[4] We can predict how

---

3. *On the Problem of Empathy*, 110. See also chapter 1 above.

4. Stein has granted the point that there can be nothing in our individual form that is not allowed by the human form, and thus—in some sense—each individual (human) form realizes possibilities already laid out as possible by the human form. Nonetheless, she emphasizes that there is something *of content* in the individual form that is not present in the human form (even if allowed by it). Here, I am arguing that the content is already in the human form, even if actualized differently (and characteristically differently) by differing individuals.

someone will behave or respond, not because there is an individual form ontologically comparable to the human form, but because there are intelligible relations among the traits of the human form and because we develop patterns and habits of how we commonly respond to various types of situations. This is certainly not to deny that we have genuine freedom and may act in unpredictable ways, but it does explain why so much of our behavior is in fact so predictable, or at least intelligible, for each of us qua individual.

~

It seems to me that a further epistemological issue is implicitly at work here. If, as Stein argues, grasping an intelligible structure requires that there be a distinct even if inseparable structure, and that that structure have a distinct being (essential being), then any grasp of our intelligibility *qua individuals* would require an individual form with essential being. Stein could grant that insofar as material, social, and historical conditions are important for setting the conditions for the "arrival" of certain individual forms rather than others, there is an a posteriori element important for each of our individual forms. Our various "a posteriori" conditions are significant for the kind of essential structure each of us has qua individual. Nonetheless, each of us genuinely does have an individual form with its own essential being. There must be such an individual form precisely because we do have genuine knowledge of people in their individuality. Further, insofar as essential being always accompanies either actual or mental being, we would expect such a mutual relationship between (i) the essential structure and being of each of us qua individual and (ii) our actual conditions in real being.

I take the position I am putting forward in this and the previous chapter to differ subtly from such an account. If, however, the position for which I am arguing is to offer any substantive philosophical alternative, it will need to address Stein's position on the level of knowledge claims. What kinds of acts and what kind of being are involved in our coming to understand or know anything? Does a genuine grasp of intelligibilities require distinct essences and a distinct being for those essences? Addressing these questions, although important, is beyond the scope of this text, although I will return briefly to these questions in the final chapter.

Evolution

I believe that the intelligibility of our individuality can be accounted for on a classic Thomistic model. I am not convinced, however, that the classic Thomistic account of the static form (which may or may not be the best reading of Thomas himself)[5] is easily compatible with Darwinian evolution. Stein is right that Thomism needs to rethink in some manner the account of the inner species-form if it is to accept the possibility of some form of evolution. Stein proposes both an account of the species-form "with leeway," or flexibility, and individual forms. She claims that the species-form is not quite as static as Aristotle claims and that there thus might be a range of expressions all of which rightly count as expressions of that species. She further argues that, in the case of human beings, we each have an individual form which offers different specifications of the species-form as well as our common species-form.

We could, however, accept her account of the flexibility of the species-form articulated for non-personal animals and simply apply that account to human beings, without positing individual forms. Stein writes in *Der Aufbau* (also quoted above in chapter 2):

> The type of appearance and the inner form do not coincide. They stand indeed in an internal relationship in which nothing in the appearance type can come to be that is not delimited in the form as *possible*. But not everything delimited in the form is *necessary;* the form allows leeway [literally, "rooms to play"].[6]

It is not wholly clear to me all that Stein has in mind in claiming that "the form allows open leeway," but it is clear that she intends

5. I am grateful to Bill Murion for emphasizing this point at the Lonergan Workshop, Boston College, June 2007.

6. *Der Aufbau*, 68.

for that leeway to account for how we can affirm a common species-form and yet also acknowledge evolutionary change among
the individuals of that form. Presumably at least part of what she
wants to claim here is that there is a single type of species structure
characterizing all members of the species, but that that species lawfulness may—given differing material conditions, histories, etc.—
express itself in a whole range of ways.

This claim regarding leeway raises many questions about the
nature of forms. The form is the principle of lawfulness and intelligibility. What, however, does it mean to be a *law*? Does lawfulness require necessity, or is there a lawfulness that is statistical and
probabilistic?[7] The phenomenological tradition has certainly recognized a wide range of types of essences and intelligibilities, and
Stein's comments in her 1932 *Der Aufbau* reveal that she is open to
understanding the species-form in a broader way than Thomists
have traditionally done.

I do not yet know how we should best articulate such a "loos-
ened" account of the species-form; it is clear, however, that Stein—
in order to respond to the Darwinian challenge—appeals to this
strategy. I take Stein to claim, first, that non-human living, corporeal beings are members of the same biological species in virtue of
sharing in a common metaphysical species structure. That structure, however, is not static in its expression, and may even express
itself in quite strikingly structurally different ways. These variations do not, however, undermine the claim that all the members
are indeed members of the same species, but it does point to the
variety of ways in which the same species-form may present itself
and to the importance of material conditions and material history
to those differing expressions.

In addition to this flexibility in the species-form, Stein also
thinks that human beings each possess an individual form. Presumably, the flexibility in the more general species-form is what al-

7. Perhaps the best-developed account of such non-classical lawfulness is in
Bernard Lonergan's *Insight: A Study of Human Understanding,* ed. Frederick E.
Crowe and Robert M. Doran (Toronto: University of Toronto Press, 1992).

lows Stein so easily to posit individual forms for human beings. Because Stein's conception of species-form already allows for a wide range of expressions, including what might appear to be quite distinct structural expressions, individual forms fit nicely into her scheme. Although the move to individual forms is plausible in light of Stein's understanding of species-form and fits with her broader response to evolutionary theory, it is not clear that she needs to make the move to a priori content-rich individual forms in order to maintain the core of her response to Darwinian evolution. As far as I can tell, the key work is done in the loosening of the understanding of the species-form (as well as the claims regarding the history of designated matter). Whether we make the move to individual forms is an independent question.

Stein does, however, have significant reasons for wanting to make this move. Certainly key among them is her recognition of the differences between personal and non-personal beings. Stein acknowledges the possibility of an evolutionary chain linking all organic life, but she also wants to maintain a clear distinction between *personal* organic life and *non-personal* organic life, and she wants to maintain the value and distinctiveness of each and every human person. But if our unrepeatable uniqueness lies in our spirit, consciousness, and freedom, rather than our individual form per se, then Stein could preserve the clear distinction between persons and non-persons by pointing to our consciousness and freedom rather our individual form. (In the following sections, I will explore more fully whether Stein would, or we ought to, find this approach adequate.) Thus, I think that—at least on an initial reading—Stein could preserve the significance of persons and our difference from non-persons without positing individual forms. Work would, of course, need to be done to describe and defend such a distinction between non-personal and personal life—and doing so lies beyond the scope of this study—but it is not clear to me that a priori individual forms are necessary to do so.

Theological Concerns

In *The Hidden Life,* Stein claimed that divine power is necessary for us to develop as *individuals*—not simply as human beings[8]— and she describes the sheer variety of human individuals surrounding God's throne as a "garland."[9] We are not more or less complete human beings, but each is a "beautiful and unique flower." Stein might object to my suggestion regarding individual forms by claiming that—on my account—our individuality appears to be a problem, something to be more or less overcome, rather than something positive to be developed. As I have described it, the ideal (although unrealistic) situation would be to realize all the possibilities of the human form. It is unfortunate that we cannot. Our individuality—individual personality and distinctiveness—is the result of this inability. Thus, individual form as an a posteriori individual structure appears to be a kind of limitation of the human form and, in some sense, a hindrance to be overcome. It is a liability to have an individual form (i.e., to be a limited version of the more comprehensive human form), not an asset. Thus, one might object, I have denigrated the value of the individual and our individual uniqueness; humanity, or our human-ness, is the most basic category that each of us unfolds, sadly, only to varying degrees.

It seems to me that one can make a twofold response to this. First and more significantly, each of us is not simply an individual human being, but an individual human *person.* It is in our life as persons that we each have a unique place in the "garland" circling God's throne. If one values our actual being, and not simply our essential structure, then it is our actual, personal existence that is present to God, each in her own unique way. What it means to be persons includes that we are beings with the capacity[10] for self-

---

8. See the long passage quoted in chapter 1 above.

9. See EeS 464/ESG 425/FEB 508 as well as the discussion in chapter 1 above.

10. I would like to put the emphasis here on *capacity,* not the actualization of that capacity. I am not in any way requiring that—in order to "count" as a per-

conscious, free life. We are what Stein calls *spiritual* beings. Stein beautifully describes such a personal life in chapter 7 of *Finite and Eternal Being,* and she emphasizes that we are not ruled simply by instinct. We are not driven purely by our various desires.[11] We are and can become more fully self-aware in and through our various acts, and we have the freedom, albeit conditioned freedom, to make judgments and choices about our instincts, desires, motivations, and values.

Like Thomas Aquinas, Stein connects our rationality and our freedom. She says, "If the gift of reason belongs to being-a-person, then the person as such must possess reason and freedom."[12] Reason is an act of the intellect and involves the ability to consider various possibilities; connected to this is our freedom as the power to act according to our understanding (and judgment).[13] If we are rational beings, then we are also free beings. Likewise, in her notion of *spirit* and the person as a unity of body, soul, and spirit, Stein reiterates the essential role of freedom in our being.[14] Most telling is her claim that "the human being is a spiritual person because he stands freely opposite not only his body but also his soul [*Seele*], and only so far as he has power over his soul has he also power over his body."[15] I take this claim to include our power to choose which

---

son—this capacity be actualized, nor that the full material conditions for actualizing this capacity obtain. All I am requiring is a living being, developing (if not yet fully actual) in the pattern that is characteristic of such personal lives. See Patrick Byrne's "Foundations of 'The Ethics of Embryonic Stem Cell Research,'" presented at the Lonergan Workshop, Boston College, June 18, 2007, for both the inspiration for this formulation and for a much more carefully worked out articulation and defense of this view.

11. Or, taking the previous footnote into account, we might restate this to say that we are in a pattern that can come to be driven not simply by instinct or desire.

12. EeS 335/ESG 309/FEB 362. See also Stein's appendix on Teresa of Avila, *Die Seelenburg.*

13. See *Finite and Eternal Being* VII, §2.

14. See, for example, *Finite and Eternal Being* VII, §7 and §9, 1 and 2. It would be valuable to pursue the relation between her descriptions of human beings as a unity of body, soul, and spirit and her discussion of human beings as a unity of substantial soul, essence, and being. I will not, however, do that here.

15. EeS 394/ESG 362/FEB 429.

psychological *(seelische)* traits and tendencies to act upon. We can refuse, for example, to entertain envy or we may cut short an aggressive action or thought. The traits characterizing us, both bodily and psychological, need not dominate our being. We retain an independence and power (albeit not complete) over them.

Our dignity as individuals lies in our personhood, with its power to choose among mutually exclusive options, revealing us as self-determined and self-constituted beings. The freedom to choose among options, to negotiate among the possibilities available to us, is central to all personality. With that freedom, we may choose to alter our actions or thinking patterns (to greater and lesser degrees) and thus to transcend our previous limitations. Thus, while "personality" per se as a pattern of possibilities may be a limitation of the human form, we are not limited by or to our "personalities" at any one time or stage. Our set of personality traits may be a set of thus-far-realized possibilities.

In the foreword to *Finite and Eternal Being*, Stein acknowledges that Martin Heidegger's *Being and Time* made "a strong impression" on her.[16] Core to Heidegger's account in *Being and Time* is a vision of the person as non-thing-like. Persons, or Dasein, are not primarily "present-at-hand," out there now, waiting to be "hit upon." In *Being and Time*, Martin Heidegger says:

> The *"essence" of Dasein lies in its existence.* Accordingly those characteristics which can be exhibited in this entity are not "properties" present-at-hand of some entity which "looks" so and so and is itself present-at-hand; they are in each case possible ways for it to be, and no more than that. All the Being-as-it-is [So-sein] which this entity possesses is primarily Being. So when we designate this entity with the term "Dasein," we are expressing not its "what" (as if it were a table, house or tree) but its Being.[17]

But if the Self is conceived "only" as a way of Being of this entity, this seems tantamount to volatilizing the real "core" of Dasein. Any appre-

---

16. EeS xii/ESG 7/FEB xxxi.
17. *Being and Time*, trans. John Macquarrie and Edward Robinson (San Francisco: HarperSanFrancisco, 1962), 67.

hensiveness however which one may have about this gets its nourishment from the perverse assumption that the entity in question has at bottom the kind of Being which belongs to something present-at-hand, even if one is far from attributing to it the solidity of an occurrent corporeal Thing. Yet man's *"substance"* is not spirit as a synthesis of soul and body; it is rather *existence*.[18]

Heidegger focuses on our existence and argues that our being is, at base, activity and orientation toward—not a substantial soul, if what is meant by that is some "thing-like" entity similar to trees and tables. Our identity is in our activity within a world; it does not lie in an essence existing prior to our real existence or as another thing in and among the things in the world.[19]

Likewise, when Stein describes our substantial form (in contrast to our essence), she focuses on it as a principle of actuality and as an activity.[20] It is not a *thing* like a tree or a house. She says, "Form and matter cannot be without one another: the being of the form is matter-forming."[21] Form is the principle for matter-formation, and its being lies in this task.[22] Certainly there are important differences between Stein's and Heidegger's accounts (Stein's substantial form is clearly not identical in all respects with Heidegger's

18. Ibid., 153.

19. I am interested here in Heidegger's focus on the human being, Dasein, as self-determining. He makes clear, however, that this self-determination is not completely free. Thus, he distances himself from the existentialism of, for example, Sartre in "Existentialism Is a Humanism."

20. Precisely how close Stein ends up to Heidegger on this point is a topic which should be pursued. It is not yet clear to me whether substantial soul in Stein is closer to a Heideggerian notion or a Thomistic one, or whether there is a way in which to reconcile them. The language is certainly Thomistic, but as pointed out in chapter 5, n. 13, she may have been pushing toward a slightly more Heideggerian understanding. See also James Collins's review of *Finite and Eternal Being*.

21. EeS 445–46/ESG 408/FEB 486.

22. In this, we can see hints of why Stein posits a principle of potentiality for angels. I would like to leave open the question of whether the being of form is exclusively the formation of matter. See *Finite and Eternal Being* IV, esp. §3 and §4, 5 for descriptions of various relations between form and matter in different kinds of beings.

Dasein), but in her discussion of substantial form, Stein emphasizes some of the Heideggerian foci, including the import of actual existence, activity, and (in the case of humans) choice and freedom. Given these emphases, it is not clear to me that Stein needs to proceed to a notion of individual form, rather than, like Heidegger, focusing on the self-determining, free nature of human beings. It strikes me that giving an account of the distinctiveness and value of such personal, spiritual life is critical, and that Stein has done this.[23] It is not clear to me, however, that Stein needs individual forms in addition to the free, choosing activity of the substantial soul in order to preserve the distinctive uniqueness and dignity of personal beings.

I worry in addition that Stein's decision to posit a principle of individual distinctiveness possessing essential being is part of a slight playing down of the value, significance, and dignity of actual being. Stein can certainly not be accused of strongly denigrating actual being (our actual being is, after all, central to our unrepeatable uniqueness and dignity). But there may be a slight playing down of actual being. Insofar as each of us is valued as a distinctive part of the garland around God's throne because of what we are in our *essential* rather than our *actual* being, then our essential being becomes more important than our actual being. But we are most truly what we are in our actual being, not what we are in our essential being. Our essential being may tell us what we *ought* to be, but it is not yet clear to me that we can properly say that we *are* our essential being—at least not in the sense that we *are* our actual being. If this is right, then I am not sure that individual forms with essential being yet add to *my* unique contribution to the beauty surrounding God's throne. I do not want to make this critique too strongly. Stein argues for a distinction between essential and actual being, not a separation. But it seems to me that the distinction may be sufficient to raise at least a few questions.

23. See Mette Lebech's work, including "The Identification of Human Dignity. Hermeneutic, Eidetic and Constitutional Analyses in the Light of the Phenomenology of Edith Stein" (Ph.D. diss., Katholieke Universiteit Leuven, 2006).

Thus, it seems to me that a posteriori individual forms need not indicate a denigration of the value of our individual structure. Our individuality is valuable because it is *our* individuality, that is, the accomplishment of some person and a reflection of who that person chose to become in and amid the particular factors he or she had to face. Each person *qua person* is intrinsically valuable, and our individual structure can have tremendous value as an achievement of a person.[24]

Spiritual Development

Among the significant questions upon which this issue will have an impact is how one understands spiritual life and what can be said of an afterlife. With the notion of a priori individual form, Stein understands at least part of our spiritual life and development to include an opening up to divine grace in order to become who we are essentially and who we, as individuals, are intended to be. But if we reject a priori individual forms, then there seems, on the surface, no longer to be an account of who each of us as an individual should be. Rather, *who* we are is a responsibility and choice, but without a goal. (Certainly, we should ideally become full *human beings*, but, as individuals, there seems to be no goal different from the goal of all human beings.) Stein argues that there is an ideal for each of us not simply as human, but as this, particular, and distinct human individual.

I am not yet convinced, however, that we need lose all senses of who each of us *qua individual* ought to be in giving up the notion of a priori individual forms. Stein says that each of us has "an unrepeatable mirror of God" in our soul.[25] We could understand this phrase—on the account put forward here—as the unrepeatable and

24. Individual forms, on this account, need not all be equally valuable. Each of us must form ourselves in some way and thus create an a posteriori individual form. But some personal structures might be better than others, even if all are distinctive and valuable insofar as they are the work of a personal spirit.

25. EeS 473/ESG 433/FEB 517.

unique way in which each of us brings the same human form to different fulfillment. Presumably, the human form contains more possibilities than any one of us can unfold within our limited lifetimes. We can find joy in reflecting together different aspects of that human form. Thus, the uniqueness of our gift to God lies in each of our distinctive ways of unfolding the image God has given equally to all human beings.

Further, each of us puts a distinctive face on the human form by working through distinctive circumstances. We are corporeal beings; we develop ourselves through matter, and matter not only in the sense of material stuff (bodies, food, etc.) but also matter in the sense of the examples surrounding us, the particular ideas we are acquainted with, people we meet, our place in history, etc. Matter, in the sense of *pure matter,* is pure potency, but we can distinguish different types of formed matter, including physical stuff and the broader influences on our formation, which include more than physical elements. Our bodies grow by taking in milk, carrots, and pizza. And we learn to read by opening books about Jack and Jill, or Peter Rabbit. We learn to think more abstractly by beginning with particular situations and gradually working toward the more general claims. And so on. On the classic Thomistic account, we are and are meant to be forms or souls becoming ourselves in and through matter, understood, I take it, in at least this dual sense. There is no full human being that is not material (and thus also historical). The goal is not to overcome our matter but to become ourselves in the working through our matter and material conditions. Stein agrees with this conception. She describes us as body, soul, and spirit, not simply souls or spirits "hanging out" with particular bodies. Thus, our materiality cannot be insignificant for our spiritual life. Stein certainly acknowledges this, but it seems to me that a posteriori individual forms can emphasize the role of matter in a particularly significant way as we articulate what and who we ought to be. Our material conditions are not secondary issues, but the very ground in which we grow and become. It is not simply that we are becoming more fully *human* as we work through our matter, but that we become more fully *individual* in working through our material conditions.

Thus, the particulars of our material circumstances (understood in the broadest sense) provide opportunities for unfolding our common human form in quite different ways. On the one hand, this can include the development of certain human possibilities more fully than others. One might, for example, develop physical capacities more fully than emotional ones, and thus differing people can express different aspects of the human form. It may be that the circumstances of one's life motivate such differing development. Where there is great physical hardship, the greater need could be for physical development and survival skills; where there is an emotional desert, in contrast, other kinds of human development may be more critical. Surely both right physical and appropriate emotional development are human virtues, and both ought to be developed. But whether an individual puts greater resources into cultivating physical skill or emotional attentiveness is not unrelated to material circumstances. And thus whether one's individuality is more marked by features and habits of one sort rather than another is importantly tied to our material lives.

On the other hand, the differing development may include more than simply the development of differing traits or aspects of our common humanity. Materiality is also significant for the differing *casts* to our common human development. Even as fully developed, we are never simply form. We are corporeal beings, and thus our full development includes our materiality (in, once again, the broadest sense). Presumably, both J. S. Bach and John Coltrane developed fully their musical capacities. Both actualized and expressed that aspect of our common humanity. But their music is very different. It is hard to imagine John Coltrane writing a classic fugue, or Bach creating "A Love Supreme." The music of each reveals differing influences, histories, and choices. Thus, the same capacity—even when fully realized—can express itself quite differently, in part because of the quite differing material conditions under which it is developed. These differences can, it seems to me, be

AN ALTERNATIVE ACCOUNT REVISITED

accounted for not by a priori individual forms, but by our materiality (and our choices within those material circumstances). There were particular customs regarding musical patronage, venues for playing, instruments available, as well as styles of music thus far explored, available as matter for Bach's development in the late seventeenth and early eighteenth centuries. These differed from the musical patronage, venues, instruments, and styles available to Coltrane. These influences, although not determining their music, conditioned their choices, creativity, and thus the ways in which their musical abilities were developed.

On this account of a posteriori individual forms, we can understand both discovery of self and discovery of who we ought to be (if we want to distinguish these two) by turning to the particulars of our own circumstances. "Discovery of self" would involve discovering how we have already developed and how we can continue to develop the human possibilities, given the circumstances of our lives. There are particular patterns and habits characterizing how we have thus far developed, and thus, discovery of self means discovering who we have become. We can also, moreover, speak of discovering who we as individuals *ought* to be. Each of us is to be human, to fully develop our humanity, but we can still ask: What among the human possibilities ought *I* become, what gifts and opportunities have *I* been given, and what responsibilities do *I* have in light of my particular family, history, culture, material conditions, etc.? A posteriori individual forms allow us to retain the notion that each of us—not simply as human beings, but also as individuals—has a very individual goal for our development. But figuring this out, on this account, would not involve searching for some essential individual structure, but living in our particular contexts, that is, "vaulting to our times" and recognizing the struggles, cultural challenges, needs, etc., of our day. Given our material circumstances and given the ways in which we have developed ourselves and can continue to do so, what can we contribute to the world? (I take it that this is part of why the college years have so often been a time in which students try to "find themselves." Finding ourselves is importantly about finding out about our history, our broader world and the needs of that world, and thus *who* we ought to be in relation to that greater whole.) Who we as individuals ought to be is not unrelated to our material conditions. Who we ought to be is precisely to be and develop fully within our very particular contexts, with the particular needs of our time.

Part of the attraction of many people to Stein is the way in which her own life is itself a model of someone who lived rightly in her own day and found her calling (and thus who she was) in and amid the challenges of her day. Her autobiography reveals the deep impact of her family on the cultivation of her personal traits and distinctiveness. She speaks beautifully of her own struggles with her education. Her particular kind of passionate activity, unmotivated by revenge in the face of injustices, was surely forged in the kiln of deep disappointment (including, among other disappointments, her repeated failures to get a university post).[26] She was clearly shaped and formed in her changing patriotism and love for her country as she lived during both world wars. She embraced many of the feminist concerns of her time, reflecting carefully about what it means to be feminine and masculine, and forming herself according to that which she identified as genuinely feminine. And she cultivated her Jewish identity, responding forcefully to the anti-Semitism of her time. Part of what makes Stein's story and personality so attractive is the way in which she developed herself in "dialogue" with her very particular social, cultural, and historical world.

The present is always informed and shaped by its history, and one cannot know oneself or one's time without appreciating the historical character of each. Similarly, to act in the present always involves acting for the sake of some future possibility, some ideal of who we want to be. It is inevitable that we aim toward some goal. Those goals may be the mere "taking over" of the ideals of our

---

26. See particularly Steven Payne's "Edith Stein: A Fragmented Life," *America*, October 10, 1998, 11–14. See also http://www.americapress.org/articles/Payne.htm.

culture, or they may be involved in a more reflective, intentional life. But acting for the sake of some future is unavoidable. Heidegger has articulated so well the challenge and necessity of living in time, as temporal beings.[27] Thus, living in our time is not opposed to a past and future orientation. On this model, we can speak of discovering ourselves and discovering who each of us as individuals ought to be. Neither of these would involve finding some eidetic structure characterizing oneself as an individual but, rather, living in light of our history where we find ourselves, negotiating and becoming ourselves in and amid the challenges that mark each of our particular situations.

I am not convinced that affirming a posteriori individual forms rather than a priori individual forms need change our conception of the spiritual life in all respects—both positions affirm the need to become ourselves as individuals (and not simply as human beings), both can affirm the significance of our material life, both can speak of a need to discover the self, and both can speak of what each of us as individuals ought to be. But there would be some slight differences in the meaning of each of these if we accept a posteriori rather than a priori individual forms. We would need further examples and investigation in order to defend fully one account over the other, but it seems to me at least plausible that a posteriori individual forms can preserve some substantive account of the spiritual life that maintains many of the things Stein emphasizes in her own descriptions of our spiritual growth and development. There would probably need to be a few adjustments to the account if one accepts a posteriori rather than a priori individual forms. For example, the particulars of her account of our soul as an interior castle might need minor adjustment and the notion of what it means to reach our individual perfection in glory may need to be reconsidered.[28] But I do not think that a posteriori individual forms would

27. In endorsing here much in Heidegger's descriptions from *Being and Time* of our nature as temporal, I am not endorsing his claims either about this aspect of our being as most fundamental or his understanding of *being* as time in general.

28. See EeS 213/ESG 199/FEB 226, quoted in n. 49 in chapter 1.

be guilty of creating an account of spiritual life inattentive to our significance as distinct and valuably different individuals.

Defending Thomas on Individuation

I suspect that Stein's explicit critiques of Thomas on individuation are less significant than their broader differences regarding being and essence. Thus, I think that the real debate between Stein and Thomas needs to occur at the level of discussion of types of being and the nature of essence. (See the next chapter for a few brief comments on these topics.) But I would like to address her explicit critiques very briefly.

There are a few ways a Thomist might respond to Stein. First, Stein's paradigm for what it means to be an individual includes both *impredicability* and *internal unity.* One might simply separate these two and argue that insofar as an entity is individual in the sense of *impredicable,* designated matter is responsible. Insofar as an entity is individual in the sense of *internally unified,* substantial form is responsible. Taking this route would require careful language, and one could not simply speak of the "principle of individuation," as if being impredicable were sufficient for being an individual. But, nonetheless, the basic Thomistic scheme would be retained.

A second route might be to claim that *impredicability* alone is the criterion for being an individual. Thus, both the pile of sand and the bird are individuals. They are very different types of individuals, but both are individuals. We can move, however, beyond talk of being merely an individual to different types of individuals, and in doing so, we need to move to the question of form.

I am not fully sure which of these two alternatives to prefer, or what would be at stake in preferring the one to the other. Certainly an account of the transcendentals—especially *unum*—would be relevant here.[29]

29. See Stein's *Finite and Eternal Being* V.

Questions of what counts as an individual, however, are not the only points Stein raises. She claims as well that matter, in order to be matter, must be that in virtue of something. She contrasts *matter* as space-filling with *spirit,* and she claims that some form must make matter precisely matter. I am not, however, convinced that this is so. Matter, for Thomas, is that which is formed. It is not clear that being "that which is formed" need be so through a positive principle of intelligibility. I am not sure that matter in order to be matter requires a positive form. Might matter not be, as Thomas understands it, the potency to be formed? We can distinguish between (a) the intelligible pattern according to which formation is occurring and (b) that there is "something" with the potency to be so formed. But need we claim that the potency of matter has any intelligibility other than "to be formed"? Thomas does not claim that form and matter are each individual *things.* They are *principles.* As such it is not clear that we should expect to understand them in identical manners. Thomas distinguishes the two principles precisely because they are understood in different manners: the one as that which can be accessed in a positive act of understanding, and the other as that which is understood to have undergone the formation by that first principle. As a pure potency, there would be nothing *in act* to be understood as "matter."[30] As actualized by form,[31] there is then something to be understood—i.e., the formal elements. Matter is simply that in which certain kinds of intelligibility occur.[32]

30. This argument itself presumes a slightly different cognitional theory than Stein posits. Once again, I think that major issues may lie at a deeper level than individual form itself, and in this case must be settled at the level of method and cognitional theory.

31. It is worth noting that there are two senses of potency in Thomas: the potency of matter in relation to form, and the potency of the essence in relation to the act of existence. See especially *Summa contra gentiles* II, 54, 9.

32. In *Insight,* Bernard Lonergan writes: "Let 'act' denote what is known inasmuch as one affirms; let 'form' denote what is known inasmuch as one understands; let 'potency' denote what is known inasmuch as one experiences the empirical residue" (510). If an account like this is correct, then form and matter

Stein spends a good deal of time in *Finite and Eternal Being* discussing the nature of matter, and she thinks—in light of contemporary science and quantum physics—we need to think carefully about our understanding of matter.[33] This is surely right, and my brief defense of Thomas here is far too short, given her broader concerns. Insofar, however, as those concerns were not directly and explicitly raised in the context of Stein's most explicit critique of Thomas on individuation, I will leave a more substantive discussion and evaluation of Stein's position on matter to a more thorough investigation of that topic. But, at least on an initial look, there seems to me to be a plausible Thomistic response to Stein's most explicit critiques. And, given how close Stein's position on individuation is, ultimately, to Thomas's, I am not sure that she intended her critiques to be as much of a challenge to Thomas's position as they might first appear.[34]

Conclusion

Husserl distinguishes facts from essences. Facts are contingent insofar as a fact could just as well not be. In contrast, essences are necessary. The essence must have such and such traits and structures in order to be *this type* of essence. Insofar as individual forms are essences with eidetic necessity, they cannot be changed or have been otherwise. But if individuality is due to facts rather than eidetic necessity, then Stein can preserve real and fundamental eidetic commonality among all human beings in our common human form. Individuality may be real, but without compromising our fundamental eidetic commonality.

Further, because of the role of personhood and its tie to our actual existence (rather than any feature of our essential being), the dignity of each person can be preserved without appealing to dis-

---

would not be accessed in comparable manners, and thus it is not clear that a further form making matter to be matter would be necessary.

33. See especially *Finite and Eternal Being* IV.

34. See n. 43 in chapter 5 above.

tinct individual forms. Finally, it seems to me that nearly all that Stein wants to gain by positing a priori content-rich individual forms can be preserved with an a posteriori account of individuality. Stein convincingly argues that we do, in fact, need to articulate such an account. Individuality—and not merely individuation and identity—is a philosophically significant topic. In contrast to Stein's position on individuality, however, it seems to me that we should posit as the most basic essential structures the human form, and not an individual one. Individuality and our individual form result not from a distinct formal principle, but from a posteriori considerations, including our matter, social and cultural influences, material situation, and, most significantly, our choices and free, self-determining actions amid these conditions. We might be able to speak of an a posteriori individual form insofar as we can articulate the patterns and habits among the human possibilities characteristic of an individual, but this would not be an individual comparable to our species-form and thus not an a priori content-rich individual form.

Ten ~ CONCLUSION

Stein's conception of the human individual is beautiful, and she articulates well an experience all of us have had of the uniqueness of each person we truly love. We do not love *a* human being, but *this* particular person. Stein's focus on individuality—and what it means to be oneself—is exceedingly valuable and challenging. There is certainly an emphasis (and a right and good one) in our culture, both philosophical and social, on individual uniqueness and "being true" to oneself. There is something convincing about the idea that there is a predictable structure to our personalities, and I have certainly seen in myself and others willful strivings both to develop and to repress personal traits, with both good and bad results. These descriptions surely get at something philosophically significant. Stein's metaphysical positions regarding essence and being, and her related understanding of the nature of potency and act, are theoretically powerful and ought to have a place in our contemporary philosophical discussions.

Nonetheless, I am hesitant about her a priori individual forms. Stein can, through Husserl's mereological theory and her own claims regarding essences and essential being, account for the integrity of both the individual form and the common form while also insisting that the two are irreducibly united. Her theory exhibits genuine conceptual progress. Despite her success in this and her admirable concerns regarding the value of individuality, I am not yet ready to affirm with Stein her particular account of individual forms, first, because I am not yet convinced that they are necessary to account for our experiences of ourselves and others, and second, because they pose significant challenges which may prove difficult to address fully. My leaning at the moment is to follow Thomas more closely than Stein in accounting for the positive value of our individual uniqueness in terms of our freedom and existence in our particular historical, social, and cultural formations, rather than through a priori content-rich individual forms. As noted in chapter 8, there are a few texts that suggest Stein may have been willing to go in this direction, but the majority of her texts articulate a less Thomistic position on individual distinctiveness.

But even if one follows Thomas more closely than Stein on questions of individuality, Stein has mounted substantive challenges which will require us to update and modify our Thomism, both in its emphases and in its understanding of the lawfulness of the species-form. Stein, it seems to me, has rightly raised questions that will call for, if not a significant modification in our understanding of species-form, at the very least different emphases in our account of the species and the individual. I have attempted to sketch briefly the lines for such work, but my position is woefully underdeveloped. The arguments made in the previous chapters are insufficiently fleshed out to account for all that needs to be accounted for in order to be fully defensible. I have hopes that such development is possible, but these are still promissory notes.

Further, however, and more significantly, a full evaluation of Stein's position on individuality and individual forms will require greater discussion and evaluation of more foundational issues, in particular, the key questions of philosophy: being and method. What is being, what is *ousia*? And how do we have access to being? Stein can posit a priori individual forms in part because she affirms a kind of being distinctive in all formal structures. Individual forms (in relation to finite beings) have first and properly essential being, and they may also come to have actual or mental being. In that essential being, individual forms may timelessly retain their identity and distinctness from the common human form. Stein's tripartite division of being into actual, mental, and essential, as well as her account of essence and its relation to potency and act, is central to her account of individual forms. And significantly tied to Stein's account of being and essence is an account of how we are in communion with each.

As far as I can tell, Stein, like Scotus, thinks that there must

CONCLUSION

be something about the *essence* that enables us to grasp its intelligibility, in contrast to its actual existence. Essential being is that which ensures the "unscathed-ness and virginity" of the essence in both actualization and intellectualization;[1] essential being is that which guarantees the reliability of our knowledge. Perhaps, however, Stein wants such a guarantee because she has not adequately distinguished various cognitional acts. Phenomenologists focus on the centrality of our acts and operations, distinguishing differing types of acts in relation to the same content. If we can preserve the "unscathed-ness and virginity" of the essence by distinguishing differing acts, then differing types of being would not be necessary. We perceive, for example, the color of a single, unified rose through sight, while we perceive the smell of that same rose through our faculty of smell. There is not something different in kind or exceedingly special about the color which allows the act of smelling to perceive both the color and the scent. Each of these elements of the rose is perceived via different acts. Perhaps analogously we might grasp intelligible structures through acts of understanding, while we grasp existence through acts of judgment. Intelligible structures would then not need to have some special being by means of which they preserve their identity in both actual and mental being. Perhaps we do not through acts of understanding perceive first the essence in its essential being and then the actual existence. Perhaps instead the acts by which we grasp essence differ in kind from those by which we grasp being. If one does not, however, adequately distinguish acts of understanding from acts of judging, one might be tempted to think that there must be *something* about the item in virtue of which one type of act can give us intelligibility and another act *of the same type* can give us actual existence.

Thus, it seems to me that critical questions for evaluating Stein's position on individual forms require us to investigate carefully accounts of human cognition. And having a fully phenomenologically evidenced and adequately complex cognitional theory is importantly related to a right account of being and essence. As Stein

1. See EeS 97/ESG 95–96/FEB 100–101 and chapter 4 above.

articulates and defends essential being, she appeals to our cognitional acts and to the ways in which we come to understand ourselves and others. Thus, implicit in her account of being is also an account of human knowing. (Although Stein does not discuss this correlation of being and knowing in detail, she openly acknowledges it in the introduction to *Finite and Eternal Being*.) Thus, the key issues in evaluating individual forms are ultimately not ones regarding human freedom, evolution, the intelligibility of individuality, etc.—as important as these things may be—but the classic foundational philosophical questions.

Evaluating Stein's position on these issues is a large task. Stein is a subtle thinker, deeply involved in contemporary concerns, well read in the history of philosophy, aware of developments in the sciences, adept in many philosophical languages, and thoroughly immersed in the early phenomenological school. She articulates a metaphysical account in her later work that is, as far as I can tell, unique in the history of philosophy, even if in important conversation with major philosophical debates. Investigation of Stein's positions on fundamental philosophical questions is well worth doing, both for those inclined to agree with Stein about individual forms and those, like myself, who would like to articulate a more Thomistic response to Stein's challenge.

Stein's position is worth investigating not only because of its sophistication and distinctiveness in the history of philosophy, but also because—like all substantive philosophical positions—it is importantly tied to how we live. Much is at stake in where we come down on issues of individuality, uniqueness, being, and essence; the various aspects of our lives are deeply interconnected. Our evaluation of the nature and role of reason, the value of the arts and the various natural sciences, the role of our materiality, sociality, and historicality in conditioning our individuality, the role and meaning of the good life and its tie to social, political, and economic organization, etc., are all affected by and tied to our positions in these seemingly abstract debates. But, perhaps most significantly, the debate is about who each of us is as an individual and what it means to be true to ourselves.

Selected Bibliography

Primary Works by Edith Stein

In German

*Der Aufbau der menschlichen Person: Vorlesung zur philosophischen An-
thropologie.* Edith Stein Gesamtausgabe 14. Freiburg: Herder, 2004.

Briefe an Roman Ingarden 1917–1938. Edith Steins Werke 14. Freiburg:
Herder, 1991.

Endliches und ewiges Sein: Versuch eines Aufstiegs zum Sinn des Seins.
Edith Steins Werke 2. Louvain: E. Nauwelaerts, and Freiburg: Herder, 1950.

Endliches und ewiges Sein: Versuch eines Aufstiegs zum Sinn des Seins.
Edith Stein Gesamtausgabe 11/12. Freiburg: Herder, 2006.

Die Frau: Fragestellungen und Reflexionen. Edith Stein Gesamtausgabe
13. Freiburg: Herder, 2000.

"Husserls Phänomenologie und die Philosophie des hl. Thomas von
Aquino." *Jahrbuch für Philosophie und phänomenologische Forschung,* supplementary volume, Festschrift for Edmund Husserl
(1929): 315–38.

"Lateinisch-Deutsches Wörterverzeichnis" (index for Stein's translation
of *De veritate*). In *Übersetzung: Des hl. Thomas von Aquino Untersuchungen über die Wahrheit "Quaestiones disputatae de veritate,*
Edith Steins Gesamtausgabe 4, ed. Andreas Speer and Francesco
Valerio Tommasi, 875–918. Freiburg: Herder, 2008.

"La Phénoménologie." *Journées d'Études de la Société Thomiste* (September 12, 1932): 101–11.

Potenz und Akt: Studien zu einer Philosophie des Seins. Edith Steins
Werke 18. Freiburg: Herder, 1998.

Potenz und Akt: Studien zu einer Philosophie des Seins. Edith Steins
Gesamtausgabe 10. Edited by Hans Rainer Sepp. Freiburg: Herder,
2005.

Potenz und Akt. Manuscript corrected by Stein; copies available at Archivum Carmelitanum Edith Stein, Würzburg, Germany, and the
Edith-Stein-Karmel, Tübingen, Germany.

SELECTED BIBLIOGRAPHY

"Was ist Phänomenologie?" *Wissenschaft/Volksbindung—Wissenschaftliche Beilage zur Neuen Pfälzischen Landes-Zeitung* 5 (May 15, 1924). Reprinted in *Theologie und Philosophie* 66 (1991): 570–73.

Welt und Person: Beitrag zum christlichen Wahrheitsstreben. Edith Steins Werke 6. Louvain: E. Nauwelaerts, and Freiburg: Herder, 1962.

In English

Essays on Woman. Translated by Freda Mary Oben. Washington, D.C.: Institute of Carmelite Studies Publications, 1996, revised edition.

Finite and Eternal Being. Translated by Maria Augusta Gooch (unpublished). Copy available at the Edith Stein Center for Study and Research at Spalding University, Louisville, Ky.

Finite and Eternal Being: An Attempt at an Ascent to the Meaning of Being. Translated by Kurt F. Reinhardt. Washington, D.C.: Institute of Carmelite Studies Publications, 2002.

The Hidden Life: Essays, Meditations, Spiritual Texts. Translated by Waltraut Stein. Washington, D.C.: Institute of Carmelite Studies Publications, 1992.

"Husserl's Phenomenology and the Philosophy of St. Thomas Aquinas: Attempt at a Comparison," translated by Mary Catharine Baseheart. In *Person in the World,* by M. C. Baseheart, 129–44. Boston: Kluwer, 1997. See also the translation available in Stein's *Knowledge and Faith.*

An Investigation Concerning the State. Translated by Marianne Sawicki. Washington, D.C.: Institute of Carmelite Studies Publications, 2006.

Knowledge and Faith. Translated by Walter Redmond. Washington, D.C.: Institute of Carmelite Studies Publications, 2000.

Life in a Jewish Family. Translated by Josephine Koeppel. Washington, D.C.: Institute of Carmelite Studies Publications, 1986.

On the Problem of Empathy. 3rd ed. Translated by Waltraut Stein. Washington, D.C.: Institute of Carmelite Studies Publications, 1989.

Philosophy of Psychology and the Humanities. Edited by Marianne Sawicki, translated by Mary Catharine Baseheart and Marianne Sawicki. Washington, D.C.: Institute of Carmelite Studies Publications, 2000.

Self-Portrait in Letters, 1916–1942. Translated by Josephine Koeppel. Washington, D.C.: Institute of Carmelite Studies Publications, 1993.

"Ways to Know God: The 'Symbolic Theology' of Dionysius the Areopagite and Its Factual Presuppositions," translated by Rudolf Allers. *The Thomist* 9 (July 1946): 379–420.

SELECTED BIBLIOGRAPHY

Secondary Works on Edith Stein

Allers, Rudolf. Review of *Endliches und ewiges Sein*, by Edith Stein. *New Scholasticism* 26 (1952): 480–85.

———. Review of *Endliches und ewiges Sein*, by Edith Stein. *Stimmen der Zeit* 151 (1952–53): 153.

Bardzik, Renata. *Das Bild der Frau: bei Edith Stein und heute* (Magisteriumarbeit, Uniwersytet Wrocławski, Instytut Filologii Germańskiej, Wrocław, 1996). Copy at Edith-Stein-Karmel, Tübingen.

Baseheart, Mary Catharine. "The Encounter of Husserl's Phenomenology and the Philosophy of St. Thomas in Selected Writings of Edith Stein." Ph.D. diss., University of Notre Dame, 1960.

———. "Edith Stein's Philosophy of Person." In *Edith Stein Symposium/Teresian Culture*, Carmelite Studies 4, 34–49. Washington, D.C.: Institute of Carmelite Studies Publications, 1987.

———. "Edith Stein's Philosophy of Woman and Women's Education." *Hypatia* 4, no. 1 (1989): 120–31.

———. *Person in the World: Introduction to the Philosophy of Edith Stein*. Boston: Kluwer, 1997.

Baseheart, M. C., Linda Lopez McAlister, and Waltraut Stein. "Edith Stein." In *A History of Women Philosophers*, vol. 4. Edited by Ellen Waithe, 157–87. Boston: Kluwer, 1995.

Beckmann-Zöller, Beate. "Edith Stein's Theory of the Person in Her Münster Years (1932–1933)." *American Catholic Philosophical Quarterly* 82, no. 1 (Winter 2008): 47–70.

Bejas, A. *Vom Seienden als solchen zum Sinn des Seins. Die Transzendentalienlehre bei Edith Stein und Thomas von Aquin*. New York: Peter Lang, 1994.

Borden, Sarah. *Edith Stein*. Outstanding Christian Thinkers. London: Continuum, 2003.

———. "Edith Stein and Individual Forms: A Few Distinctions Regarding Being an Individual." *Yearbook of the Irish Philosophical Society* (2006): 49–69.

———. "Edith Stein's Understanding of Woman." *International Philosophical Quarterly* 46, no. 2 (June 2006): 171–90.

———. "What Makes You You? Edith Stein on Individual Form." In *Contemplating Edith Stein*. Edited by Joyce Berkman, 283–300. Notre Dame: University of Notre Dame Press, 2006.

Borden Sharkey, Sarah. "Edith Stein and Thomas Aquinas on Being and Essence." *American Catholic Philosophical Quarterly* 82:1 (Winter 2008): 87–103.

SELECTED BIBLIOGRAPHY

Börsig-Hover, Lina. "Die Beschäftigung Edith Steins mit Dionysius Areopagita in 'Endliches und ewiges Sein.'" In *Ein Leben für die Wahrheit: zur geistigen Gestalt Edith Steins*. Edited by Lina Börsig-Hover, 227–42. Fridingen an Donau: Börsig, 1991.

Brenner, Rachel Feldhay. "Ethical Convergence in Religious Conversion." In *The Unnecessary Problem of Edith Stein*. Studies in the Shoah 4. Edited by Harry J. Cargas, 77–102. Lanham, Md.: University Press of America, 1994.

———. *Writing as Resistance: Four Women Confronting the Holocaust*. University Park: Pennsylvania State University Press, 1997.

Bryk, Dariusz. "Die Person als Träger des Ethos." Diplomarbeit, Bayerische Julius-Maximilians-Universität, Würzburg, 1994. Copy at Bibliotheca Carmelitana, Würzburg, Germany.

Calcagno, Antonio. "*Persona Politica*: Unity and Difference in Edith Stein's Political Philosophy." *International Philosophical Quarterly* 37, no. 2 (1997): 203–15.

———. "*Die Fülle oder das Nichts?* Edith Stein and Martin Heidegger on the Question of Being." *American Catholic Philosophical Quarterly* 74, no. 2 (2000): 269–85.

———. *The Philosophy of Edith Stein*. Pittsburgh, Pa.: Duquesne University Press, 2006.

Collins, James. "Edith Stein and the Advance of Phenomenology." *Thought* 17 (1942): 685–708.

———. Review of *Endliches und ewiges Sein*, by Edith Stein. *Modern Schoolman* 29 (1952): 139–45.

———. "Edith Stein as a Phenomenologist." In *Three Paths in Philosophy*, 85–105. Chicago: Henry Regnery, 1962.

Conrad-Martius, Hedwig. "Edith Stein." *Archives de Philosophie* 22 (April–June 1959): 163–74.

Coreth, E. Review of *Endliches und ewiges Sein*, by Edith Stein. *Zeitschrift für Katholische Theologie* 75 (1953): 110–12.

Crosby, John. "The Individuality of Human Persons: A Study in the Ethical Personalism of Max Scheler." *Review of Metaphysics* 52, no. 1 (September 1998): 21–50.

de Miribel, Elisabeth. *Edith Stein: 1891–1942*. Paris: Éditions du Seuil, 1956.

Dempf, Alois. Review of *Endliches und ewiges Sein*, by Edith Stein. *Philosophisches Jahrbuch der Görresgesellschaft* 62 (1953): 201–4.

Deneffe, A. Review of *Untersuchungen über die Wahrheit*, translation by Edith Stein. *Scholastik* 11 (1936): 131–32.

SELECTED BIBLIOGRAPHY

Devaux, André A. "Introduction bibliographique à l'étude d'Edith Stein." *Les etudes philosophiques* 11 (1956): 447–50.

De Vries, J. Review of *Untersuchungen über die Wahrheit,* translation by Edith Stein. *Scholastik* 7 (1932): 451, and 8 (1933): 131.

Dougherty, Jude. "Edith Stein's Conversion: How a Jewish Philosopher Became a Catholic Saint." *Crisis,* December 1992, 39–43.

Dubois, M.-J. "L'itinéraire philosophique et spirituel d'Edith Stein." *Revue Thomiste* 73 (1973): 181–210.

Fischer, Josef. "Endliches Sein in Edith Steins Buch: Endliches und ewiges Sein." Seminar paper for course under J. Stallmach, "Was ist Metaphysik?" 1978/79, at Johannes Gutenberg-Universität Mainz. Copy at Bibliotheca Carmelitana, Würzburg, Germany.

Garcia, Laura. "The Primacy of Persons: Edith Stein and Pope John Paul II." *Logos: A Journal of Catholic Thought and Culture* 1, no. 2 (Summer 1997): 90–99.

Geiger, L. B. Review of *Endliches und ewiges Sein,* by Edith Stein. *Revue des sciences philosophiques et théologiques* 38 (1954): 275–77.

Gooch, Augusta Spiegelman. "Metaphysical Ordination: Reflections on Edith Stein's 'Endliches und Ewiges Sein.'" Ph.D. diss., University of Dallas, 1982.

Gosebrink, Hildegard. "Meister Thomas und sein Schüler Husserl. Gedanken zu einem fiktiv Dialog zwischen Thomas von Aquin und Edmund Husserl von Edith Stein." *Erbe und Auftrag* 71, no. 6 (1995): 463–85.

———. "'Wissenschaft als Gottesdienst' Zur Bedeutung Thomas' von Aquinas für Edith Stein in ihrer Speyerer Zeit (1923–1931)." In *Edith Stein Jahrbuch* 4 [*Das Christentum,* part 1], 511–30. Würzburg: Echter, 1998.

Graef, Hilda. *The Scholar and the Cross: the Life and Works of Edith Stein.* Westminster, Md.: Newman Press, 1955; New York: Longmans, Green, 1955.

Graf, Thomas. Review of *Untersuchung über die Wahrheit,* translation by Edith Stein. *Divus Thomas: Jahrbuch für Philosophie und spekulative Theologie,* series 3 (1933): 100–103.

Granderath, Käthe. *From Finite to Eternal Being: Edith Stein's Philosophical Approach to God* (Master's thesis, Loyola University, Chicago, March 1961). Typescript in Archivum Carmelitanum Edith Stein in Würzburg, Germany.

Guilead, Reuben. *De la Phénoménologie à la science de la croix: l'itinéraire d'Edith Stein.* Louvain: Nauwelaerts, 1974.

SELECTED BIBLIOGRAPHY

Heimpel, Franz-Josef. *Der Aufstieg zum Sinn des menschlichen Seins.*
Anthropologie und Kreuzeswissenschaft bei Edith Stein (Zulassungs-
sarbeit zur Abschlußprüfung in katholischer Theologie, Studien-
haus St. Lambert, Trier, August 1995). Copy at Edith-Stein-Karmel,
Tübingen, Germany.

Herbstrith, Waltraud. *Edith Stein, a Biography.* Translated by Bernard
Bonowitz. New York: Harper & Row, 1985.

———, ed. *Denken im Dialog: Zur Philosophie Edith Steins.* Tübingen:
Attempt Verlag, 1991.

Höfliger, A. *Das Universalienproblem in Edith Steins Werke "Endliches
und ewiges Sein."* Fribourg: Universitätsverlag, 1968.

Hughes, J. "Edith Stein's Doctoral Thesis on Empathy and the Philosophical Climate from Which It Emerged." *Teresianum* 36 (1985):
455–84.

Ingarden, Roman. "Edith Stein on her Activity as an Assistant of Edmund Husserl," translated by Janina Makota. *Philosophy and Phenomenological Research* 23 (1962): 155–75.

Kalinowski, Georges. "Edith Stein et Karol Wojtyla sur la personne."
Revue Philosophique de Louvain 82, no. 4 (1984): 545–61.

Kaufmann, Fritz. Review of *Endliches und ewiges Sein,* by Edith Stein.
Philosophy and Phenomenological Research 12 (1952): 572-77.

Kavunguvalappil, Anthony. *Theology of Suffering and Cross in the Life
and Works of Blessed Edith Stein.* New York: Peter Lang, 1998.

Knoche, Eva-Maria. "Philosopisch [*sic*]-theologische Anthropologie
bei Edith Stein mit dem Schwerpunkt auf 'Endliches und ewiges
Sein—Versuch eines Aufstiegs zum Sinn des Seins-.'" Diplomat-
keit, Eberhard-Karls-Universität Tübingen, 1988/89. Copy at Edith-
Stein-Karmel, Tübingen, Germany.

Lebech, Mette. "Edith Stein's Philosophy of Education in *The Structure of the Human Person.*" *REA: Religion, Education and the Arts* 5
(2005): 55–69.

———. "The Identification of Human Dignity. Hermeneutic, Eidetic
and Constitutional Analyses in the Light of the Phenomenology of
Edith Stein." Ph.D. diss., Katholieke Universiteit Leuven, 2006.

Lembeck, Karl Heinz. "Die Phänomenologie Husserls und Edith Stein."
Theologie und Philosophie 63, no. 2 (1988): 182–202.

———. "Zwischen Wissenschaft und Glauben: die Philosophie Edith
Steins." *Zeitschrift für Katholische Theologie* 112, no. 3 (1990): 271–87.

Lindblad, Ulrika. "Rereading Edith Stein: What Happened?" *Theology*
99 (July–August 1996): 269–76.

SELECTED BIBLIOGRAPHY

MacIntyre, Alasdair. *Edith Stein: A Philosophical Prologue 1913–1922.* Lanham, Md.: Rowman & Littlefield, 2006.

Maier, Friederike. "Den Menschen denken. Die Seele im Werk Edith Steins." Diplomarbeit, Albert-Ludwigs-Universität, Freiburg im Br., 1995.

Maskukak, Marian. *Edith Stein and the Body-Soul-Spirit at the Center of Holistic Formation.* New York: Peter Lang, 2007.

Matthias, Ursula. *Die Menschliche Freiheit im Werk Edith Steins* (Thesis ad Doctoratum in Philosophia totaliter edita, Pontificium Athenaeum Sanctae Crucis Facultas Philosophiae, Rome, 1997).

McAlister, Linda Lopez. "Edith Stein: Essential Differences." *Philosophy Today* 37 (Spring 1993): 70–77.

McInerny, Ralph M. "Edith Stein and Thomism." In *Edith Stein Symposium/Teresian Culture.* Carmelite Studies 4, 74–87. Washington, D.C.: Institute of Carmelite Studies, 1987.

Morard, M.-St. Review of *Endliches und ewiges Sein,* by Edith Stein. *Divus Thomas: Jahrbuch für Philosophie und spekulative Theologie* 30 (1952): 369–75.

Müller, Andreas Uwe. *Grundzüge der Religionsphilosophie von Edith Stein.* Freiburg: Alber, 1993.

Neyer, Maria Amata. "Edith Steins Werk 'Endliches und ewiges Sein'. Eine Dokumentation." In *Edith Stein Jahrbuch* 1 [*Die menschliche Gewalt*], 311–343. Würzburg: Echter, 1995.

Nink, C. Review of *Endliches und ewiges Sein,* by Edith Stein. *Scholastik* 26 (1951): 246–49.

Nota, Jan. "Edith Stein and Martin Heidegger." In *Edith Stein Symposium/Teresian Culture.* Carmelite Studies 4, 50–73. Washington, D.C.: Institute of Carmelite Studies Publications, 1987.

———. "Misunderstanding and Insight about Edith Stein's Philosophy." *Human Studies* 10 (1987): 205–12.

Ott, Hugo. "Die Randnotizen Martin Honeckers zur Habilitationsschrift Potenz und Akt." In *Studien zur Philosophie von Edith Stein.* Internationales Edith-Stein-Symposium Eichstätt 1991/Phänomenologische Forschungen, vol. 26/27. Edited by Reto Luzius Fetz, Matthias Rath, and Peter Schulz, 140–46. Freiburg: Alber, 1993.

Payne, Steven. "Edith Stein: A Fragmented Life." *America,* October 10, 1998, 11–14.

Posselt, Teresia Renata de Spiritu Sancto. *Edith Stein.* Translated by C. Hastings and Donald Nicholl. New York: Sheed & Ward, 1952.

Redmond, Walter. "A Nothing That Is: Edith Stein on Being without Essence." *American Catholic Philosophical Quarterly* 82, no. 1 (Winter 2008): 71–86.

Rodeheffer, Jane Kelley. "On Spiritual Maternity: Edith Stein, Aristotle, and the Nature of Woman." *American Catholic Philosophical Quarterly* 72 [Supplement] (1998): 285–303.

Salmen, Josef. "Personverständnis bei Edith Stein." Ph.D. diss., Pontificia Universitas Gregoriana, Rome: Mödling, 1968.

Sawicki, Marianne. *Body, Text and Science: The Literacy of Investigative Practices and the Phenomenology of Edith Stein.* Boston: Kluwer, 1997.

———. "Empathy Before and After Husserl." *Philosophy Today* 22 (1997): 123–27.

———. "Personal Connections: The Phenomenology of Edith Stein," www.nd.edu/~colldev/subjects/catholic/personalconn.html. (This was also given as a lecture at St. John's University, New York, in October 1998, and at the Baltimore Carmel, November 1998.)

———. Editor's Introduction to *Philosophy of Psychology and the Humanities,* by Edith Stein. Edited by Marianne Sawicki, translated by Mary Catharine Baseheart and Marianne Sawicki, xi–xxiii. Washington, D.C.: Institute of Carmelite Studies Publications, 2000.

Schudt, Karl C. "Faith and Reason in the Philosophy of Edith Stein." Ph.D. diss., Marquette University, 2001.

———. "Edith Stein's Proof for the Existence of God from Consciousness." *American Catholic Philosophical Quarterly* 82, no. 1 (Winter 2008): 105–126.

Schulz, Peter. *Edith Steins Theorie der Person: Von der Bewußtseinsphilosophie zur Geistmetaphysik.* Freiburg: Alber, 1994.

———. "Toward the Subjectivity of the Human Person: Edith Stein's Contribution to the Theory of Identity." *American Catholic Philosophical Quarterly* 82, no. 1 (Winter 2008): 161–76.

Secretan, Philibert. "Personne, individu et responsibilité chez Edith Stein." In *The Crisis of Culture.* Analecta Husserliana 5, 247–58. Dordrecht, Holland: D. Reidel, 1976.

———. "The Self and the Other in the Thought of Edith Stein." In *The Self and the Other: The Irreducible Element in Man, I.* Analecta Husserliana 6, 87–98. Dordrecht, Holland: D. Reidel, 1977.

———. "Essence et personne: Contribution à la connaissance d'Edith Stein." *Freiburger Zeitschrift für Philosophie und Theologie* 26 (1979): 481-504.

———. "Edith Stein on the 'Order and Chain of Being,'" translated by E. M. Swiderski. In *The Great Chain of Being and Italian Phenom-*

enology. Analecta Husserliana 11, 113–23. Dordrecht, Holland: D. Reidel, 1981.

———. *Erkenntnis und Aufsteig: Einführung in die Philosophie von Edith Stein.* Innsbruck: Tyrolia-Verlag, 1992.

———. "Individuum, Individualität und Individuation nach Edith Stein und Wilhelm Dilthey." In *Studien zur Philosophie von Edith Stein* [Internationales Edith-Stein-Symposium Eichstätt 1991/Phänomenologische Forschungen, vol. 26/27]. Edited by Reto Luzius Fetz, Matthias Rath and Peter Schulz, 148–69. Freiburg: Alber, 1993.

Seidl, Horst. "Über Edith Steins Vermittlungsversuch zwischen Husserl und Thomas v. Aquin." *Forum Katholische Theologie* 2 (1999): 114–33.

Spiegelberg, Herbert. "Edith Stein." In *The Phenomenological Movement: A Historical Introduction,* 3rd ed., revised and enlarged. Boston: Nijhoff, 1982.

Stallmach, Josef. "The Work of Edith Stein: The Tension between Knowledge and Faith," translated by Stephen Wentworth Arndt. *Communio* 15 (Fall 1988): 376–83.

Stein, Waltraut J. Translator's introduction to *On the Problem of Empathy,* by Edith Stein. Washington, D.C.: Institute of Carmelite Studies Publications, 1989.

Suda, Johannes. Review of *Endliches und ewiges Sein,* by Edith Stein. *Franziskanische Studien* 35 (1953): 116–23.

Tilliette, Xavier. "Edith Stein et la philosophie chretienne: À propos d'Être fini et Être eternal." *Gregorianum* 71 (1990): 97-113.

Van den Berg, M. Regina. "Community in the Thought of Edith Stein." Ph.D. diss., The Catholic University of America, 2000.

Volek, Peter. *Erkenntnistheorie bei Edith Stein* [Europäische Hochschulschriften, series 20, vol. 564]. New York: Peter Lang, 1998.

Vonhögen, Roderick. "Die menschliche Person bei Edith Stein." In *Ein Leben für die Wahrheit: zur geistigen Gestalt Edith Steins.* Edited by Lina Börsig-Hover, 176–97. Fridingen an Donau: Börsig-Verlag, 1991.

Wright, Terrence. "Artistic Truth and the True Self in Edith Stein." *American Catholic Philosophical Quarterly* 82, no. 1 (Winter 2008): 127–42.

Other Literature

Adams, M. M. "Universals in the Early Fourteenth Century." In *The Cambridge History of Later Medieval Philosophy: From the Rediscovery of Aristotle to the Disintegration of Scholasticism, 1100-1600.*

SELECTED BIBLIOGRAPHY

Edited by Norman Kretzmann, Anthony Kenny, and Jan Pinborg, 411–39. New York: Cambridge University Press, 1982.

Apollinaris. "On the Union in Christ of the Body with the Godhead." In *The Christological Controversy*. Edited and translated by Richard A. Norris Jr., 103–11. Philadelphia: Fortress Press, 1980.

Aquinas, Thomas. *On the Truth of the Catholic Faith*. Translated by James F. Anderson. Garden City, N.Y.: Image Books, 1956.

———. *On Being and Essence*. In *Selected Writings of St. Thomas Aquinas*. Translated by Robert P. Goodwin, 33–67. Indianapolis: Bobbs-Merrill, 1965.

———. *Summa Theologica*. Translated by Fathers of the English Dominican Province. Allen, Tex.: Christian Classics, 1981.

———. *Truth*. Translated by Robert W. Mulligan. Albany, N.Y.: Preserving Christian Publications, 1993.

Athanasius. "Orations against the Arians." In *The Christological Controversy*. Edited and translated by Richard A. Norris Jr., 83–101. Philadelphia: Fortress Press, 1980.

Augustine. "The Spirit and the Letter." In *Augustine: Later Works*. Edited by John Burnaby, 182–250. Philadelphia: Westminster Press, 1960.

———. *The Confessions of St. Augustine*. Translated by Rex Warner. New York: Penguin, 1963.

Bell, David. *Husserl*. The Arguments of the Philosophers. New York: Routledge, 1990.

Bernet, R., I. Kern, and E. Marbach. *An Introduction to Husserlian Phenomenology*. Evanston, Ill.: Northwestern University Press, 1993.

Bettoni, Efrem. *Duns Scotus: The Basic Principles of His Philosophy*. Edited and translated by Bernardine Bonansea. Washington, D.C.: The Catholic University of America Press, 1961.

Bobik, Joseph. "Matter and Individuation." In *The Concept of Matter in Greek and Medieval Philosophy*. Edited by Ernan McMullin, 281–92. Notre Dame, Ind.: University of Notre Dame Press, 1965.

Bocheński, I. M. *Contemporary European Philosophy*. Translated by Donald Nicholl and Karl Aschenbrenner. Berkeley: University of California Press, 1956.

Byrne, Patrick H. "Evolution, Randomness, and Divine Purpose: A Reply to Cardinal Schönborn." *Theological Studies* 67 (2006): 653–65.

Cairns, Dorian. *Guide for Translating Husserl*. The Hague: Martinus Nijhoff, 1973.

Clark, Mary T. "An Inquiry into Personhood." *Review of Metaphysics* 46 (September 1992): 3–28.

Clarke, W. Norris. *Person and Being.* Milwaukee, Wis.: Marquette University Press, 1993.

———. *The One and the Many: A Contemporary Thomistic Metaphysics.* Notre Dame, Ind.: University of Notre Dame Press, 2001.

Cobb-Stevens, Richard. "Being and Categorial Intuition." *Review of Metaphysics* 44 (September 1990): 43–66.

Crosby, John. "The Individuality of Human Persons: A Study in the Ethical Personalism of Max Scheler." *Review of Metaphysics* 52, no. 1 (September 1998): 21–50.

Darwin, Charles. *The Origin of Species by Means of Natural Selection or the Preservation of Favored Races in the Struggle for Life and The Descent of Man and Selection in Relation to Sex.* New York: The Modern Library, n.d.

Drummond, John. "Synthesis, Identity and the *a priori.*" *Recherches Husserliennes* 4 (1995): 27–51.

Elliston, F. A. "Husserl's Phenomenology of Empathy." In *Husserl: Expositions and Appraisals.* Edited by Frederick A. Elliston and Peter McCormick, 213–31. Notre Dame, Ind.: University of Notre Dame Press, 1977.

Farber, Marvin. "A Review of Recent Phenomenological Literature." *Journal of Philosophy* 27, no. 13 (June 19, 1930): 337–49.

Farrington, Benjamin. *What Darwin Really Said.* New York: Schocken Books, 1966.

Fine, Kit. "Part-Whole." In *Cambridge Companion to Husserl.* Edited by Barry Smith and David Woodruff Smith, 463–85. New York: Cambridge University Press, 1995.

Gadamer, Hans-Georg. *Truth and Method.* 2nd rev. ed. Translated by Joel Weinsheimer and Donald G. Marshall. New York: Continuum, 1993.

Gould, Stephen Jay. *Ever Since Darwin: Reflections in Natural History.* New York: W. W. Norton, 1977.

Gracia, J. J. E. *Introduction to the Problem of Individuation in the Early Middle Ages.* Washington, D.C.: The Catholic University of America Press, 1984.

———. *Individuality: An Essay on the Foundations of Metaphysics.* Albany: State University of New York Press, 1988.

———. "Introduction: The Problem of Individuation." In *Individuation in Scholasticism.* Edited by Jorge J. E. Gracia, 1–20. Albany: State University of New York Press, 1994.

———. "The Legacy of the Early Middle Ages." In *Individuation in*

Scholasticism. Edited by Jorge J. E. Gracia, 21–38. Albany: State University of New York Press, 1994.

Grajewski, M. J. *The Formal Distinction of Duns Scotus: A Study in Metaphysics.* Washington, D.C.: The Catholic University of America Press, 1944.

Haught, John F. *Science & Religion: From Conflict to Conversation.* New York: Paulist Press, 1995.

Heidegger, Martin. *Being and Time.* Translated by John Macquarrie and Edward Robinson. San Francisco: HarperSanFrancisco, 1962.

Hering, Jean. "Bemerkungen über das Wesen, die Wesenheit, und die Idee." *Jahrbuch für Philosophie und phänomenologische Forschung* 4 (1921): 495–543.

Hume, David. *A Treatise of Human Nature.* Edited by L. A. Selby-Bigge and P. H. Nidditch. New York: Oxford University Press, 1978.

Husserl, Edmund. *Briefe an Roman Ingarden. Mit Erläuterungen und Erinnerungen an Husserl.* Edited by Roman Ingarden. The Hague: Martinus Nijhoff, 1968.

———. *Logical Investigations.* Volumes 1 and 2. Translated by J. N. Findlay. New York: Humanities Press, 1970.

———. *Zur Phänomenologie der Intersubjektivität: Texte aus dem Nachlass Zweiter Teil: 1921–1928.* Husserliana 14. The Hague: Martinus Nijhoff, 1973.

———. *Husserl: Shorter Works.* Edited by Peter McCormick and Frederick Elliston. Notre Dame, Ind.: University of Notre Dame Press, 1982.

———. *Ideas Pertaining to a Pure Phenomenology and to a Phenomenological Philosophy: First Book [General Introduction to a Pure Phenomenology].* Translated by F. Kersten. The Hague: Martinus Nijhoff, 1983.

———. *Ideas Pertaining to a Pure Phenomenology and to a Phenomenological Philosophy: Second Book [Studies in the Phenomenology of Constitution].* Translated by Richard Rojcewicz and André Schuwer. Boston: Kluwer, 1989.

———. "Natural Scientific Psychology, Human Sciences, and Metaphysics," translated by Paul Crowe. In *Issues in Husserl's Ideas II.* Edited by Thomas Nenon and Lester Embree, 8–13. Boston: Kluwer, 1996.

Kelly, J. N. D. *Early Christian Doctrines.* Rev. ed. San Francisco: HarperSanFrancisco, 1978.

Locke, John. *An Essay Concerning Human Understanding.* Edited by Peter H. Nidditch. New York: Oxford University Press, 1975.

Lonergan, Bernard. *Insight: A Study of Human Understanding.* Edited by Frederick E. Crowe and Robert M. Doran. Toronto: University of Toronto Press, 1992.

Manser, Gallus. "Das Wesen des Thomismus." *Divus Thomas. Jahrbuch für Philosophie und spekulative Theologie* 2 (1925): 2–23, 196–221, 411–31.

Melle, U. "Nature and Spirit." In *Issues in Husserl's Ideas II.* Edited by Thomas Nenon and Lester Embree, 15–35. Boston: Kluwer, 1996.

Mensch, James. "Ego." In *Encyclopedia of Phenomenology.* Edited by Lester E. Embree, Elizabeth A. Behnke, et al., 163–68. Boston: Kluwer, 1997.

Miller, Joshua. "Scheler on the Twofold Source of Personal Uniqueness." *American Catholic Philosophical Quarterly* 79, no. 1 (Winter 2005): 163–81.

Miller, Kenneth R. *Finding Darwin's God: A Scientist's Search for Common Ground Between God and Evolution.* New York: Cliff Street Books, 1999.

Nenon, Thomas. "Husserl's Theory of the Mental." In *Issues in Husserl's Ideas II.* Edited by Thomas Nenon and Lester Embree, 223–35. Boston: Kluwer, 1996.

Noone, T. "Individuation in Scotus." *American Catholic Philosophical Quarterly* 69, no. 4 (1995): 527–42.

Null, Gilbert T. "Formal and Material Ontology." In *Encyclopedia of Phenomenology.* Edited by Lester E. Embree, Elizabeth A. Behnke, et al., 237–41. Boston: Kluwer, 1997.

Owens, Joseph. "Thomas Aquinas." In *Individuation in Scholasticism.* Edited by Jorge J. E. Gracia, 173–94. Albany: State University of New York Press, 1994.

Scotus, John Duns. "Six Questions on Individuation from His *Ordinatio* II. d. 3, part 1, qq. 1–6." In *Five Texts on the Mediaeval Problem of Universals: Porphyry, Boethius, Abelard, Duns Scotus, Ockham.* Edited and translated by Paul Vincent Spade, 57–113. Indianapolis: Hackett, 1994.

Smith, Barry. "Realist Phenomenology." In *Encyclopedia of Phenomenology.* Edited by Lester E. Embree, Elizabeth A. Behnke, et al., 586–90. Boston: Kluwer, 1997.

Smith, Barry, and Kevin Mulligan. "Pieces of a Theory." In *Parts and Moments: Studies in Logic and Formal Ontology.* Edited by Barry Smith, 15–109. Munich: Philosophia Verlag, 1982.

Sokolowski, Robert. "The Logic of Parts and Wholes in Husserl's *In-*

vestigations." *Philosophy and Phenomenological Research* 28 (1968): 537–53.

Stern, William. *General Psychology from the Personalistic Standpoint.* Translated by Howard Davis Spoerl. New York: Macmillan, 1938.

Suarez, F. *On the Various Kinds of Distinctions.* Translated by Cyril Vollert. Milwaukee, Wis.: Marquette University Press, 1947.

Weisheipl, James A. "Discussion [of Bobik's article]." In *The Concept of Matter in Greek and Medieval Philosophy.* Edited by Ernan Mc-Mullin, 293–97. Notre Dame, Ind.: University of Notre Dame Press, 1965.

Wolter, Allan B. Introduction to *Duns Scotus: Philosophical Writings,* by John Duns Scotus. Edited and translated by Allan Wolter. Edinburgh: Nelson, 1962.

———. "The Formal Distinction." In *Studies in Philosophy and the History of Philosophy.* Vol. 3. Edited by John K. Ryan and Bernardine M. Bonansea, 45–60. Washington, D.C.: The Catholic University of America Press, 1965.

———. "John Duns Scotus." In *Individuation in Scholasticism.* Edited by Jorge J. E. Gracia, 271–98. Albany: State University of New York Press, 1994.

Zahavi, Dan. *Self-Awareness and Alterity: A Phenomenological Investigation.* Evanston, Ill.: Northwestern University Press, 1999.

Index

Adam, 42, 175
angels, xv, xxiii, 26, 39, 40, 46, 93, 117,
    154–60, 162–63, 165, 188, 201, 222
Aquinas, Thomas, xi, xvii–xx, xxii–xxiii,
    xxxi, 4, 7, 11, 17, 19, 22–23, 27, 30, 34,
    36–39, 48–53, 55–56, 58, 62–65, 75–77,
    81–85, 89–90, 92, 95–98, 102, 105, 107,
    109, 116, 118, 126–27, 138, 143–44, 145–
    46, 154–55, 157–58, 175, 188, 192, 201–2,
    211, 216, 220, 230–32, 234–35, 248, 251
Apollinarianism, 176, 248
a priori, 63, 71, 101, 120, 121, 159, 160, 168,
    172, 180–81, 186, 189, 192, 195, 202, 205;
    adverb, 209, 211, 249; assumption,
    169–70, 208; conditions, 24; (content-
    rich) individual form, xxiv, 184–85, 187,
    191, 199, 201, 204–5, 208–12, 218, 224,
    227, 229, 233–35; individuality, 152, 203;
    laws, 131, 137; universality, 171
Arianism, 176, 248
Aristotle, ix, xxiv, xxxi, 4, 7–9, 11–12, 17–18,
    20, 30, 32, 54–55, 57, 59, 61–63, 83, 85, 94,
    105–12, 125, 130, 156, 185, 187, 201–2, 216
Athanasius, 176, 248

being: essential being, xxxi, 47, 65, 71, 81,
    82–98, 100–110, 113, 115, 118, 121–26,
    139–40, 143, 146, 151–52, 158, 164, 185–
    86, 188–89, 192–93, 195–96, 199–200,
    207–8, 214–15, 223, 232, 234–37; mental
    being, xxix, 82, 85, 90–93, 101–2, 151,
    215, 235, 236; real being, xxxi, 63, 73–74,
    78, 82, 84, 90–98, 100–5, 108–13, 115, 118,
    121–26, 137–39, 142–43, 188, 195–96, 215
being-Socrates, 4, 98–99, 110, 121, 124,
    136, 188
breath of God, 41, 163

Calcagno, Antonio, xii, 16, 24, 81, 161,
    174, 242
categories, 61–62, 70, 101, 110–11
Clarke, W. Norris, xiii, 50, 249
conceptual distinction, 89, 150–51
Conrad-Martius, Hedwig, x, xxv, xxix,
    xxxi, 48, 200, 242

constitution, 15, 61, 137, 140, 161, 182, 193,
    223

Darwin, Charles, xvii, 30–42, 216–18, 249
Dasein, xxix, 58, 98–99, 109, 121, 221–23
democracy, xxiv, 171–75
Descartes, Rene, 127
divine ideas, 95–96, 102, 109
divine intervention, 12

empathy, 7, 11–12, 15–16, 28, 119, 121, 139,
    161, 163–64, 178–80, 182–84, 193–94,
    207, 214, 240
empty form, xxx, 78, 119, 139–40
essentiality, xxii, xxxi, 3, 56, 58, 65–77,
    79–81, 92–96, 101–2, 104–5, 116, 137
essential what, xxxi, 2, 65, 82, 84, 86, 91,
    93, 95, 97, 104, 108, 113, 143, 152
evolution, xxii, 27, 30–43, 54, 163, 211,
    216–218, 237, 248, 251

formal distinction, 87, 128, 148–53, 250,
    252
full what, xxx, 143

Gracia, Jorge, 17, 249–50

haecceitas, ix, x, xxi, xxiii, 17, 21, 118, 126,
    128–29, 153
Hegel, G.W.F., 60, 164
Heidegger, Martin, xiii, xxvii, xxix, 44, 68,
    107, 161, 174, 221–23, 229, 250
Hering, Jean, xxii, 65, 67–68, 71, 73–74, 79,
    99, 136–37, 200, 250
Honecker, Martin, xix, 245
Hume, David, xvi, 59–61, 84, 101, 250
Husserl, Edmund, x–xi, xiii, xvii–xx, xxiii,
    xxvi, xxix–xxx, 1, 5, 9–10, 16, 23–24,
    28, 35, 57–66, 70–72, 79, 101, 119, 122,
    128–38, 141, 143, 146–47, 151–53, 177, 186,
    199–200, 232, 234, 250

identity, xxi, 16, 19, 20–23, 38, 50, 52, 54,
    71, 74, 82, 128, 132, 141, 146, 149–52, 174,
    186, 222, 228, 233, 235–36, 246, 249

INDEX